Idealistic Thought
in
Indian Philosophy

Contemporary Researches in Hindu Philosophy & Religion, no. 1

Idealistic Thought in Indian Philosophy

Rise and growth from the *Vedic* times
to the *Kevalādvaita Vedānta* up to Prakāśānanda
of 16th century, including
as propounded in the *Mahāyāna* Buddhism

Shuchita C. Divatia

DK PRINTWORLD
Publishers of Indian Traditions

Cataloging in Publication Data — DK
[Courtesy: D.K. Agencies (P) Ltd. <docinfo@dkagencies.com>]

Divatia, Shuchita C. (Suchita Chittaranjanbhai), 1957 -
Idealistic thought in Indian Philosophy.
(Contemporary researches in Hindu philosophy & Religion, no. 1).
Includes bibliographical references. (p.).
Includes Index.

1. Idealism. 2. Philosophy, Indic. 3. Philosophy, Buddhist. I. Title. II. Series: Contemporary researches in Hindu philosophy and religion ; no. 1.

ISBN: 9788124600214

First published in India in 1994
Reprinted in 2017

Printed and published by:
D.K. Printworld (P) Ltd.
Regd. Office : *Vedaśrī*, F-395, Sudarshan Park
(Metro Station: Ramesh Nagar)
New Delhi - 110 015
Phones : (011) 2545 3975; 2546 6019
e-mail : indology@dkprintworld.com
Web : www.dkprintworld.com

Preface

THE alluring phenomena of the world have been a subject of inquiry from time immemorial. Could the world with its diversities have been created by some Almighty Ominiscient Lord? Or has it always been there and will continue to exist even though changes may occur? Or is it a big illusion? And also is it, that is deluded? How many ultimate entities could be there? Such questions certainly compel an inquisitive mind to think that there should be at least two entities — sentient and non-sentient, or consciousness and matter. But at the same time doubt arises, how could there be any inter-relation between entities so opposed to each other? Now, if there is only one ultimate entity, it should necessarily be sentiency, which could appear to be matter also. Further, another inquiry may arise, could this one eternal sentient principle be capable of modification or change? Or is it eternally unchanging?

If the first alternative is accepted, it should either be divisible and so non-eternal, or it should cease to exist giving place to something else. And if it is eternally unchanging, how could the world phenomenon be accounted for? So far as the world phenomenon is concerned, we all experience it with its dealings and so they have to be accepted. But at the same time, what proof or warranty is there for their existence, except that they appear in our perceptions, or are known through other means of knowledge based on perception. But this does not necessarily prove the reality of the world around. We experience things in a dream. Which do not exist as a matter of fact, being a fiction of our imagination. Similarly, could the world of the waking state also be a fiction of our imagination? But we all experience the same world phenomenon. Could it then be the imaginary construct of one supreme being? How then would we individual selves be related to that supreme being of the nature of Existence-Consciousness-Bliss?

Indian philosophical thought tried to tackle such problems in different ways with the result that a number of philosophical systems came into existence and developed by virtue of mutual influence. As a student of *Vedānta Darśana,* I was much interested in studying carefully how *Kevalādvaita Vedānta* has handled this problem of the unreality of the phenomenal world. I have tried to detect the slightest hint in *Vedāntic* works beginning with the *Upaniṣads,* which could gradually show the way to the doctrine of *Dṛṣṭi-Sṛṣṭi.* I have taken up some pre-Śaṅkara and post-Śaṅkara *Vedāntic* works as well as Idealistic schools of Buddhism, and have tried to trace the line of development leading to *Dṛṣṭi-Sṛṣṭi-vāda.*

In this book I have treated the rise and growth of Idealistic thought from the *Vedic* times till the final establishment of *Dṛṣṭi-Sṛṣṭi-vāda* in *Kevalādvaita Vedānta vis-a-vis* the *Sṛṣṭi-Dṛṣṭi-vāda* of the same school. The *Ṛgveda* represents a very primary stage of Idealistic thought. Glimpses of Idealism are certainly found in the *Upaniṣads,* which assert in clear terms the reality of the non-dual sentiency. On the other hand, some minor *Upaniṣads* emphasise the subjective trend of thinking which can lead towards the type of Idealism that demolishes the reality of the phenomenal world. The *Brahma-sūtra* declares the one non-dual sentiency as the Ultimate Reality. Both the *Mādhyamika* as well as the *Vijñānavāda* schools do not regard the objective world as real. The *Mādhyamika* school points out the faultiness of each one of our empirical concepts and the unreality of the organs of proof. The *Vijñānavāda* school clearly supports the subjectivistic thought and this appears to have helped the Idealistic thought of *Vedānta* in its onward development. Besides, it is noteworthy, that the law of simultaneous apprehension

(*Sahopalambhaniyama*) presents a theory which brings it very near to the *Dṛṣṭi-Sṛṣṭi-vāda*. Though *Yoga-vāsiṣṭha* is a *Purāṇa* it is replete with Idealistic thought and the actual use of the term *Dṛṣṭi-Sṛṣṭi* is found. The confutation of the theory of causation and the emphasis on the doctrine of Acosmism (*Ajātivāda*) also help in the progress of Idealistic thought. Like the *Gauḍapādakārikā*, the *Vivekacūḍāmaṇi* compares the empirical world with the dream world and asserts the mind's leading role in the projection of the world. This positively leads towards subjectivism. So far as the world phenomenon is concerned, Śaṅkara asserts its objective reality from the empirical standpoint, but emphasises its unreality from the transcendental standpoint. Maṇḍana Miśra, the author of the *Brahma Siddhi* is considered to be a pioneer of *Dṛṣṭi-Sṛṣṭi-vāda*. He is the first *Vedāntin* who has boldly emphasised the *jīva* as the locus of *Avidyā*. This revolutionary mode of thinking has paved the way for *Dṛṣṭi-Sṛṣṭi-vāda*. On the other hand the thoughts of the Śaṅkarites bifurcated in two directions, viz., those of *Sṛṣṭi-Dṛṣṭi-vāda* and *Dṛṣṭi-Sṛṣṭi-vāda*. The main thesis of the *Vedānta-Siddhānta-Muktāvalī* is *Dṛṣṭi-Sṛṣṭi-vāda*. Prakāśānanda, the author of this work is the expounder of *Dṛṣṭi-Sṛṣṭi-vāda*. He has very logically elucidated that *Sṛṣṭi* takes place simultaneously with its percipi (*Dṛṣṭi*) or that *Sṛṣṭi* and *Dṛṣṭi* are identical. We find *Dṛṣṭi-Sṛṣṭi-vāda* as an established theory in the works of Madhusudana Sarasvati and Appaya Dikṣita.

Here I have worked out a few points in my own way which I would like to mention. It is true that the *Vedic* thought does not assert the phenomenal world as unreal. On the contrary it worships Nature in all its aspects. I have tried to show that this could be interpreted in the light of Idealism. It cannot be stated that the unreality of the world is meant here. Yet the doubts presented here in the book could be considered later on as suggesting that the world has never been created, and so must be an unreal projection of some power. Also I have tried to be very clear and careful in the interpretation of *Upaniṣadic* statements and not jumped to conclusions which could clearly favour *Dṛṣṭi-Sṛṣṭi-vāda*. I have attempted to present a striking similarity between the law of simultaneous apprehension

(*Sahopalaṁbhaniyama*) and *Dṛṣṭi-Sṛṣṭi-vāda* and to show how both these concepts represent the culmination of the Idealistic thought. From my study I have derived that *Dṛṣṭi-Sṛṣṭi-vāda* is not a direct development of the views of Śaṅkara. Besides, I have tried to make it clear that *Ekajīvavāda* is not identical with *Dṛṣṭi-Sṛṣṭi-vāda* though in the *Siddhāntabindu, Ekajīvavāda* is considered as an identical theory of *Dṛṣṭi-Sṛṣṭi-vāda.*

Before I end here, I would like to acknowledge my indebtedness to the *Ṛṣis* of the Sanskrit lore for the knowledge I have been able to attain from the original Sanskrit works. I also express my gratitude to the great scholars, from whose works I have been benefited much. I must express my deep gratitude to *Padmaśrī* Prof. Dr. Esther A. Solomon who has been my inspiration throughout. I should also not forget to mention my loving parents and husband who encouraged me throughout my work. And last but not the least, I am extremely thankful to the management of D.K. Printworld, New Delhi, who took the task of publishing my book. Besides, my heart-felt gratitude is certainly there to all who have helped me in various ways in my research.

Shuchita C. Divatia

Contents

Table of Transliteration

अ	a	आ	ā	इ	i	ई	ī	उ	u
ऊ	ū	ए	e	ऐ	ai	ओ	o	औ	au
				ऋ	ṛ	ऌ	ḷ		
क	ka	ख	kha	ग	ga	घ	gha	ङ	ṅa
च	ca	छ	cha	ज	ja	झ	jha	ञ	ña
ट	ṭa	ठ	ṭha	ड	ḍa	ढ	ḍha	ण	ṇa
त	ta	थ	tha	द	da	ध	dha	न	na
प	pa	फ	pha	ब	ba	भ	bha	म	ma
य	ya	र	ra	ल	la	ळ	ḷa	व	va
श	śa	ष	ṣa	स	sa	ह	ha		

ं = ṅ or m

: = ḥ

Abbreviations

Ad. Si	*Advaitasiddhi*
Ait. Up.	*Aitareya Upaniṣad*
Bra. Sid	*Brahmasiddhi*
Br. Sū	*Brahma-sūtra*
Bṛ. Up.	*Bṛhadāraṇyaka Upaniṣad*
Br. Sū. Śā. Bhā.	*Brahma Sūtra Śāṅkara-Bhāṣya*
Chā. Up	*Chāndogya Upaniṣad*
G. K.	*Gauḍapādakārikā*
L. S.	*Laṅkāvatārasūtra*
M. K.	*Madhyamaka Kārikā*
M.K.V	*Mdhyamaka Kārikā Vṛtti*
Mund. Up.	*Muṇḍaka Upaniṣad*
P. D.	*Pañcadaśī*
S. L. S.	*Siddhāntaleśasaṁgraha*
Si. Bi.	*Siddhāntabindu*
Śve. Up.	*Śvetaśvatara Upaniṣad*
Tai. Up.	*Taittirīya Upaniṣad*
Tejo. Up.	*Tejobindu Upaniṣad*
Up.	*Upaniṣad*
Vi.	*Vivekacūḍāmaṇi*

V. M. S.	*Vijñāptimātratāsiddhi*
V. P. S.	*Vivaraṇāprameya Saṁgraha*
V. S. M.	*Vedānta Siddhānta Muktāvalī*
Yoga. Up.	*Yogaśikhopaniṣad*
Yv.	*Yoga-Vāsiṣṭha*

Introduction

A COMMON-SENSE view of the world tells us that it can be classified into two divisions : Mind or consciousness and Matter. Matter could further be classified into Solid, Liquid and Gaseous or Substance, Quality, Action, etc. (as the *Nyāya-Vaiśeṣika* system has attempted to do). On deeper thought it is felt that the worldly poenomena could be traced back to just one final or Ultimate Principle — either Matter or Consciousness. Philosophical thinkers have exercised their thinking in both these directions. Most thinkers having an idealistic tendency have felt that Matter could emerge from consciousness if its potencies are suppressed, but consciousness could certainly not emerge from matter which has no innate potency for it. Moreover, Matter can never be established apart from consciousness. We know, the existence of material things only through our knowledge of them, whereas knowledge or consciousness is self-established or self-luminous. Two totally diverse things can have no relation, so it is consciousness that is the prime thing from which all Matter gradually emerges, and is illuminated by it. This consciousness is a transcendental Universal Entity of which our apprehensions are diverse modes.

Another question that arises in regard to consciousness is whether this consciousness is one, or there are as many consciousness-units as there are living beings, and if there be innumerable such units, whether these are integrally related to the Supreme Consciousness or the Supreme Consciousness does not exist at all, these consciousness-units being the sole factors manipulating Matter and its numerous modifications which have evolved in dependence on them.

Philosophers all over the world have deeply thought about such problems. In India, *Vedic* thought passing through gradual stages got stabilised in the concept of one Eternal-Transcendental-Consciousness as the Ultimate Reality and explained the emergence of the worldly phenomena from it. The *Sāṃkhya* thought recognised a plurality of ubiquitous principles (*puruṣas*) and along with it ubiquitous Matter (*Prakṛti*) which undergoes modification as *Mahat* (Intellect), *Ahaṁkāra* (Ego principle) and so on up to the five *mahābhūtas*.

The Buddhists, like other thinkers, accepted this to some extent. But they started thinking on a different line. If a thing is modified, how could it still retain its original identity? Either there is no change or there is total change and a new entity comes into existence every moment. Of course depending on the previous one and also on supporting conditions. Only this could change be accounted for. Thus if any eternal thing is to be recognised, it is just the continuum that is eternal and not any substance-sentient or non-sentient. There is no eternal soul but an eternal continuum of consciousness (*Vijñāna*). But as thought progressed, some felt that such consciousness exists by itself and there is no need to hypostatise the existence of any Matter along with it as apart from consciousness there is no proof of its existence. In a dream we see things outside us without there really being any external objects.The same could be the truth about the external world. The things we feel outside are nothing but projections of our own ideas and have no existence apart from them.

The only distinguishing factor here is the common experience of the world that people have. A table is a table for all. How could it be said to be a construct of any individual mind? This the Buddhists explained in numerous ways — all by chance having the same idea, or one mind influencing other minds and so on. This they had to resort to as they did not recognise Transcendental-Universal Consciousness.

Another line of approach of the Buddhists was that no means of knowledge or proof can be said to be valid and to yield true knowledge as all our concepts and definitions are faulty and suffer from the faults of self-dependence, interdependence, argument in a circle and so on. Thus our knowledge cannot vouchsafe for the existence of anything. Put to the test of Reason, everything including that of bondage and liberation topples down like a house of cards. These *Mādhyamikas* are called *Śūnyavādins* as according to them all empirically recognised entities are void of essence. But they were not Nihilists, for *Śūnyavāda* also signified that what is beyond the realm of all empirical proof is devoid of what we know as empirical realities. (Only they did not stress this sufficiently as it is beyond empirical proof and verbal usage).

The *Vedāntins* with their firm belief in *Advaita* — an ultimate-non-dual sentient principle; regarded consciousness as evolving in two different directions — individual souls and Matter, both these being non-different from the Ultimate and yet having some identity of their own. This could be regarded as some type of *bhedābheda* but some among the *Vedāntins,* who were very open in their outlook and could appreciate the reasoning of others and even imbibe their views, felt that this was not in the true spirit of *Upaniṣadic* thought which recognised one non-dual eternally immutable sentient principle as the Ultimate Reality.

The Buddhist argument that an ubiquitous entity cannot undergo any change or perform any successful activity, and that change or activity is possible only if things are recognised as momentary must have appealed to these thinkers, so also the argument that the external world need not be accepted as real on account of its knowledge. Some Absolutist *Vedāntins* therefore felt that the world has to be looked upon as unreal even as a mental construct like the dream-world. The authors of the *Yoga-vāsiṣṭha* and the *Gauḍapādakārikā* adopted this line of thought in conformity with the *Upaniṣadic* doctrine of the non-dual Absolute principle.

Śaṅkarācārya realised that even then a number of difficulties would have to be faced, as the common-sense view compels us to admit the existence of the external objects, of a plurality of souls, and of God who can be regarded as the cause of the creation, sustenance and dissolution of the world. He recognised all this from the empirical point of view, and propounded the view that from the transcendental point of view, the Ultimate Reality — Brahman is eternally unchanging sentiency, and it is due to *Avidyā* that the world-phenomenon is brought about. *Brahman* conditioned by *Avidyā* can be said to be the cause of the phenomenal world, which is experienced by the individual souls, which themselves are really non-different from *Brahman* but seem to be different due to the functioning of *Avidyā* in its various capacities. Thus the external world was recognised as something superimposed upon *Brahman* by virtue of cosmic *Avidyā* and this could justify the common experiences of living beings. This theory was later more precisely systematised by the followers of Śaṅkara, and given the name of *"Sṛṣṭi-Dṛṣṭi-vāda"* — the doctrine that held that there is perception of things that have already been created. That is to say, things can exist even when not apprehended by individual views, as they are the creation of God.

Other followers of Śaṅkara, notable among them — Prakāśānanda seemed to hold that this could not be regarded as a faithful representation of Śaṅkara's philosophy. Things could be either real (*Brahman*) or unreal (dream). There could not be something that is, in addition to these; empirically real but transcendentally false, and there is no need to distinguish between ephemeral existence and empirical existence which are both equally unreal. In a way these thinkers were right, because the early *Śūnyavādins* and even Śaṅkara seem to admit two grades of existence, of course the unreal one can be further subdivided into empirical and ephemeral, to account for universal illusion (the outer world) and illusions that are only in the case of individual views (e.g., rope-serpent, dream). But these are both unreal. The Buddhist theory of *Sahopalambha* (that a thing and its knowledge are always apprehended simultaneously; and so knowledge which is self-luminous and self-established is alone real, and not also its object which cannot be established independently of its apprehension), greatly influenced such thinkers and *Dṛṣṭi-sṛṣṭi-vāda* came to have a footing in Śāṅkara *Vedānta*.

The term *'Dṛṣṭi-sṛṣṭi '* signifies that the creation is a product of the perception. This would mean that existence consists in being perceived; and there are no durable things existing independently of the conscious being. Things do not exist while unperceived.

Obviously, this theory seems shocking as we are very sure of the existence of the things which are perceived by our sense-organs. Of course, to a lay man this seems absurd to consider a thing as existing only when it is perceived. But philosophers all over the world have deeply thought about this problem; wheteher things exist independently of mind or not? Some have arrived on conclusion that things of the world are in some sense dependent on the mind or consciousness which perceives them. On the other hand some do believe that things exist independently of the mind or consciousness. The former who hold that perceptions are in some sense dependent upon the mind of the perceiver may be broadly called Idealists.

Idealism and its Different Shades

What is meant by the term 'Idealism'? As there are two words namely — Idea and Ideal, it can be assumed that 'Idealism' must be a theory or doctrine related to Idea. This term is so variedly applied that it is very difficult to present a precise definition. In The chief currents of contemporary philosophy, D.M. Datta writes. "Idealism, in the metaphysical sense is the theory that ultimate reality is spiritual, and it is thus opposed to materialism and even neutralism. In its epistemological sense, Idealism is the view that objects of knowledge are not independent of the knower, and it is thus opposed to epistemological realism".[1]

Thus, Idealism and Realism are rival trends of philosophy, which have developed in opposition to each other. On the one hand, Idealism denies the independent existence of the world from its percipi, and on the other, Realism propounds the independent existence of the world from its percipi. *The Dictionary of Philosophy and Psychology* gives the definitions of Idealism as "In metaphysics any theory which maintains the universe to be throughout the network or the embodiment of reason or mind. In epistemology: the view which holds in opposition to Realism, that the reality of the external world is perceptibility".[2]

In short, Idealism considers the mind or idea or the spiritual entity as the projector of this worldly phenomenon, and emphasizes that it does not exist independently of the mind or idea.

We find different shades of Idealism, defined in the *Dictionary of Philosophy* edited by Dagobert Runes,[3] of which mention may be made of some that are relevant to our discussion.

Metaphysics

Pure Idealism or Immaterialism identifies ontological reality (substance, substantives, concrete individuality) exclusively with the ideal, i.e., Mind, Spirit, Soul, Person, Archetypal Ideas, Thought.

Impersonalistic Idealism

Identifies ontological reality essentially with non-conscious spiritual principle, unconscious psychic agency, pure thought, impersonal or "pure" consciousness, pure Ego, subconscious will, impersonal logical mind, etc.

Monistic Idealism (Pantheistic Idealism)

Teaches that the finite self is a part, mode, aspect, moment, appearance or projection of the one.

With respect of cosmology, pure Idealism is either subjective or objective.

Subjective Idealism (Acosmism)

Holds that nature is merely the projection of the finite mind, and has no external, real existence.

Objective Idealism

Identifies an externally real nature with the thought or activity of the world mind.

Epistemological Idealism

Derives Metaphysical idealism from the identification of objects with ideas. In its nominalistic form the claim is made that "To be is to be perceived". From the standpoint of rationalism it is argued that there can be no object without subjects, relations, sensations and feelings are mental, and since no other type of Analogy remains by which to characterize a non-mental thing in itself, pure Idealism follows as the only possible view of being. Epistemological Idealism teaches that all entities other than egos or subjects of experiecne are exclusively noetic objects, i.e., have no existence or reality apart from the of being perceived or thought.

It is difficult to show through parallelism between the views of Indian Philosophers and Western Philosophers having an Idealistic trend. But it may be pointed out that while Idealism developed in its different shades after the 16th century in the West, we find philosophers in India, who from very early times adduced sound reasons in support of Idealism of some sort.

The idealism of the *Upaniṣads* can be said to be Realistic Deism at places, but more characteristically mystical or Impersonal Idealism. The world substratum *Brahman* is identified with the universal soul (*Ātman*) which is the core of each individual living being. As a matter of fact, according to the *Upaniṣads* the whole universe is the product of the Absolute. All things are therefore the final modes of the non-dual Ultimate Reality and have no independent existence.

The Realistic Buddhists even while admitting the reality of the external world regarded everything as momentary. According to the *Sautrāntikas* among them, there is a similarity (*Sārūpya*) between the form of an object and its congnition, for a formless congnition cannot apprehend an external object. The external objects can only be inferred from impressions. The

Vijñānavādins put the external world on a par with the dreaming world, as in a dream perceptual cognitions are possible without any external object. They hold that sensations arise from within the mind, due to the variety of subconscious impressions. Thus the *Vijñānavādin* is a thorough going subjectivist. This Idealism is very near to Berkeley's Idealism, but unlike Berkeley it does not believe in God.

The *Mādhyamika* Buddhism (*Śūnyavāda*) negated the reality of all empirical objects, as they are relative and essenceless by nature.

Influenced by the *Mādhyamika* and the *Vijñānavāda* Buddhism, the author of the *Yoga-vāsiṣṭha* seems to be emphasizing Subjective Idealism. But at the same time owing to his Brāhmaṇical affiliation admits the Ultimate Reality of the non-dual consciousness. His philosophy can be termed Subjective Monistic Idealism.

Gauḍapāda, also perhaps influenced by the Buddhist logic put forth Acosmism (*Ajātivāda*) in the *Gauḍapādakārikā*. An eternal cosmic entity could not change its nature and yet eternally remain what it was, with the result that it could not do anything, or it should be momentary. Impressed by such logic of Buddhist thought, Gauḍapāda established the doctrine of non-origination. Nothing is ever produced. Whatever is perceived, is merely a projection of the mind. At the same time, adhering to the *Upaniṣadic* philosophy, he propounded Absolute, Non-dual, Unchanging *Brahman* as the Ultimate Reality. Hence, Gauḍapāda's philosophy is also subjectivistic. Monistic Idealism like that of the *Yoga-vāsiṣṭha*.

Śaṅkara's philosophy is a wonderful combination of objective and Absolute Idealism. From the transcendental standpoint, he holds that nothing exists besides non-dual unchanging eternal *Brahman*. But from the empirical point of view he positively establishes the objective reality of the phenomenal world.

The same can be said of his followers who are directly concerned with establishing the sole reality of the non-dual unchanging eternal consciousness, and put forth their own explanations of the world appearance, locus of *Avidyā*, concept of *Jīva* and *Īśvara* and so on in consonance with this final teaching of theirs. Most of them recognise the reality of the external world from the empirical point of view and thus they can be said to be adherents of *Sṛṣṭi-Dṛṣṭi-vāda*, which may be lebelled as objective Idealism.

On the other hand Prakāśānanda, the only exception amongst the Śaṅkarites has established *Dṛṣṭi-Sṛṣṭi-vāda*, the culmination of Idealistic thought. According to it, perception itself is creation, or creation is simultaneous with perception, and a thing cannot exist unapprehended. This is allied to Subjective Idealism.

It can only be said that *Dṛṣṭi-Sṛṣṭi-vāda* is a theory solving the puzzle of the world appearance in its unique way. According to it, Ultimate Spiritual Reality is the non-dual entity, while everything else is just an illusion. The universe consisting of individual beings after all disappears in the serene Bliss of the eternal unchanging Absolute Sentiency! This huge dream of the phenomenal world dissolves in the Ultimate Sentiency proving itself as illusory (*prātibhāsika*).

References

1. Datta, D.M., *The Chief Currents of Contemporary Philosophy*. ch.I, p.1, second edition (1961), The University of Calcutta.
2. James Mark Baldwin (ed.), *The Dictionary of Philosophy and Psychology*, Vo.I, p.500, (1940), Peter Smith, New York.
3. Dagobert, D. Runes, *The Dictionary of Philosophy*, Fourth edition (1942) Phiosophical Library, New York.

1

Idealistic Thought in the *Vedas* and the *Upaniṣads*

IN the construction of a building, the foundation stone is of great importance. This is true of every construction. In the build-up of Indian Philosophy, the early thoughts of the *Vedas* and *Upaniṣads* are considered as the foundation stone. The *Ṛgveda* is the oldest sound literary record of Indian thought, which reflects the continuous endeavour of the intellect to solve the mystery of the world that is before us.

The Philosophical Hymns of the *Ṛgveda*

The mundane world with all its alluring complexities was an enchanting topic for the *Vedic* seers. They were all aware of Nature in its various aspects, which they believed to have their presiding deities and so dedicated hymns to them.

Gradually, they became curious about the creator of this fascinating world of appearance. In the course of their sincere inquiry about the creator, various trends like henotheism, pantheism, monotheism and monism emerged.

A student of *Ṛgveda* can easily see how the simple naturalistic hymns, replete with poetry, developed into the highest type of monistic thought. Of course, though the monistic ideas are not found in a full-fledged form, one can clearly see that the *Vedic* seers were conscious enough about a single sentient principle as the Ultimate Reality, from which everything emerges. Hence, it can be said that a belief in a spiritual Reality is found, and this can lead ahead in the direction of Idealism in its different shades.

The philosophical hymns of the *Ṛgveda* represent the early Indian thought. Some of the hymns of the first and the tenth *Maṇḍalas* are replete with philosophical views. When the seer was not content with polytheism, he turned gradually towards monotheism. He felt that over and above these numerous seemingly great deities, there should be one Ultimate Reality, or these deities should be but different aspects or powers of that one all powerful God.

In the *Asya vāmīya Sūkta*, it is stated that the different gods are manifestations of one Ultimate Reality. "To what is one, sages gives many titles".[1] This suggests that the *Vedic* seer was conscious about a non-dual Ultimate Reality. Though we cannot state with certainty whether this concept was strictly monistic, there is certainly the germ of monism in it. It is further evident that the *Vedic* seer has realised that the Ultimate Reality is of the nature of existence-cum-consciousness.

We find the idea of non-dual Reality emphasized in the *Puruṣa-Sūkta* also. Its seer has put forth this concept through a fine metaphor: "The *puruṣa* was thousand-headed, thousand eyed and thousand footed, having covered the earth on all sides, he stood beyond it to the length of ten *aṇgulas*" . . . "*Puruṣa* himself is all this, that has been and that will be, and he is the ruler of immortality" . . . "Thus far extended is his greatness and greater than this is the *puruṣa* himself, a quarter of him is all the creatures, three quarters of him are the immortals in the heaven."[2] This clearly indicates the inability of human intellect to describe fully the omnipresent character of the Ultimate Reality, the Supreme Lord. This shows that the *Vedic* seer is conscious enough about the characteristics of the Ultimate Reality, which cannot be described by human intellect.

Another hymn, viz. the *Hiraṇyagarbha sūkta* also contains monotheistic ideas. In this *Sūkta, Hiraṇyagarbha* is considered to be the non-dual Reality. It is stated, "*Hiraṇyagarbha* existed in the beginning, as soon as he was born, he became the sole lord of the created world. He supported the earth and also this heaven. What god shall serve with an oblation?"[3]

Besides, hymns like the *Skambha sūkta* of the *Atharvaveda* put forth monistic views. Here are *Skambha*, that is to say, the supporter supreme self is declared as prevading the whole universe. It is depicted as the only thing comprising everything in itself.[4] So, recognising one spiritual Reality, the *Vedic* thought was gradually progressing ahead on the path of Idealism.

The *Nāsadīya Sūkta* can be helpful to us in the direction of Monistic Idealism. In this *Sūkta*, the seer's inability to explain the creation is conspicuous. Since time immemorial, the quest of the human mind to solve the riddle of creation is going on. It is a thirst, which is never slaked. This hymn represents and over-awed human mind, which is not able to arrive at a concrete conclusion. It is rightly stated by A.B. Keith, "It is the hymn of creation, and exhibits not merely the putting of the question of the nature of the universe, but an effort to enter into detail, followed by confession of doubt as to the value of the result achieved."[5] A very deep inquiry of the human mind to find out the beginning of the universe is expressed in the very first *Ṛc* of the *Nāsadīya Sūkta*, "There was neither non-existent, nor existent then . . . "[6] Here, the seer's embarassment is easily seen, as he cannot find out appropriate words to describe the state of this universe in the beginning. But in the second *Ṛc*, the word *'Tad Ekaṁ'*[7] shows that the *Vedic* seer was fully aware about the non-dual sentient Ultimate Reality. Then the third *Ṛc* states, "In the beginning, darkness was concealed by darkness."[8] Here, the seer seems to be struggling to find some expression to describe the initial state, when there was nothing distinct. It was all a mass. As there was merely darkness in the beginning, it was difficult to differentiate. Of course, it was not the darkness that we experience, it was something else. Hence it is stated, "darkness was concealed by darkness." Further, as the fourth *Ṛc* states, "It was desire, which was the first seed of the mind, that took possession of that in the beginning."[9] As Sāyaṇa states, "In the beginning of this manifold world, at first, desire (*kāma*) arose in the mind of God."[10] Thus, 'desire' is considered to be responsible for this complex network of this world. Of course, desire for something is the very root cause of the mental effort which prompts physical activity for the creation or the attainment of the desired entity. But those, who believe that nothing exists except the sentient entity, can interpret this statement to mean that we imagine the external objects or the world of appearance as we desire them. The last *Ṛc* confesses the inability to arrive at a definite answer to the problem of creation. "That God who is the supervisor of this in the highest heaven, indeed known; or may be, even he does not know from whom this varied creation arose, and whether he created it or not."[11]

Thus, this hymn indicates that the mystery of the world creation cannot be solved. No one is able to arrive at a specific answer. One can only satisfy oneself with different types of hypothesis. On the one hand, this hymn could be interpreted to mean that the world is beginningless (*anādi*); and there was no first creation. On the other hand, it could also be interpreted to mean that there has never been any creation at all. Those, who propounded later the philosophy of the unreality of the world, point this out as one of the *Vedic* sources, which could support their line of thought, though this does not seem to be what the *Vedic* seer really meant.

We may say, the *Nāsadīya Sūkta*, which is a land mark in the history of Indian Philosophy, can guide us towards Idealism. Though, there is no definite view expressed about this world of appearance, we can interpret it in a way which could support Idealism. Holders of the unreality of the world appearance could interpret it to mean that there is no creation at all. But it is a hazardous to make such a bold statement as coming from a seer of the Vedic times. Nevertheless, we can take this idea, rather an expression as a germ of the later development of Idealism. We can only say that the expressions employed in the *Sūkta*, and the sense of mystery displayed helped considerably in the development of Idealistic thought.

Idealistic Views Expressed in the *Upaniṣads*

The *Upaniṣads,* presenting the acme of *Vedic* thought have been illuminating Indian culture since time immemorial. According to Deussen, "The *Upaniṣads* teach that this universe is not the *Ātman,* the proper 'self' of things, but a mere *Māyā,* a deception or an illusion."[12] While Dr. Radhakrishnan holds "There is hardly any suggestion in the *Upaniṣads* that the entire universe of change is a baseless fabric of fancy, a mere phenomenal show or a world of shadows . . . ".[13] Whatever it be, the germ of Monistic Idealism planted in the *Ṛgveda,* later sprouted forth in the *Upaniṣads.* That the Ultimate Reality is sentient is the fundamental belief of the *Upaniṣads;* and hence the *Upaniṣadic* thought can safely be said to be of the type of Idealism.

At first, we shall try to examine the Idealistic thought of the *Upaniṣads* according to which 'the self' viz. *Brahman* is the Ultimate Spiritual Reality and then we shall try to concentrate on the type of Idealism, which asserts that this world of appearance is unreal, merely a fiction, or a projection of the mind and having no reality of its own. It can be said with confidence that this latter type of Idealism was not prevalent during the *Upaniṣadic* period, though, some *Upaniṣads,* which are considered as minor and later, present scattered traces of the thought that the world of appearance is an imaginary construct.

There are more than one hundred *Upaniṣads,* but only a few of them are considered as the principal ones, those on which Śaṅkara commented. As Dasgupta states in the *History of Indian Philosophy,* "The earliest and most important are probably those that have been commented upon by Śaṅkara, namely *Bṛhadāraṇyaka, Chāndogya, Aitareya, Taittirīya, Īśā, Kena, Kaṭha, Praśna, Muṇḍaka* and *Māṇḍūkya.*"[14] Besides these, three more *Upaniṣads,* viz, *Kauśītaki, Śvetāśvatara* and *Maitrāyaṇī* are found added to the list of principal *Upaniṣads.* The *Maitrāyaṇī Upaniṣad* is regarded as the latest one among these *Upaniṣads.* Mostly, the major *Upaniṣads* are considered pre-Buddhistic. As Deussen, Max-Müller, Winternitz are not unanimous about the chronological order of the *Upaniṣads,*[15] we do not mention here their chronological order.

In the *Upaniṣads*, we find two types of concepts regarding this phenomenal world. Some passages emphasize creation in very clear term.[16] On the other hand we do find passages which deny plurality and difference, and regard the Ultimate Principle viz. *Brahman* as the only reality.[17] This Ultimate Sentient Reality is said to be devoid of characteristics such as colour, taste, size, etc.[18] Now, most of the *Ācāryas* have interpreted this latter class of passages to mean that the phenomenal world cannot exist apart from *Brahman*, the Ultimate Reality of the nature of sentiency. *Brahman* is devoid of the characteristics found in the mudane world. The world has emerged from *Brahman*, and it is to *Brahman*, that the world owes its existence. So it is unwise to consider the world as absolutely non-existent. But on the other hand, there have been *Ācāryas* like Gauḍapāda and Śaṅkara, who interpreted these passages to mean that the one Ultimate Reality alone exists. It is neither a knower nor a doer. It is one without a second, eternally and absolutely unchanging; it alone is real, and nothing else exists. So naturally, the reality of the world is denied.

We cannot make the bold statement that the *Upaniṣads* declare that this world of appearance is a fiction. But they certainly have expressions and ideas which could be interpreted as leading to full-fledged Idealism. They contain glimmerings of Idealism, which shone forth brightly afterwards. Hence such passages can be interpreted as containing the germ of Idealism.

In the *Chāndogya Upaniṣad*, (VI.1), we find the view, which emphasizes that everything except the Supreme spirit is a modification, a verbal creation, but a name. This has been interpreted to mean that this phenomenal world, which contains duality, is a verbal creation; and hence it must be considered to be unreal. The Supreme self is the sole Reality.

In the sixth *Prapāṭhaka* of the *Chāndogya Upaniṣad*, Uddālaka instructs his son Śvetaketu about the Supreme Reality. He presents analogies of clay, gold, iron and their modifications as follows : "Just as, my dear, by one clod of clay, all that is made of clay becomes known, the modification being only a name arising from speech, while the truth is that it is just clay."[19] This signifies that clay is the only reality, and its transformations such as pot, jar, etc. are unreal, apart from their cause viz. clay. Various shapes viz. pot, jar etc. are nothing but clay only. Clay is the very essence, without which no pot, jar etc. exists. Clay always remains the same in its various transformations. Whether one calls a thing pot or jar; it is really clay. The same is the cause with the world of appearance, and its very essence, viz. the non-dual sentient Ultimate Reality. This phenomenal world is a modification, a verbal construct or a name, which does not exist independently without its very essence. It is the Ultimate Reality, which appears as the manifold world. So it can be said that this phenomenal world, a verbal modification is unreal independently of its very essence. The final cause alone is ultimately real.

In the third chapter namely, *Advaita Prakaraṇa* of the *Gauḍapādakārikā*, Gauḍapāda has mentioned these analogies of clay, iron etc.;[20] which could be interpreted to mean that there is no difference between the cause and effect, and hence both are real. This interpretation can be taken as supporting, what was later styled as *Pariṇāmavāda* the one cause modifying itself in the form of various effects; and this would not allow to say that the phenomenal world is unreal, an appearance only. But, Gauḍapāda, himself holds that the illustrations of clay, iron, etc. are meant to be stepping stones leading to the Ultimate Truth viz. the world is unreal and that they should not be taken at their face value.

All that could be said is that apart from the final cause, the phenomenal world has no reality. What is meant is that this manifold world does not exist independently of the Ultimate Reality. viz. *Brahman*, just as the various transformations of clay do not exist independently of clay. Perhaps this is what the *Upaniṣadic* thinker wanted to say; but the expression employed is such as could support the belief of the unreality of the world, which is regarded as a fiction, created by speech. We may consider it as a step ahead in the direction of Idealism.

The *Bṛhadāraṇyaka Upaniṣad* occupies a remarkable place in the history of early Indian thought. Its seer Yājñavalkya is thought to be a great Idealist.[21] According to Deussen, Yājñavalkya's Idealism is the very kernel of the *Upaniṣads*.[22] Yājñavalkya has gifted the greatest truth to human race, which is a land mark in the history of Indian Idealism. He says: "Verily, not for the sake of all is all dear but all is dear for the sake of the self."[23]

This could indicate that each and every human being perceives the external world according to his own liking, according to his own satisfaction. It is rightly said that the thing is not good or bad by itself. Its perceiver makes the thing good or bad. Spinoza has stated: "We desire nothing because it is good. We call it good, because we desire it."[24] This could mean that we like things not because the things are inherently dear, but we like them for our own pleasure, we love ourselves and love other things only for our sake. Goodness or badness does not reside in the thing, but depends on the mood of its perceiver. Both the primary qualities such as figure, solidity, motion, as well as the secondary qualities such as colour, sound, taste, smell, etc. remain in the mind of its perceiver.[25] The same thing is viewed differently by different persons. In the exhibition of photographs, each person likes photographs according to his taste. A book of philosophy gives pleasure to a philosopher; on the other hand, that very book is worthless for an uneducated person. Cruelty is avoided by a good person, while it gives pleasure as well as satisfcation to a cruel person. Thus goodness or badness is determined by our attitude and state of mind towards it. This may not challenge the reality of the basic thing, but certainly questions the validity of various characters especially goodness, badness, pleasantness etc. in the same thing. This passage can also be interpreted as signifying that things are dear by virtue of the *Ātman* which is their very essence. We like things as much as we like the *Ātman* our very essence. The *Upaniṣadic* seer could have also meant this, in which case it could not be interpreted as Subjective Idealism. Nevertheless the expression and even Śaṅkara's commentary on it[26] would lead us a step ahead in the direction of Subjective Idealism. It would be out of place to mention that there is a great resemblance between this expression of the *Bṛ. Up.* and ideas expressed by the Western philosopher — Berkeley, which has already been mentioned.

Now, in this very same *Upaniṣad,* there is a passage which states that this seeming duality does not appear when the Ultimate Truth is realised. In the second *adhyāya,* while instructing Maitreyī about the Supreme Reality, Yājñavalkya says, "Where there is duality as it were, there one sees another, smells another, hears another, addresses another, knows another, but where everything else has become one's self, how should one see anybody?[27]

This passage shows that when the Ultimate Reality is experienced, this world of appearance becomes as good as non-existent. The use of the word *iva* shows that duality does not exist as a matter of fact. Duality seems as if it exists. Such a state is experienced only during the state of self-realisation or of deep meditation. Nevertheless, this expression certainly favours the onward march towards Idealism; and it has been accordingly interpreted by later thinkers.

In the *Kaṭhopaniṣad,* this very idea is expressed very clearly. It is stated, "Whoever perceives anything like manyness here, goes from death to death."[28] This suggests that non-dual sentiency alone is the Ultimate Reality. Nothing else exists apart from the Supreme Entity.

Besides, the *Aitareya Upaniṣad* puts forth an Idealistic thought in the third *adhyāya,* where it is said, "This god Brahmā, and this God Indra . . . these five great elements . . . creatures born from the egg, from the womb, and from perspiration, sprouting plants, horses, cows, men, elephants and whatsoever breathes, whether moving or flying, and in addition, whatsoever is immovable; all this is led by intellect, and is supported on intellect. The world is led by intellect. Intellect is the support. Intellect is the highest Reality."[29] Here, the intellect is considered as a cosmic power, from which the universe has emerged. According to Belvalkar and Ranade this passage is replete with Idealism,[30] and provides a root for the *Vijñānavāda.*[31]

The term *Prajñā* perhaps signifies consciousness in an

individual, and consciousness is *Brahman*. Nevertheless, Idealistic thinkers could interpret such passages as propounding the unreality of the world which is but a projection of the intellect. Such passage pave the way to Idealistic thought, and the view that the phenomenal world is devoid of Reality.

Thus, in the *Upaniṣads,* one is taken a step ahead in the direction of the progress of Idealism. Later Idealistic thinkers could interpret such passages as propounding the unreality of the world of appearance.

It would not be out of place to examine the concept of *Māyā*, as used in the *Upaniṣads.* Here, we would not like to enter into details as to when and where the word *Māyā* is used for the first time. The word *Māyā* is used in various ways. It is used in the sence of 'uncommon intellectual power'. in the *Bṛ. Up.* where it is stated, "Through *Māyā*, Indra assumed various forms."[32] Generally, in early Indian thought, the word *Māyā*. is used in the sense of extraordinary power of God. It does not have the sense of illusion. Gradually, the word acquired the meaning of illusion, and the power to give rise to illusion.[33]

The philosophical concept of *Māyā* is clearly found in the *Śvetāśvatara Upaniṣad*. It is stated, "*Māyin* (God) creates all this universe, and the other (the individual self) is confined by *Māyā*."[34] Here, the word *Māyā* is used in the sense of 'extraordinary power'. Furthermore it is stated, "Know then that *Prakṛti* is *Māyā* and the wielder of *Māyā* is the great Lord. This whole world is pervaded by beings that are parts of Him."[35] According to A.B. Keith, the word *Māyā* in this verse expresses the sense of illusion. He says, "The *Śvetāśvatara* certainly does not mean that God is a real creator and that matter is his real creation; the sense of delusion or illusion is paramount."[36] It is difficult to agree with Keith though this would be a great leap in the direction of Idealism. *Māyā* can be taken here also in its original sense, the power of God which serves as the original matter out of which the phenomenal world is created and God is the wielder of this *Māyā*. Nevertheless, it is noteworthy that the individual soul is said to be confined by *Māyā*, which is a power of the Lord serves to hamper and confine the individual soul.

Now, so far as the concept of creation is concerned, the *Bṛ. Up.* IV. 3.10 is interesting. It is started, "There are no chariots, nor animals to be yoked to them, no roads but he created (projects for himself) chariots, animals to be yoked to them and roads. There are no joys, no pleasures, no delights, but he creates joys, pleasures and delights. There are no tanks, no lotus pools, no rivers, but he creates tanks, lotus pools and rivers. He, indeed, is the agent (maker or creator)."[37] Thus, the *Jīva* is said to create or imagine the dream world. When no such objects really exist.[38] Here a curiosity may arise : As the *Jīva* creates the dream world, similarly, could it not create the waking world also? But it is not possible to get its answer from the *Upaniṣads* as such inquiries came later.

Idealistic Views Expressed in some minor *Upaniṣads*

Some minor *Upaniṣads* have some passages, that seem to propound the unreality of the phenomenal world. It may be mentioned that this is not meant to suggest that these fall immediately in the line of the development of Idealistic thought. They are much later, but are considered here only inasmuch as they are termed *Upaniṣads* and so that their divergent trend is later *Upanisạdic* thought could be properly noticed.

We have seen that the major *Upaniṣads* emphasize the non-dual Ultimate sentient Reality, and thus they can be said to be idealistic in the broad sense of the term. There are a few passages which can be interpreted as declaring the world as unreal and merely a fiction of the mind. There is no doubt that the *Upaniṣads* deny the seeming diversity of this phenomenal world, apart from *Brahman*.

Besides these major *Upaniṣads* there are some minor *Upaniṣads*, which seem to contain scattered glimmerings of Idealism in the sense that the objective world is unreal.

It is difficult to say anything specifically about the date of these minor *Upaniṣads*. Jadunath Sinha says, "Hence the minor *Upaniṣads* cover a period of several centuries from the third century to the seventh century or later".[39] Perhaps, for this reason they seem to be influenced by Buddhistic thought.

Here, we shall discuss some of these *Upaniṣads,* which could help us in tracing the *Dṛṣṭi-Sṛṣṭi-vāda.* Of course, they do not emphasize this concept clearly, but they have some expressions, which can lead us onwards in the direction of the *Dṛṣṭi-Sṛṣṭi-vāda.*

The *Tejobindu Upaniṣad* shows considerable development towards a bold type of Idealism, which stresses the sole reality of the Supreme self. It reiterates that everything is just consciousness and nothing else.[40] So, from the highest point of view, everything other than the self is negated. Even the scriptures, bondage, liberation, happiness, sorrow etc. do not exist.[41] It says, "This phenomenal world does not exist. Whatever is of the form of perception and perceived, is unreal like the horns of hare."[42] While denying the world, it emphasizes the great role of the mind in the world construction.[43] It also states that sound, touch, form, taste, colour, the five sheaths, the waking, dreaming and dreamless sleep are products of the mind.[44]

In the sixth *adhyāya,* the *Tejobindu Upaniṣad* has boldly denounced the reality of the world. It has very clearly stated, "If anything exists except *Brahman,* it is unreal (*mithyā*) like mirage water. If anyone fears because of the statement of a barren woman's son, then a thing exists."[45] Further, presenting the analogies of hare's horn, *gandharvanagara,* mother of pearl, rope-snake, etc. It has emphasized the unreality of the world.[46]

We find a few verses in the *Yogaśikhopaniṣad* also regarding the unreality of the world. They put forth the similes of *gandharvanagara,* phantom, double moon, barren woman's son, mirage etc. to explain the unreality of the world.[47] Whatever appears, is *Brahman* only. So obviously the world apart from *Brahman* is unreal like a barren woman's son or mirage-water.

We may say that some of the minor *Upaniṣads* contain much thought of the type of Idealism, which strongly denies the reality of the phenomenal world. Perhaps under Buddhistic influence, these minor *Upaniṣads* have emphasized the rule of the mind (*citta*) as a creative factor so far as the concept of world creation is concerned. In the later *Upaniṣads,* we find a clear-cut distinction between the two rival trends of philosophy, namely — Realism and Idealism. No doubt, none of the *Upaniṣads* asserts the reality of the world apart from the Ultimate Reality viz. *Brahman,* and in this sense they plainly put forth Idealism.

Thus it may concluded that in the early *Upaniṣads* especially the major *Upaniṣads,* which are believed to be pre-Buddhistic, do not find much to support the unreality of the world. As Dasgupta states in *Indian Idealism,* "On the whole the central doctrine of the *Upaniṣadic* philosophy seems to be an Idealism of a mystical type, in which the Innermost Self is regarded as the highest Reality, from which the world has somehow come into being or of which the world is a manifestation, and which is also somehow to be regarded as the inner controller of all natural forces."[48]

Hence, the main purport of the *Upaniṣads* is to declare the Ultimate Reality as the original cause and the sole ruling force of the universe. In this sense they are Idealistic in thought. But the type of Idealism is not found, which holds the world to be unreal like a mirage, as this is a later philosophical development. Nevertheless, we do find some expressions which can serve as a germinal force, and which sprouted forth in full bloom as Subjective Idealism at a later stage. Some of the later minor *Upaniṣads* propound Idealism and stress the unreality of the world-phenomena, both personal and universal. But since these seem to be of quite a later date, they would not be of much help in tracing the development of Idealistic thought immediately after the *Upaniṣadic* period. Neverthless, the Idealistic thoughts contained in them are interesting inasmuch as they herald the entry, into the Brāhmaṇical or *Vedāntic* current of philosophy, of Idealistic thought which denies outright the reality of the world-phenomena. These *Upaniṣads* would provide a complete picture along with the *Yoga-Vāsiṣṭha* and *Gauḍapādakārikā.*

References

1. एकं सद् विप्रा बहुधा वदन्ति।

   Ṛgveda I. 164.46.

2. सहस्रशीर्षा पुरूषः सहस्राक्षः सहस्रपात् ।
   स भूमिं विश्वतो वृत्वात्यतिष्ठद्दशाङ्गुलम् ॥१॥
   पुरूष एवेदं सर्वं यद्भूतं यच्च भव्यम् ।
   एतावानस्य महिमातो ज्यायाँश्च पुरूषः ।
   पादोऽस्य विश्वो भूतानि त्रिपादस्यामृतं दिवि ॥३॥

   Ṛgveda X. 90.

   Velankar, H. D., Ṛksūktaśatī, English Translation, pp. 277-78 (1972), Bharatiya Vidya Bhavan.

3. हिरण्यगर्भः समवर्तताग्रे भूतस्य जातः पतिरेक आसीत् ।
   स दधार पृथिवीं द्यामुतैमां कस्मै देवाय हविषा विधेम ॥१॥

   Ṛgveda X. 121.1.

   Velankar's Translation, p. 294.

4. *Atharvaveda* X.7, 8.

5. Keith, A. B., *Religion and Philosophy of the Veda and the Upaniṣads*, Vol. 32, Ch. 26, p. 435 (1970), Motilal Banarsidass.

6. नासदासीन्नो सदासीत् ।

   Ṛgveda X.129.1 (ab).

7. आनीदवातं स्वधया तदेकं तस्माद्धान्यन्न परः किं चनास ॥

   Ṛgveda X 129.2 (cd).

8. तम आसीतमसा गूलहमग्रे ....

   Ṛgveda X 129.3 (ab).

   Velankar's Translation, p. 300.

9. कामस्तदग्रे समवर्तताधि मनसो रेतः प्रथमं यदासीत् ।

   Ṛgveda x. 129.4

10. Sāyaṇa on *Ṛgveda* X.129.4.

11. इयं विसृष्टिर्यत आबभूव यदि वा दधे यदि वा न ।
    यो अस्याध्यक्षः परमे व्योमन् सो अङ्ग वेद यदि वा न वेद ॥७॥

    Ṛgveda X. 129.7

    Velankar's Translation, p. 302.

12. Deussen Paul, *The Philosophy of the Upaniṣads*, Ch. IX, p. 227, (Reprint, 1980) Banarasidass & Co.

13. Radhakrishnan, *Indian Philosophy*, Vol. I, Ch. IV, p. 186, (Eighth Impression, 1958), George Allen & Unwin.

14. Dasgupta, S. N., *History of Indian Philosophy*, Vol. II, Ch.III, p. 39 (1975), Motilal Banarsidass.

15. *Ibid.* Footnote on p. 39.
    Belvalkar S.K., Ranade R.D., *History of Indian Philosophy (Creative period)*

Ch.III, p. 87, 2nd Edition (1974), Oriental Reprint.

16. तस्माद्वा एतस्मादात्मनः आकाशः संभूतः।

Tai. Up. II.1.

स इमांल्लोकानसृजत।

Ait. Up. II.

स प्राणमसृजत प्राणच्छ्रद्धां खं वायुर्ज्योतिरापः पृथिवीन्द्रियं
मनोऽन्नमन्नाद्वीर्यं तपो मन्त्राः कर्म लोका लोकेषु च नाम च ॥४॥

Praśna. Up. VI. 4.

17. मनसैवेदमाप्तव्यं नेह नानास्ति किंचन ।
मृत्योः स मृत्युं गच्छति य इह नानेव पश्यति ॥२२॥

Kaṭha Up. II.1.11.

सर्वं खलु इदम् ब्रह्म ।

Chā.Up. III 14-1.

वाचारम्भणं विकारो नामधेयं मृत्तिकेत्यैव सत्यम् ।

Chā. Up. VI.1.4.

सदेव सौम्येदमग्र आसीदेकमेवाद्वितीयम् ।

Chā. Up. VI.2.1.

18. अशब्दमस्पर्शमरुपमव्ययं तथाऽरस्यं नित्यमगन्धवच्च यत् ॥

Kaṭha. Up. 1.3.15 (ab).

19. यथा सौम्येकेन मृत्पिण्डेन सर्वं मृण्मयं विज्ञातं
स्याद्वाचारम्भणं विकारो नामधेयं मृत्तिकेत्यैव सत्यम् ॥४॥

Chā. Up. VI. 1.4.

Radhakrishnan, (ed.), *The Principal Upaniṣads*, English Translation, pp. 446-47 (1953), George Allen & Unwin Ltd.

20. मृल्लोहविस्फुलिङ्गाद्यैः सृष्टिर्या चोदितान्यथा ।
उपायः सोऽवताराय नास्ति भेदः कथञ्चन ॥१५॥

G. K. III.15.

21. "The teaching of Yājñavalkya is a daring, uncompromising, essentric idealism . . ."
Deussen, Paul, *The Philosophy of the Upaniṣads*, Ch. XVII, p. 399 (1972), Oriental Publishers.

22. Radhakrishnan, (ed.), *Principal Upanisads*, Ch.XIII, p. 84 (1953), George Allen & Unwin;
Hiriyanna, M., *Outline of Indian Philosophy*, Ch. II, p. 60 (Fourth Impression, 1958), George Allen & Unwin.

23. न वा अरे सर्वस्य कामाय सर्वं प्रियं भवत्यात्मनस्तु कामाय सर्वं प्रियं भवति ॥

Bṛ. Up. II. 4-5.

24, Durrant, Will, *Pleasures of Philosophy*, Ch. XIII, pp. 192-93 (1952).

25. Berkeley's Point of View.

26. तस्मात् लोकप्रसिद्धमेतदात्मैव प्रियो नान्यत्......
तस्मादात्मप्रीतिसाधनत्वाद्गौणी अन्यत्र प्रीतिरात्मन्येव मुख्या ।

Śaṅkara's Com. on *Bṛ. Up.* II 4-5. p. 760;

Ten Principal Upaniṣads (1978), Motilal Banarsidass.

27. यत्र हि द्वैतमिव भवति तदितरं इतरं जिघ्रति तदितर इतरं पश्यति ।

Bṛ. Up. II. 4.14.

28. मृत्योः स मृत्युमाप्नोति य इह नानैव पश्यति।

Kaṭha Up. II 10 (cd).

29. एष ब्रह्मैष इंद्र एष प्रजापतिरेते सर्वे देवा इमानि च पंच महाभूतानि पृथिवी वायुराकाश आपो ज्योतींषीत्येतानीमानि च क्षुद्रमिश्राणीव बीजानीतराणि चेतराणि चाण्डजानि च जारुजानि च स्वेदजानि चोद्भिज्जानि चाश्वागावः पुरूषा हस्तिनो यत्किंचेदं प्राणि जंगमं च पतत्रि च यच्च सथावरं सर्व तत्प्रज्ञानेत्र प्रज्ञाने प्रतिष्ठितं प्रज्ञानेत्रो लोकः प्रज्ञाप्रतिष्ठा प्रज्ञानं ब्रह्म ।।३।।

Ait. Up. IV 3.

30. Belvalker, S.K. and Ranade, R.D., *History of Indian Philosophy*, Ch. V, p. 164 (1974), Oriental Reprint.

31. Ranade, R.D., *A Constructive Survey of Upaniṣadic Philosophy*, Ch.IV, p. 181 (1926), Oriental Book Agency, Poona.

32. इन्द्रो मायाभिः पुरुरूप इयते ।

Bṛ. Up. II.5.19.

33. अस्मान्मायी सृजते विश्वमेतत्तस्मिंश्चान्यो मायया संनिरूद्धः ।

Śve. Up. IV.8 (cd).

34. Shastri, Prabhudatta, *Doctrine of Māyā*, (Luzac, 1911); Solomon, E.A., *Avidyā, A problem of Truth and Reality* (first edition, 1969), Gujarat University, Ahmedabad.

35. मायां तु प्रकृतिं विद्यान्मायिनं तु महेश्वरम् ।
तस्यावयवभूतेस्तु व्याप्तं सर्वमिदं जगत् ।।१०।।

Śve. Up. IV. 10.

36. Keith, A.B., *Religion and Philosophy of the Veda and the Upaniṣad*, Vol. 32, Ch.28, p. 532 (1970), Motilal Banarsidass.
Radhakrishnan, (ed.), *History of Philosophy : Eastern and Western*, Vol. I, Ch.III, p. 67 (1952), George Allen & Unwin.

37. न तत्र रथा न रथयोगा न पंथानो भवन्त्यथ रथान्रथयोगान्पथः सृजते न तत्रानंदा मुदः प्रमुदो भवन्त्यथानंदान्मुदः प्रमुदः सृजते न तत्र वेशान्ताः पुष्करिण्यः स्रवन्त्यौ भवन्त्यथ वेशान्ता पुष्करिणीः स्रवन्तीः सृजते स हि कर्ता ।।

Bṛ. Up. IV. 3. 10.

38. Śaṅkarācārya is apt to regard the *Jīva* (individual soul) as the creator of the dream world. Of course, he bows to the traditional view and says that God can be regarded as the creator of even the dream inasmuch as he is the monitor of all.

Bṛ. Sū. Śāṅkara Bhāṣya, III, 2.4.

39. Sinha, Jadunath, *History of Indian Philosophy*, Vol. I, Ch. III, p. 124 (1956), Sinha Publishing House, Calcutta.

40. *Tejo. Up.* II, IV, V.

41. *Tejo. Up.* V. 43, 44.

42. इदं प्रपञ्चं यत्किंचिद्यद्यज्जगति विद्यते ।
दृश्यरूपं च दृग्रूपं सर्वं शशविषाणवत् ॥७५॥
Tejo. Up. V. 75.

43. *Tejo. Up.* V. 98-105.

44. स्पर्शो रूपं रसं गन्धं कोशाः पञ्च मनोभवाः ।
जाग्रत्स्वप्नसुषुप्त्यादि मनोमयमितीरितम् ॥१०३॥
Tejo. Up. V. 103.

45. मत्तोऽन्यदस्ति चेन्मिथ्या यथा मरुमरीचिका ।
वन्ध्याकुमारवचने भीतिश्चेदस्ति किंचन ॥७३॥
Tejo. Up. VI. 73.

46. *Tejo. Up.* VI. 74-99.

47. यथैव शून्यो वेतालो गन्धर्वाणां पुरं यथा ।
यथाकाशे द्विचन्द्रत्वं तद्वत्सत्ये जगत्स्थितिः ॥१६॥
जगन्नाम्ना चिदाभाति सर्वं ब्रह्मैव केवलम् ।
यथा वन्ध्यासुतो नास्ति तथा नास्ति मरौ जलम् ॥१८॥
Yoga Up. IV. 16, 18.

48. Dasgupta, S.N., *Indian Idealism*, Ch. III, pp, 54-55, (1962), Cambridge.

2

Idealistic Thought in the *Brahma-Sūtra*

THE *Upaniṣads* present the views of different philosophical thinkers and thus offer glimpses of early Indian thought, but not one clear-cut *Vedāntic* thought. After that period, it was Bādarāyaṇa, who interpreted and brought together the *Vedāntic* thought in the form of aphorisms, giving it the shape of a system of philosophical thought. This work, which focuses on the main rudiments of the *Vedāntic* thought, is known as the *Brahma-sūtra.*

Brahman, the *Jīva* and its nature, its relation to *Brahman,* the creation of the world, attainment of knowledge, the means of liberation and its process are the topics which are dealt with on the basis of the *Upaniṣads*. Besides, the refutation of the other Indian systems viz. *Sāṁkhya, Vaiśeṣika,* Buddhism, Jaina, Śaivism and others also form a part of the *Brahma-sūtra.*

About the date of the *Brahma-sūtra* Dasgupta writers, "It is difficult to ascertain the time when the *Brahma-sūtra* were written, but since they contain a refutation of almost all the other Indian systems, even of the *Śūnyavāda,* they cannot have been written very early. I think it may not be far from the truth in supposing that they were written sometime in the second century B.C."[1]

It becomes rather difficult to take out the precise meaning of the *Sūtras* without the help of commentary. Various *ācāryas* have commented upon them from their point of view.

Prima facie, most of the *Sūtras* seem to present the Realistic view in general. In the second *adhyāya*, the process of creation is described.[2] It is stated that at first *ākāśa* was created, then *vāyu* was created. After that, *tejas, āp* and *pṛthivī* were created. And at the time of dissolution, they dissolve in the reverse order.

The *sūtrakāra* has not denied the Objective Reality of the world. While refuting *Yogācāra* Buddhism (Subjective Idealism) he has stated, "The non-existence (of external objects) cannot be maintained on account of perception.[3] Furthermore, he has differentiated the waking state from the dreaming state.[4] Thus, he does not seem to deny the Objective Reality of the world. Besides, several *Sūtras* of the third and the fourth *adhyāyas* reveal the realistic view while presenting the actual process of getting liberation. From this it appears that the *sūtrakāra* himself believes that bondage and liberation actually take place accordingly. In the fourth chapter of the fourth *adhyāya*, while describing the state of a released soul, it is stated, "In the presence (of a body the fulfilment of desire is) as in the waking state."[5] This signifies that in the waking state, the body, the sense-organs, mind and the objects of enjoyment are all real. Thus Bādarāyaṇa clearly holds that there is the existence of objects of the external world, apart from their perception. In short, they cannot be believed to be unreal. But at the same time they are not the Ultimate Reality, which *Brahman* alone is.

Idealistic Views of the *Brahma-Sūtra*

There are a few *Sūtras* which assert the non-dual consciousness viz. *Brahman* as the Ultimate Reality. And in this respect, they come close to Idealism, as Idealism believes in Sentient Reality from which everything emerges.

The *Brahma-sūtra* admits the non-dual spiritual Reality viz. *Brahman* as the cause of the origination, sustentation and destruction of this universe.[6] This manifold world emerges from *Brahman*, it persists in *Brahman* and is dissolved in *Brahman*. *Brahman* is considered to be the material as well as the efficient cause of the world.[7] *Brahman* itself in the material cause from which this world is created, and it is the efficient cause also, in as much as it creates the world. This universe results from *Brahman*.[8]

Thus the *Brahman-sūtra* clearly emphasizes *Brahman* as the Ultimate Sentient Reality. But this does not mean that the phenomenal world and souls are unreal or illusory.

In the third chapter of the second *adhyāya,* after describing the systematic process of the creation of the five elements, the *sūtrakāra* turns his attention towards the *Jīva* (individual self). The question may arise as to whether like these five elements, The *Jīva* is created or not. The *sūtrakāra* declares that the *Jīva* is not created because the scriptures declare it to be eternal (*Nitya*).[9] The *Jīva* is a knower, i.e., sentient.[10] It is stated that the *Jīva* is a part (*aṁśa*) of the lord on account of the statements regarding the difference of the individual soul from *Brahman* as also among themselves. But they are not absolutely different from *Brahman*. Some (recensions of the *vedas*) record that (*Brahman*) is of the nature of slaves, fishers and so on,[11] which shows that *Brahman* assumes the from of the individual souls; which are non-different from *Brahman*. *Ācāryas* have interpreted this *sūtra* according to their own philosophical views. Śaṅkara has inserted the term *iva* after *aṁśa* to derive a meaning in accordance with *Kevalādvaita*. Rāmānuja holds that the souls are in reality parts of *Brahman,* in the sense that they are the qualifiers of *Brahman*. He upholds their reality. On the other hand, Nimbārka emphasizes that the *Jīva* is different as well as non-different from *Brahman*. The *sūtrakāra* also seems to hold this view later known as the *svābhāvika-bhedābhedavāda* (Doctrine of difference and non-difference both being natural).

Now, so far as the reality or the unreality of the *Jīva* is concerned, another *Sūtra* namely. *Ābhāsa eva ca* is noteworthy.[12] It would not be out of place to mention the different views of the *ācāryas* regarding this *Sūtra*. Śaṅkara, while explaining this *Sūtra,* interprets the word *Ābhāsa* as signifying 'unreality' and presents the analogy of the reflection. The reflection of the sun in one vessel of water may be moving as the water is moving. But the actual sun remains unaffected. The reflection of the sun in other vessels full of water also does not move. So the sun appearing on the water is just an appearance and not the real one.[13] Similarly, *Brahman* is not affected by the seeming affliction of the individual soul, nor is one soul affected by the happiness or misery of another. On the other hand, Bhāskara, negates the view of Śaṅkara and criticises it. Rāmānuja interprets the word *Ābhāsa* as *hetvābhāsa*. Vallabha does not take the *Jīva* as unreal and emphasizes that the *Jīva* is known as *Ābhāsa* of *Brahman* so far as its virtue of Bliss is suppressed.

We can only state here that whatever the interpretation of this *Sūtra* be, its main concern seems to be to show that *Brahman* is the only reality and everything else apart from it is just an appearance. As E. A. Solomon states, "The intention is to show that *Brahman* is the Ultimate Reality and everything else visualised apart from it, is merely an appearance."[14]

We cannot get a clear idea as to what was in the mind of the *sūtrakāra* as the *ācāryas* have tried to interpret the *sūtra* according to their point of view. But the *sūtrakāra* does not seem to propound the unreality of the *Jīvas* (individual souls).

In the third *adhyāya*, there are *sūtras* about the dreaming state. The first *sūtra* seems to present the view of *Pūrva Pakṣa*. "In the intermediate state there is creation, because the *śruti* says so."[15] But in answer to this it is stated, "But (the dream world) is a mere illusion, on account of its nature not being manifest in its totality."[16] Here, for the first time the word *Māyā* is used. According to the *sūtrakāra*, the dream world is merely *Māyā*, an appearance only. It would be essential to state that eventhough the sord *Māyā* is used, it only indicates illusory character of the things of the dreaming state and not the unreality of the external world, that is experienced during the waking state. It may be mentioned that Rāmānuja even here explains the word *Māyā* as signifying extraordinary power and its creation.

Thus it may be surmised that in the *Brahmasūtra*, there is no hint that could lead towards a view which regards the external world as unreal. The *Sutrakāra* has not stated a word against the Objective Reality of the phenomenal world. So he does not seem to be in favour of its unreality. Since the concept of the unreality of the external world is a later development, which took place under the spell of the full-fledged *Yogācāra* Idealism, naturally it is not found in the *Brahmasūtra*.

References

1. Dasgupta, S.N., *History of Indian Philosophy*, Vol. I, Ch.X. p.418 (1975), Motilal Banarsidass.
2. *Br. Sū.* II, 3.1-15.
3. नाभाव उपलब्धेः ।
   Br. Sū. II. 2. 28.
4. वैधर्म्याच्च न स्वप्नादिवत् ।
   Br. Sū. II, 2.29.
5. भावे जाग्रद्वत् ।
   Br. Sū. IV. 4.14.
6. जन्माद्यस्य यतः ।
   Br. Sū. I.1.2.
7. प्रकृतिश्च प्रतिज्ञादृष्टान्तानुपरोधात् ।
   Br. Sū. I.4.23.
8. आत्मकृतेः परिणामात्।
   Br. Sū. I.4.26.
   योनिश्च हि त्रीयते ।
   Br. Sū. I.4.27.
9. नात्मा श्रुतेनित्यत्वाच्च ताभ्यः ।
   Br. Sū. II, 3.17.
10. ज्ञोऽत एव ।
    Br. Sū. II. 3.18.
11. अंशो नानाव्यपदेशादन्यथा चापि दाशकितवादित्वमधीयत एके ।
    Br. Sū. II. 3.43.
12. *Br. Sū.* II. 3.50.
13. This has led some later thinkers to say that Śaṅkara recognised the *Pratibimbavāda*.
14. Solomon, E. A., *Avidyā — A Problem of Truth and Reality*, Ch.III, p.120 (1969), Gujarat University, Ahmedabad.
15. संध्ये सृष्टिराह हि ।
    Br. Sū. III. 2. 1.
16. मायामात्रं तु कात्स्र्त्येनानभिव्यक्तस्वरूपत्वात् ।
    Br. Sū. III. 2. 3.

3

Idealistic Thought in the *Mādhyamika* and the *Vijñānavāda* Schools of Buddhism

IN spite of the risk of going astray from *Dṛṣṭi-Sṛṣṭi-vāda,* Buddhism — especially *Mahāyāna* Buddhism which is clearly Idealistic — has been examined here. So far as the unreality of the worldly phenomena is concerned, the philosophical schools of *Mahāyāna* Buddhism, namely the *Mādhyamika (Śūnyavāda)* and the *Yogācāra (Vijñānavāda)* propound it forcefully.

The continuous chain of birth and death, sorrow etc. compels a person to think about the substantiality of human life and the world in which one lives. Any sensitive mind would experience that nothing in this world remains permanent. Animate bodies are born only to die. Green leaves on a tree are fast seen changing into dryness. Even non-animate substances perish. In short, everything in this world keeps on changing continuously and rushing towards its ultimate destiny — viz. extinction.

Influenced by the hard facts of human life such as birth, pain, sorrow, death etc. Buddha renounced worldly life in search of truth. Buddha's way of solving the riddle of life was not Objective but rather Subjective.[1] The main concept on the basis of which the Pāli canon and later works announce the world as essenceless and impermanent is of "dependent origination"—(*pratītya samutpāda*); which we shall examine later on.

In this chapter, our study is confined to examine Idealistic thought in the *Mādhyamika* as well as in the *Yogācāra* schools to determine to what extent it could be said to be allied to the *Dṛṣṭi-Sṛṣṭi-vāda* of *Vedāntic* thought.

As a result of realistic, logical, critical and psychological ways of thinking; Buddhism is found to be split up into the — *Vaibhāṣika,* the *Sautrāntika,* the *Mādhyamika* and the *Yogācāra* schools of philosophical thought. Amongst these four trends, since the *Vaibhāṣika* and the *Sautrāntika* schools admit in some form the reality of the external world, they do not enter into the realm of our inquiry, and, hence, the other two schools are to be appropriately studied.

Mādhyamika Buddhism

Nāgārjuna (100 A.D.), the pioneer exponent of the *Mādhyamika School (Śūnyavāda),* has established the external world or rather everything as essenceless with his unique dialectic. He recognises neither the *Śāśvatavāda,* nor the *Ucchedavāda* but follows the middle path that reality is neither positive nor negative.[2] A thing is not explained either by itself or by any other entity. As everything is relative and has dependent origination, it is necessarily essenceless and indescribable.

It has been stated before that the theory of 'dependent origination' is the main basis, on which the concept of the unreality of the phenomenal world is formed. That is to say, not a single thing exists independently but always depends on some other factors for its existence. To find out a possible solution for the mundane life, Buddha preached the twelve-fold chain of causation that this *saṁsāra* appears due to *Avidyā,* depending on which *saṁskāra, vijñāna, nāmarūpa, ṣaḍāyatanas,. sparśa, vedanā, tṛṣṇā, upādāna, bhava, jāti-jarā-maraṇa* come-about. In this way, the vicious circle of birth and death goes on.

Widening the scope of this theory of dependent origination, it can be understood that one thing is known and established in relation to another. So things do not seem to have any distinct existence or character or nature of their own. And what does not exist independently, cannot be a real thing. From this point of view, it becomes difficult to put the world of appearance under the category of reality. A chair is known as a chair due to its relation with a table; and the table is known as a table, due to its relation with a chair. And a chair or table is so known in relation to the person sitting on or at it. In this context it is stated in *Indian Idealism* — " . . . without making any reference to any other entity no entity is intelligible by itself. That being so, every entity involves all other entities for its own support."[3] Thus, all the things are dependent and relative. A line is considered as big or small only in relation to another line. If a bigger line is put next to it, it is considered as a small line; while it is considered as a big line, if a smaller line is beside it. Besides, its being a line also is in relation to other things. Thus all concepts are interdependent. Moreover, the very same entity is looked upon differently in different circumstances. A fire seems soothing in winter, while in summer it is unbearable. Hence, all the things are relative, and so are essenceless. Things do not possess a character of their own; but appear relatively, or their conception is always relative. And this is the reason, why things should be considered unreal.

On the basis of relativity, Nāgārjuna establishes the essencelessness (*niḥsvabhāvatā*) of all entities. In the *Madhyamaka Kārikā,* Nāgārjuna has demolished the reality of each and every phenomenon such as causality, motion, time, space, 'thinghood', qualities, relations, attributes, substance, soul, God, *nirvāṇa* etc. on the basis of dependent origination.

Some of the concepts put forth in the *Madhyamaka Kārikā;* which may have connection with the topic we discussed below.

Rejection of the Theory of Causation

The theory of Causation has no place in the realm of Idealism. It is noteworthy that the Buddhistic Idealism as well as the *Vedāntic* Idealism reject the theory of Causation in their own ways. On the one hand, the *Mādhyamika* School of Buddhism refutes it on the very basis of logic, while *Kevalādvaita Vedānta* negates it taking the metaphysical standpoint. That is to say, as *Kevalādvaita Vedānta* emphasizes that nothing exists apart from the eternally unchanging Ultimate Spiritual Reality viz. *Brahman,* nothing is ever born. Of course, the very same argument is put forth by the *Mādhyamika* School. But there is this difference that it does not admit any permanent reality.

In the *Madhyamaka Kārikā*, Nāgārjuna has forcefully demolished the theory of causation, while establishing the doctrine of no-origination. At the very outset he declares, "There is neither destruction, nor production, neither nihilism nor eternalism; there is neither unity nor plurality; neither coming in nor going out."[4]

After putting forth the main thesis of his work, Nāgārjuna proceeds to refute the theory of Causation — "Never and nowhere can anything be produced. A thing can originate neither out of itself nor out of not-self nor out of both nor out-of neither."[5] A thing, which is already existent, has no purpose for re-origination from itself. On the other hand, it does not originate from something else, as there is absence of the other thing.[6]

Nāgārjuna shows the uselessness of finding out the cause : "The talk of finding out the cause of ever-existing and non-existing objects, is illogical. If a thing is non-existing, whose cause is to be found out? And if it is ever-existing, what is the use of cause?"[7] That is to say, if a thing is ever-existing, then there is no use of establishing its cause, as the thing is already there. On the other hand, if a thing is non-existing, it is futile to seek out its cause. There is no use of finding out the cause of a round square, as it is not existing. Hence, it is not possible to establish any theory of causality. The theories of causality that the propounded by the different schools of philosophical thought cannot stand the test of Reason.

Further, the author explains that the effect cannot be present in the cause. "The effect does not remain in the causes singly or in their totality. Hence how can an effect arise from a cause, where it did not remain?"[8] Further it is stated, "And if the effect (which is not found to exist in the causes) can be imagined as arising out of causes, then why should not the effect arise out of non-causes?"[9] Nāgārjuna very cleverly states that the effect, which does not exist in the cause, cannot be produced. Suppose it is imagined as being produced from the cause, then it can as well be stated that the effect arises from non-cause. Nāgārjuna then shows the logical inconsistency of the theory of Causation: "An effect is of the nature of cause and a cause is not of its own nature. How can an effect coming from one, that is not of its own nature be said to be full of the nature of the cause."[10] While concluding he asserts, "Thus effect is neither constructed of the cause, nor different from cause. In the absence of an effect therefore the problem of cause and non-cause cannot arise at all."[11] In other words, it is not possible to establish the nature of cause and effect. From the logical point of view, the relation of cause and effect is inexplicable, and relative.

On the basis of relativity and inexplicability; Nāgārjuna thus rejects the theory of Causation. In no way could the theory of Causation be established. It may be noted that the rejection of the theory of Causation can culminate in the doctrine of non-origination or Acosmism (*Ajātivāda*).

We shall see in a later chapter that Gauḍapāda perhaps under the great influence of Nāgārjuna's way of thinking has forcefully rejected the theory of Causation and has established *Ajātivāda* in his *Gauḍapādakārikā*.

Thus, the logical refutation of the theory of Causation leads one to negate production. That is to say, as the cause-effect relation is impossible to establish, it is also not possible to be sure about production of things. Then what about the creation of the world? The answer to this question would compel to conclude logically that it must be unreal and as fictitious as *Māyā*, dream, *gandhrvanagara* etc. It is said, "Things do not exist, nor are they produced or destroyed. Origination, existence and destruction are of the nature of *Māā*, dreams or *gandharvanagara*."[12]

Confutation of all Concepts

Not only the theory of Causation, but every phenomenon is demolished by Nāgārjuna.

No one is able to find out who was in the beginning of the

world, and what is at its end also cannot be determined. Thus, the world is regarded as beginningless and endless. Very rationally Nāgārjuna states, "If a thing does not have a beginning and an end, it cannot have a middle also."[13] Thus, a thing is clearly established as unreal. On this very basis, Nāgārjuna emphasizes all things as middleless and hence as unreal. "Not only is the Mundane existence beginningless; but all objects are beginningless and hence middleless and endless."[14]

As everything is relative, it becomes devoid of reality. So every phenomenal entity is compared with a dream, *gandharvanagara* etc. "Afflictions, actions, bodies, doers and results are like *gandharvanagara*, a mirage and a dream."[15]

Even Buddha (*Tathāgata*) is declared to the inexplicable by Nāgārjuna. While stating this, the author has put the nature of the world on a par with Buddha.[16]

Not only Buddha, but bondage and liberation are also stated to be relative and unreal. "There is no bondage and no liberation. Both are relative and unreal. When *saṁsāra* is not snatched away nor *nirvāṇa* superimposed, then why should they both be imagined."[17] Thus, Nāgārjuna states the uselessness of imagining bondage as well as liberation.

In short, the worldly phenomena are relative and as a result inexplicable. It is not possible to ascertain their exact nature. Hence, everything is declared to be unreal by Nāgārjuna.

Though everything is declared relative and unreal, Nāgārjuna does not condemn the world in all its aspects from the empirical standpoint. Only from the ultimate point of view he rejects the world. So, we can compare his philosophical views with Śaṅkara's philosophy; as Śaṅkara also accepts the empirical reality of the world and negates it from the ultimate standpoint.

Acceptance of two-fold Truth

In order to save the practical life of people from collapsing, the empirical reality of things is accepted by almost all the thinkers. Eventhough the world is considered unreal from the ultimate point of view, its empirical reality is admitted.

Nāgārjuna, in his *Mūla-Madhyamaka Kārikā* declares his acceptance of two-fold truth viz. *saṁvṛti satya* (empirical truth) and *pāramārthika satya* (Ultimate Truth). It is stated, "Buddha's instruction is based on two-fold truth, namely, *lokasaṁvṛti satya* (empirical truth) and *pāramārthika satya* (Ultimate Truth)."[18]

Here, Candrakīrti defines the term *Saṁvṛti* as "*Ajñāna* concealing the object from all the sides."[19] Thus, *Ajñāna* (Nescience) is the root-cause of the phenomenal dealings. (Only the concealing power of *Ajñāna* is emphasized here, and not its projecting power).

Emphasizing the importance of the two-fold truth it is stated, "Those, who do not recognise two-fold division of truth, they do not understand the deep essence of Buddha's instruction."[20]

Further, Nāgārjuna shows that it is not possible to dispense with the empirical truth. "The Ultimate Reality cannot be taught without resorting to the empirical usage, and without realising the Ultimate Reality, liberation is not gained."[21] So, it can be said that the empirical truth is a means to attain the knowledge of the Ultimate Reality. Candrakīrti states in his *Madhyamakakārikāvṛtti*, "Therefore, the empirical truth must be recognised as a means to the attainment of *nirvāṇa*, just as a person, who wants water, must have a pot for it."[22]

Thus, the empirical reality of the world is accepted by Nāgārjuna. Though he compares the worldly phenomena with *gandharvanagara*, dream, a mirage etc. he admits them from the common-sense point of view. From the ultimate point of view everything is essenceless, relative and unreal.

Now, if one tries to dig out an expression, that can lead towards the type of Idealism, which *Dṛṣṭi-Sṛṣṭi-vāda* emphasizes cannot get a satisfactory link. As a matter of fact, the *Mādhyamika* School did not want to establish any theory as no theory can stand the test of Reason and all theories are equally misleading. We shall see later on that *Dṛṣṭi-Sṛṣṭi-vāda* forcefully negates the empirical reality of the world; while the *Mādhyamika*-Buddhism does accept the conception of the empirical reality if only as a means to the attainment of liberation.

Nevertheless, as everything is considered relative and essenceless by its nature, such an expression can be regarded as leading one towards the unreal character of the world, which the *Dṛṣṭi-Sṛṣṭi-vāda* also establishes.

Yogācāra Buddhism : (Vijñānavāda)

Vijñānavāda was not a sudden outburst, rather the *Sautrāntika* School itself paved the way for *Vijñāavāda* by its theory of Representative Perception. As mentioned in *The Central Philosophy of Buddhism*, "The *Sautrāntika* by its insistence on the creative work of thought and the doctrine of Representative Perception directly led to the Idealism of the *Yogācāra*."[23]

Now, a question arises as to what is meant by 'Representative Perception'. It can be stated that, according to the *Sautrāntikas*, the phenomenal world is not directly perceived; but the existence of the world is inferred on the basis of its knowledge that we have. In the process of congnition, at first indefinite sensation (*nirvikalpa*) is produced; and then a definite image or idea (*savikalpaka*) about an object takes place.[24] Thus, we do not perceive a thing directly; but our mental images or ideas are imposed on it. On the basis of the Representative Perception of the *Sautrāntika* Buddhism the *Vijñānavāda* emphasises that the world does not exist independently of the mind. Our images or ideas alone construct the external world, or appear as if they were outside.

Such a type of Idealism resembles the views put forth in the *Dṛṣṭi-Sṛṣṭi-vāda.* The *Vijñānavāda* propounds Subjective Idealism that nothing exists independently of the mind. Whatever we perceive is imagined or constructed by the mind. This mode of thinking declares the outer objective world as unreal.

Some Idealistic views expressed in the *Laṅkāvatārasūtra,* the *Vijñaptimātratāsiddhi* and some other works; which seem to resemble the views put forth by the *Dṛṣṭi-Sṛṣṭi vāda* have been discussed here.

The Unreality of the World, and the Mind's Projecting Power

The *Laṅkāvatārasūtra,* which can be said to be the oldest work of the *Vijñānavāda* School, very lucidly establishes the unreality of this world of appearances and emphasizes the mind as the factor projecting the external world.

In order to establish the unreality of the external world; similes of a dream, sky flower, mirage, *gandharvanagara* etc. are employed. It is said, "Things are not originated as a matter of fact. But as the *gandharvanagara,* dream, illusion etc. appear without any cause; So this world appears."[25] It is further said, "As a dream, hair floating in the air, *Māyā, gandharvanagara,* and the mirage appear without any cause; So this world appears."[26] In short, the world is devoid of any substance; it is essenceless. It is the mind (*citta*) which assumes the form of the external world. In the *Laṅkāvatāra* it is stated, "This appearance is nothing else but the mind,. which takes the form of the congnised and cogniser."[27] Emphasizing the constructive role of the mind it is said, "Nothing exists outside; but it is the mind only which appears outside in the form of objects."[28] Everything up to Brahmā is nothing else but the mind only. So when the mind is emancipated, Brahmā and the like are not apprehended."[29] In short, "The mind alone functions, and the mind alone is liberated. The mind itself is originated, and nothing else but the mind itself is suppressed."[30]

Now, in this context, a question may arise as to how the mind operates and how varieties of things occur. In answer to such a question, it is stated that the only factor responsible for such a delusion is residual impression (*vāsanā*). From the rsidual impressions, various forms emerge. Describing the process, it is stated, "From the store-consciousness (*Ālaya Vijñāna*), proceed the minds like waves. These (the minds) are caused by the residual impressions in accordance with their causes."[31] Stating the analogy of a mirror it is stated, "As a form appears on the surface of mirrors but does not exist inside it; similarly on the surface of the mirror of the residual impressions, the mind is seen as subject and object to the people with a poor intellect."[32]

Besides emphasizing the mind's creative power the *Laṅkāvatārasūtra* puts forth the doctrine of Acosmism that "Everything is non-originated. What appears is an illusion only."[33] Declaring the imaginary character of the objects it is stated, "Nothing whatsoever is originated from causes nor is it suppressed by causes. Only imaginary causes are originated and suppressed."[34] That is to say, only imaginary things seem to be produced and destroyed.

Idealistic Views Expressed in the *Vijñaptimātratāsiddhi*

The name of Vasubandhu s remarkable in the history of the *Vijñānavāda* school of Buddhism, Vasubandhu, as it is believed, started as a *Vaibhāṣika,* showed leanings towards the *Sautrāntika* schooland finally emerged as a *Vijñānavādin.* His *Vijñāptimātratāsiddhi*[35] is an important work propounding Subjective Idealism. The main theme of this work is to reject the reality of the external world and to assert consciousness as the Ultimate Reality.

At the very outset, Vasubandhu announces in the *Viṁśatikāvṛtti,* "In the *Mahāyāna* School, the three-fold world — viz. *Nāmadhātu, Rūpadhātu* and *Arūpadhātu* is instructed to be *Vijñapti* only, through the aphorism — *Jinaputrā-* "what is perceived as the three-fold world, is only of the form of *citta.* Mind, *Vijñāna* and *Vijñapti* are identical."[36] Considering everything as not real but as consciousness only he states, "As a man with defective eyes has the false perception of hairs floating in the air; so everything that appears is not real but consciousness only."[37]

Here, a number of doubts arise. Since we are much attached to worldly things, we cannot readily consider the world as an unreal phenomenon. We perceive a number of things and events around us as occurring at a particular place and time. Hence, we feel like asking that if the external things be unreal, how things could have originated at a particular place and time.

We find such a doubt put forth in the *Vijñaptimātratāsiddhi,* "If knowledge of colour etc. arises without colour etc. that is to say without their being a corresponding external colour etc. then why is it originated at a particular place and not everywhere; and why is it originated at that particular place and time and not at all times? Further, why does it arise in the consciousness-continuum of all at that very place and time; and not in that of only one."[38]

We experience in this world that certain objects, viz. fruits etc. grow at a particular place and time. Now, if without any external object, the knowledge of external things arises, then why is such a universal law experienced? Why is everything not originated everywhere and at all times. And why do all the people at a particular place and time experience the things and not just one person?

In answer to this it is stated, "In a dream, even in the absence of objects — bee, garden, woman etc. re seen only at a particular place and time and not everywhere. In a dream, things are seen at a particular place at some time and not at all times. Thus, the restriction of place and time is established even without objects."[39]

There is absence of the external objects. It is our ideation that takes the form of the external objects. Vasubandhu, while putting the waking state on a par with the dreaming state emphasizes that as in a dream, things are apprehended at a particular place and time, though they do not exist as a matter of fact, similarly, in the waking state also, in the absence of things, they (things) are apprehended at a particular place and time.

Now, to a layman, a doubt certainly arises as to how a thing could be considered non-existing when it is actually perceived. But, Vasubandhu in his *Vijñaptimātratāsiddhi* asserts that perception cannot prove the existence of a thing.

External Thing cannot be Proved by Perception

With the help of the means of knowledge we can establish whether a thing exists or not. Perception is believed to be the most valid means of knowledge, through which we apprehend the external world and can carry on our practical dealings. Among the Buddhist thinkers, the *Vaibhāṣikas* hold that the external world is directly erceived; while the *Sautrāntikas* hold that the world is not directly perceived, but can only be inferred; on the strength of the knowledge that we have.

The *Vijñānavādins* went ahead on the same lines, and said that the perceptual knowledge of a thing need not lead us to infer its objective existence, for in a dream, knowledge arises without an external object being present.

In the *Vijñaptimātratāsiddhi*; Vasubandhu has put forth the doubt of the Realist and has refuted the realistic view of perception.

It may be asked by the Realist, "If a thing does not exist; how could one have the notion. 'This is perceived'?"[40]

In answer, the analogy of a dream is presented that as in a dream though the things are not present; perceptual cognition arises; so it happens in the waking state also.[41] Now if as the *Sautrāntika* says, an object does not remain present at the time of its perceptual cognition; then how could it be known to be perceived.[42] That is to say, when the perceptual cognition arises — "I perceive this particular thing" — at that time, that particular thing does not remain present. And through *Manovijñāna* it is decided that a thing is perceived. So how could it be said that the object is perceived ? Especially, in the case of momentary objects, their form, taste etc. have ceased to exist at that time.[43]

It may be argued that whatever is not experienced, cannot be recalled by *Manovijñāna*. So the experience of the object, must be there in the form of perception. Hence, colour etc. are considered as objects of perception.[44] In answer to such an argument, Vasubandhu says, "It is not proved that only a thing previously experienced is recalled, because it is already stated that consciousness with an image of a thing arises (even though the thing is absent). And from such consciousness; *Manovijñāna* arises with that every image in association with recollection being constructive of colour etc. Therefore, on the strength of the rise of recollection, experience of a thing cannot be proved."[45]

That is to say, even if we take for granted the reality of external things, they cannot be said to be directly known by perception. At the most their existence can be inferred from the knowledge that arises. But there is no relation of invariable concomitance between the existence of a thing and its knowledge through the sense-organs. In a dream we have perceptual knowledge of things, but they do not really exist. Similarly, in the waking state, consciousness alone is established but not the reality of the external things. It could be said that it is our consciousness that appears as if it were outside.

Thus, Vasubandhu establishes that the external thing is not actually perceived; but it is our imagination only that projects a thing as if it were outside. The object does not as a matter of fact exist.

It can be seen that Vasubandhu here puts the waking state on the same footing as the dreaming state; and proves that even in the absence of a thing, it can be apprehended.

Similarity between the Waking State and the Dreaming State

To show the unreality of a thing, it is generally compared with a dream. So, in order to establish the world as unreal; thinkers put it on a par with a dream.

Now, the *Vijñānavādin* asserts that though there is no external thing, consciousness appears as the external object, as it happens in a dream.

To a lay man, a doubt may occur, "If in the waking state, consciousness of the unreal object occurs as in a dream, then people would certainly themselves understand that in the waking state also there is absence of things as in the dreaming state. But this is not what happens. So unlike in a dream; consciousness of all thing should not be considered objectless."[46]

Such a doubt is set aside by saying that the absence of the things seen in a dream, cannot be known by the dreamer unless he wakes up from the dreaming state.[47] Similarly, the residual impression (*vāsanā*), born of the (long persistent) habit of making wrong constructions compels people to fall into a slumber as it were, and as in the case of a dream, they perceive things which do not exist as a matter of fact and do not realise their nature till they are awake. But when they wake upon attaining the knowledge just the opposite of that and develop a pure supra-empirical knowledge, then being prone to a pure empirical knowledge they realise the negation of objects.[48]

Hence, it is concluded that like dream-consciousness, (in the waking state also) it is consciousness itself which arises in the form of objects though there are no external objects.[49]

Thus, Vasubandhu denies the existence of the external objects, putting them on a par with a dream. Besides, a logical refutation of the *Vaiśeṣika* view, which recognised the external objects is found in his work.

Refutation of Atomic Realism

Since the *Vaiśeṣika* school admits the independent existence of the external objects, it forcefully propounds that since a thing exists, it is directly apprehended. There is no absence of the external objects.

Now, according to Vasubandhu, the reality could be conceived either as a single thing or as an aggregate of atoms. But both these alternatives are untenable. It is stated, "The object is (experienced) neither as a single entity, nor as many distinct atoms, nor as an aggregate of them, because the single atom is not established."[50]

Colour and other things which severally from the contents of eye-consciousness and the like, should either be one in the form of an *avayavin* (whole) as believed by the *Vaiśeṣikas* or they may be many as atoms or there may be a conglomeration of atoms.[51]

There cannot be one, since apart from the parts, nothing is perceived as a whole. Nor could there be many, as each atom is not perceived. Nor do they form the object in a conglomeration, since the atom is not established as a substance.[52] This is so because if six atoms are believed to simultaneously come into contact with a single atom, then that single atom must be said to have six spatial dimensions . . . . And if they are said to be occupying one single space then the conglomeration would remain of the size of an atom only.[53] If it is admitted that the same space that the single atom occupies can also accomodate the six other atoms; then all of them being in the same space, the whole mass would be of the same size as an atom only and they could not be perceived. Moreover; atoms being partless, cannot come into contact with each other.[54]

Now, conglomerations also cannot mutually unite, for in that case it must not be claimed that the atoms cannot unite as they are partless; even if conglomeration have parts, their contact is not recognised. Therefore, the atom cannot be established as one substance.[55]

Thus, Vasubandhu presents the logical inconsistencies in the theory that atoms construct the external world. As atoms are partless, they cannot unite with each other.

Further, "That which has different parts, cannot make a unity, (on the contrary; if it has no parts) how come it is subject to shadow and concealment? It cannot be argued that they belong to the aggregate of atoms, unless the aggregate is admitted to be different from atoms."[56]

That is to say, if spatial divisions of each single atom were not admitted, then it could not have one side with shadow and another without shadow. And where the parts of atom are not admitted, there could be no case of one atom being concealed by another, for the atom has no 'other' part. And even because there is no other part where another atom could come to unite, a resistance could not grow and in the absence of resistance, all atoms would be having the same spatial dimension, and any conglomeration would be of the size of an atom, as already discussed.[57]

Further, are blue, etc. — that get recognised as the objects of the eye and the like — unitary substances or many?[58] Neither of these alternatives can stand here. "If it is one, then no gradual movement is possible; for it cannot be that one is grasped and not grasped at the same time. (At the same time) many objects that are so different from each other, could not be held to be existing in the same locus; and the subtle one could not be perceived by us."[59]

If however, what is indivisible and not many, that only can form the object of the eye and therefore, such a thing is taken to be unitary, then there would be no scope for any gradual movement on the earth since one single foot-step would mean grasping the whole earth. It could not happen that the front part is grasped and the posterior part is not grasped at the same time. What are divisible and many; that is to say — an elephant, a horse etc. cannot co-exist. If where one exists; there you admit another as existing; how could division in that case be admitted? And how could that be one; since between what is occupied and what is not occupied, there is another region which is perceived as void. The subtle worms born in water, which are of the same form as gross animals, should not be beyond perception. If it is thought that it is the difference of characters that brings about the differences of substance and not otherwise, then this difference on the basis of atoms must be recognised and that is not established as unitary.[60] And that not being established, colour etc., would cease to be regarded as the object of eye (consciousness) and thus, consciousness alone is established as the only Reality.[61]

Thus, refuting the 'Atomic Realism' of the *Vaiśeṣika*-system, Vasubandhu establishes that no object exists but consciousness alone exists, which takes the form of the eternal objects.

It would not be out of place to mention a verse from the *Ālaṁbanaparīkṣā,* which emphasizes that consciousness takes the form of the external objects and appears as if it were existing outside. It is said, "It is the object (*artha*) which exists internally in knowledge itself as the knowledge aspect and which appears to us as if it were existing externally. Because consciousness is the essence (of the external object) and that (object, the essence of which is consciousness) acts as the condition (to consciousness)."[62]

Thus, consciousness alone is the Reality; and the external objects do not exist.

Now, a question might arise that if consciousness alone is real; and everything else is unreal, how could the world appear before us.

We find an answer to this put forth in the *Trimśikā*, wherein this world is said to be a transformation of consciousness.

World: Transformation of Consciousness

It is stated in the *Trimśikā* that the external world is a result of the three-fold transformation of consciousness, viz. *Ālaya Vijñāna* (store consciousness). *Mano Vijñāna* (thought consciousness), and *Pravṛtti Vijñāna* (active consciousness). Amongst these, *ĀlayaVijñāna* which is the seed of everything is called *Vipāka*.[63] So, *Ālaya Vijñāna*, which is the store-house of consciousness, is one of the modifications of pure consciousness, from which the worldly phenomena emerge.

In order to have the idea of *Vijñānavādin*'s view regarding the world phenomenon the three-fold transformation of consciousness has been discussed below:

Ālaya Vijñāna: *Ālaya Vijñāna* has the representation of consciousness of unknown objects and places. It is always associated with touch; attentiveness, knowledge, conception and volition."[64] Moreover, "The feeling therin is that of indifference. It is unobscured and undefined, similarly indifferent are touch, etc. And it is like a stream of water."[65]

As *Ālaya Vijñāna* is momentary, it persists not as one; but is like the flow of a stream. It is stated, "*Ālaya Vijñāna* ceases to exist when arahathood is attained."[66] When arahathood is attained, all the seeds of section are destroyed and thus, *Ālaya Vijñāna* also ceases to exist.

Mano-Vijñāna: "The consciousness called *Manas* acts dpending on *Ālaya Vijñāna*. It is an act of thinking."[67] *Ālaya Vijñāna* is considered the locus of the root-inclination (*vāsanā*) of *Mano Vijñāna*. Further, "*Mano Vijñāna* is always associated with four defilements (*kleśa*), which are themselves obscured and undefined. They are belief in self, ignorance about the self, pride in self and love of self."[68] It is associated with others like touch etc. which are all of the same nature as the region in which one is born. It does not belong to one in the state of arahathood; nor does it operate in the state of suppressed consciousness, nor in the supra-mundane path."[69]

Pravṛtti Vijñāna: "The third transformation of consciousness is the same as the perception of the six-fold object. It could be good or bad or indifferent in character."[70]

In short, "This three-fold transformation of consciousness is the distinction (between subject and object). What is thus distinguished, does not exist as such. Therefore, all this is more consciousness."[71]

It is well-known that in regard to one and the same object, contradictory consciousnesses arise amongst various people. But one and the same object cannot be logically of a contradictory nature. Therefore, in view of being of the form of something superimposed, the object-cause of the constructive imagination has to be understood as unreal."[72]

As the nature of the external object is thus self-contradictory, the thing cannot be considered as real. Therefore, everything is declared as merely consciousness, in the absence of external objects.[73]

The question arises that if everything is consciousness alone, how are such constructions possible? In answer to this it is stated, "The consciousness contains all seeds. Its transformations proceed by mutual influence, as a result different constructions arise."[74]

Hence, *Ālaya Vijñāna* is the seed of all the things. Whether it is a cosmic force or is individual, is not made clear. But Buddhism unlike the *Vedānta* would not normally admit a universal consciousness. *Ālaya Vijñāna* is compared with an ocean, from which numerous *Vijñāna* in the form of waves emerge. One wave causes another. From this, the common worldly experience can explained, "Knowledges get conditioned by each other due to mutual predominance."[75] That is to say, knowledge of all persons have a mutual predominance, that gets conditioned by each other as and when called for. Hence, from a particular consciousness of an individual, a particular consciousness develops in another individual and not an external object.[76]

Thus, no external object causes a common worldly experience, but consciousness of one individual affects another individual-consciousness, and by virtue of their being mutually affected a common world-experience comes about. As an example it is stated, "Death is a change of course caused by a particular mental representation of another being."[77] That is to say, due to the predominance of the particular consciousness of others, some change emerges which is opposed to the life force and death, which is called the disruption of the uniform continuum.[78]

It can be clearly seen that plurality of consciousness continues to be recognised. According to the *Vijñānavāda*, the soul is nothing but a continuum of consciousness-point-instants. In the commentary on the *Madhyāntavibhāgasūtra* it is stated, "Eventhough there is an absence of different objects, each stream of consciousness reveals its own world."[79]

Thus, the plurality of the individual selves is admitted by the *Vijñanavāda*. So far as the plurality of the selves is concerned the *Vijñānavāda* certainly differs from the *Dṛṣṭi-Sṛṣṭi-vāda* which, as we shall see, positively prefers the *Ekajīvavāda*.

Another query is whether the *Vijñānavāda* accepts the empirical nature (truth) of the world or not. *Dṛṣṭi-Sṛṣṭi-vāda* rejects the three-fold existence, admitting only the illusory existence *(prātibhāsika sattā)* and the ultimate existence *(pāramārthika sattā)*. In the realm of this theory, there is no place for empirical reality.

Three-fold Nature *(trisvabhāva)*

We have seen that the *Mādhyamika* Buddhism recognises

empirical truth, eventhough it rejects it from the ultimate standpoint.

Now, what about the *Vijñānavāda*? Till here, we have seen that it denounces the independent existence of external objects, and puts them on a par with the objects of a dream. So, the *Vijñānavāda* can be said to reject the empirical reality of the world. But it may be noted that the *Vijñānavāda* also recognises a three-fold nature of things. It is stated in the *Triṁśikā*, "In the *Sūtras*, three natures are spoken of imagined (*parikalpita*) dependent (*paratantra*) and absolute (*pariniṣpanna*).[80] Though everything is of the nature of consciousness, the three-fold nature can be established."[81]

Parikalpita : By whatever constructive imagination whatever thing is imagined, that is *parikalpita svabhāva* (imagined nature).[82]

Paratantra : That which is controlled or originated by other causes and conditions is known as *parataṅtra* (dependent).[83]

Pariniṣpanna : The state of ever being free from the previous one (*paratantra*) is called *pariniṣpanna*.[84]

It would not be out of place to mention that Vasubandhu, in his *Trisvabhāvanirdeśa* has explained three-fold nature of a thing.[85] When by means of a spell (*mantra*), a piece of wood is made to appear in the illusory form of an elephant, in that case, the elephant is *parikalpita*, its form is *paratantra*, while the absence of real elephant is the absolute aspect.

Hence, like the *Mādhyamika* Buddhism, the *Vijñānavāda* also recognises the dependent nature of the things. So, eventhough it rejects the nature of things from the ultimate standpoint, it affirms it empirically.[86] It can be said that the *Vijñānavādin* has tried to analyse the nature of things as they are imagined in consciousness.

Beside this, the concept that puts the *Vijñānavāda* near to *Dṛṣṭi-Sṛṣṭi-vāda* is the law of simultaneous apprehension (*Sahopalambhaniyama*). Here we shall see how this law of simultaneous apprehension resembles *Dṛṣṭi-Sṛṣṭi-vāda*.

The law of Simultaneous Apprehension (*Sahopalambhaniyama*)

Realism holds that the thing to be perceived exists independently of its perception. On the other hand, Idealism asserts that nothing is established independently of the consciousness. So, the difference between the thing to be perceived and its consciousness should be considered illusory. According to this *Vijñānavāda,* the invariably simultaneous apprehension of knowledge and its object is called the law of simultaneous apprehension (*sahopalambhaniyama*). As stated in *Indian Idealism,* "Any two things that are simultaneously manifested are identical. This is called the law of simultaneous apprehension (*Sahopalambhaniyama*).[87] This law states that there could be no difference between the thing and its cognition, that is to say, the blue thing is identical with the congnition of blue.[88]

To a layman, a thing that is apprehended seems to be different from its cognition. He cannot consider the thing and its cognition as identical, for example, he feels that the rose and the cognition of rose are two dfferent things. But Idealism has a different stand, according to which nothing is established independently of the consciousness. So everything is of the nature of consciousness.

Now, the *Vijñānavāda* recognises consciousness alone (*Vijñaptimātratā*) as the Ultimate Reality, which takes the form of subject and object. Thus, this manifold world, and its cognition are nothing else but consciousness only. Congnition itself is the illuminator of its own form like light, as there is absence of any *grāhya* other than itself.[89] The thing is to be congnised does not differ from its cognition. And the difference that appears between the thing and its congnition is just an illusion (*Bhrama*) like the illusion of twoness in the moon.[90] The law of simultaneous apprehension states that a thing and its cognition are both simultaneously apprehended, i.e., blue colour and congnition of blue colour are known at the same time. Thus, there is no difference between knowledge (*jñāna*) and the thing to be known (*jñeya*).

This very fact is emphasized in *Dṛṣṭi-Sṛṣṭi-vāda*. It asserts the existence of a thing, simultaneous with its perception. A thing does not exist when not perceived, for there is no proof for its existence. So far as the approach is concerned, both the *Vijñānavāda* and *Dṛṣṭi-Sṛṣṭi-vāda* work on the same line and do not accept the independent existence of an object.

In conclusion it may be stated that so far as the unreality of the phenomenal world is concerned, the Buddhist schools, viz. the *Mādhyamika* and the *Yogācāra (Vijñānavāda)* are Idealistic. Of course, both the trends regard the world as unreal from the transcendental point of view, while they admit some truth or nature from the empirical standpoint. On the other hand, the *Dṛṣṭi-Sṛṣṭi-vāda* makes bold to totally negate the empirical reality of the world considering it as illusory as a dream.

The point which puts the *Vijñānavāda* and the *Dṛṣṭi-Sṛṣṭi-vāda* on a par is the law of simultaneous apprehension. That is to say, both *Vijñānavāda* and *Dṛṣṭi-Sṛṣṭi-vāda* regard the object as having the form of consciousness. They assert that consciousness itself assumes the form of subject and object. This naturally establishes identity between the thing to be known and its cognition. So, there is a simultaneous process of thing's existence and its perception. Such an Idealistic way of thinking brings *Vijñānavāda* and *Dṛṣṭi-Sṛṣṭi-vāda* very close.

It seems that perhaps the Subjectivistic thought of *Vijñānavāda* has paved the way for the development of *Dṛṣṭi-Sṛṣṭi-vāda*. In the chapters pertaining to the Idealistic thought in some of the *Vedāntic* works, such as the *Yoga-Vāsiṣṭha*, the *Gauḍapādakārikā*, the *Vivekacūḍāmaṇi* etc. we shall see how they are greatly influenced by the Idealism of the *Vijñānavāda* in asserting the world as unreal and putting it on the same footing as a dream. The *Vijñānavāda* does not recognise one eternally unchanging consciousness as the Ultimate Reality, but seems to admit a plurality of continua or streams of conscious moments while *Kevalādvaita Vedānta*, whatever shape it assumes, always adheres to the *Upaniṣadic* concept of one eternally unchanging Ultimate Reality of the nature of Existence — Consciousness — Bliss.

References

1. ". . . The solution, accordingly, of this great problem is attempted by Buddhism not objectively, but subjectively."
   — Sogan, Yamakami, *Systems of Buddhistic Thought*, Ch. II, p. 47 (1912), University of Calcutta.

2. " . . . the *Mādhyamika* claims that he follows Buddha's doctrine of the mean or middle path, by holding that reality is neither positive nor negative . . . "
   — Raju, P. T. *Idealistic Thought of India*, Ch. VI, p. 243 (1973), Johnson Reprint Corporation, New York, London.

3. Dasgupta, S.N., *Indian Idealism*, Ch. V, p.126 (1962), Cambridge University Press.

4. अनिरोधमनुत्पादमनुच्छेदमशाश्वतम्
   अनेकार्थमनानार्थमनागममनिर्गमम् ।
   M. K. Ch. I (ab).
   Chatterjee, Herambanath, (ed.), *Mūla-Madhyamaka-kārikā,* Part-I (1957), Calcutta.

5. न स्वतो नापि परतो न द्वाभ्यां नाप्यहेतुत: ।
   उत्पन्ना जातु विद्यन्ते भावा: क्वचन केचन ॥
   M. K. Ch. I.1.

6. . . . . नहि स्वात्मनो विद्यमानानां पदार्थानां पुनरुत्पादे प्रयोजनमस्ति । .....परतोपि नोपपद्यन्ते भावा:, पराभावादेव ।
   Page 14, 36.
   Extracts from *M. K. V.* on *M. K.* I-1, Poussin, Louis-de-la-Valle (ed.), *Mūla-Madhyamaka Kārikā* of Nāgārjuna with *Prasanapādavṛtti* of Candrakīrti, (1903), St, Petersbourg
   (*Bibliotheca Buddhica IV*)

7. नैवासत: नैव सत: प्रत्ययोऽर्पस्य युज्यते ।
   असत: प्रत्यय: कस्य सतश्च प्रत्ययेन किम् ॥
   M. K. Ch. I.6.

8. न च व्यस्तसमस्तेषु प्रत्ययेष्वस्ति तत् फलम् ।
   प्रत्ययेभ्य: कथं तच्च भवेन्न प्रत्ययेषु यत् ॥
   M. K. I.11.

9. अथासदपि तत्तेभ्य: प्रत्ययेनेभ्य: प्रवर्त्तते ।
   अप्रत्ययेभ्योपि कस्मान्नाभिप्रवर्तते फलम् ॥
   M. K. I.12.

10. फलञ्च प्रत्ययमयं प्रत्ययश्चास्वयमया: ।
    फलमस्वयंमयेभ्यो यत्तत् प्रत्ययमयं कथम् ॥
    M. K. I.13.

11. न प्रत्ययमयं फलम् नाप्रत्ययमयं फलम् ।
    संविद्यते, फलाभावात् प्रत्ययाप्रत्यया: कुत: ॥
    M. K. I.14.

12. यथा माया यथा स्वप्नो गन्धर्वनगरं यथा ।
तथोत्पादस्तथा स्नानं तथा भंग उदाहृतम् ॥
M. K. VII.34.

13. नैवाग्रं नावरं यस्य मध्यं कुतो भवेत् ।
M. K. XI.2(ab).
Jong J. N. (ed.), *Mūla Madhyamakakrīkā* (1977), The Adyar Library and Research Centre.

14. पूर्वा न विद्यते कोटि: संसारस्य न केवलं ।
सर्वेषामपि भावानाम् पूर्वा कोटी न विद्यते ॥
M. K. XI. 8.

15. क्लेशा: कर्माणि देहश्च कर्तारश्च फलानि च ।
गन्धर्वनगराकारा मरीचिस्वप्नसन्निभ: ॥
M. K. XVII. 33.

16. तथागतो यत्स्वभावस्तत्स्वभावं इदं जगत् ।
तथागतो नि:स्वभावो नि:स्वभावं इदं जगत् ॥
M. K. XXII.16.

17. न निर्वाणसमारोपो न संसारापकर्षणम् ।
यत्र क: तत्र संसारो निर्वाणं किं विकल्प्यते ॥
M.K. XVI.10.

18. द्वे सत्ये समुपाश्रित्य बुद्धानां धर्मदेशना ।
लोकसंवृतिसत्यं च सत्यं च परमार्थत: ॥
M. K. XXIV.8.

19. अज्ञानं हि समन्तात्सर्वपदार्थत्त्वावच्छादनात्संवृतिरित्युच्यते ।
M. K. V. p. 492

20. येऽनयोर्न विजानन्ति विभागं तत्वयोर्द्वयो: ।
ते तत्वं न विजानन्ति गम्भीरं बुद्धशासने ॥
M. K. XXIV.9.

21. व्यवहारमनाश्रित्य परमार्थो न देश्यते ।
परमार्थमनागम्य निर्वाणं नाधिगम्यते ॥
M. K. XXIV.10.

22. तस्मात्मान्निर्वाणाधिगमोपायत्वादवश्यमेव यथावस्थिता
संवृतिरादावेवाभ्युपेया । भाजनमिव सलिलार्थिनेति ।
M. K. V. p.494.

23. Murti, T. R. V., *The Central Philosophy of Buddhism*, Ch. III, p. 82 (1955), George Allen & Unwin;
Radhakrishnan, *Indian Philosophy*, Vol.I, Ch. XI, p. 625, Eighth impression (1966), George Allen & Unwin.

24. Stcherbatsky, Th. F. *Buddhist Logic*, Vol. I, Ch. I, Foot-Note p. 46 (1962), Dover Publication, New York.

25. अनुत्पन्नमिदं सर्वं न च भावा न सन्ति च ।
गन्धर्वस्वप्नमायाख्या भावा विद्यन्त्यहेतुका: ॥
L. S. III.87.
Bagchi, Sitansusekhar (ed.), *Saddharmalaṅkāvatārasūtra* (1963), *Buddhist-Sanskrit texts, N:3, The Mithila Institute.*

26. स्वप्नकेशोण्डूकं माया गन्धर्वं मृगतृष्णिका ।
अहेतुकानि दृश्यन्ते तथा लोकविचित्रता ॥
L. S. III.90.

अनुत्पन्ना समी धर्मा न चैवैते न सन्ति च ।
गन्धर्वनगरस्वप्नमायानिर्माणसादृशाः ॥
L. S. X.144.

27. चित्तमात्रं न दृश्योऽस्ति द्विधा चित्तं हि दृश्यते ।
L. S. III.65 (ab)

चित्तमात्रमिदं सर्वं द्विधा चित्तं प्रवर्तते ।
ग्राह्यग्राहकभावेन आत्मात्मीयं न विद्यते ॥
L. S. III.121.

28. बहिर्धा नास्ति वे दृश्यमतो वै चित्तमात्रकम् ॥
L. S. X.101 (cd),

बहिर्धा नास्ति वै रूपं स्वचित्तं दृश्यते बाहिः ।
L. S. X.489 (ab).

29. ब्रह्मादित्स्थानपर्यन्तं चित्तमात्रं वदाम्यहम् ।
चित्तमात्रविनिर्मुक्तं ब्रह्मादिर्नोपलभ्यते ॥
L. S. III.122.

30. चित्तं प्रवर्त चित्तं वित्तमेव विमुच्यते ।
चित्त हि जायते नान्यच्चित्तमेव निरुध्यते ॥
L. S. X.145.

31. आलयात्सर्वचित्तानि प्रवर्तन्ति तरंगवत् ।
वासनाहेतुकाः सर्वे यथाप्रत्ययसंभवाः ॥
L. S. X. 871.

32. यथा हि दर्पणे रुपं दृश्यते न च विद्यते ।
वासनादर्पणे चित्तं द्विधा दृश्यति बालिशैः ॥
L. S. III.74.

33. अनुत्पन्नाः सर्वभावा भ्रान्तिमात्रं हि दृश्यते ।
L. S. X.96 (ab).

34. न ह्यत्रोत्पद्यते किंचित्प्रत्ययैर्न निरूध्यते ।
उत्पद्यन्ते निरुध्यते प्रत्यया एव कल्पिताः ॥
L. S. X.85 (ab.)

35. The *Vijñaptimātratāsiddhi* is divided into two sections:
(1) *Viṃśatikā*, (2) *Triṃśikā*.
On the *Viṃśatikā*, Vasubandhu himself has written a Commentary; while the commentary on the *Triṃśikā* is written by Sthiramati.

36. महायाने त्रैधातुकं विज्ञप्तिमात्रं व्यवस्थाप्यते:
चित्तमात्रं भो जिनपुत्रा! यदुत त्रैधातुकमिति
सूत्रात् । वित्तं मनो विज्ञानं विज्ञप्तिश्चेति पर्यायाः ।
V. M. S. Viṃśatikā Vṛtti, p.1
Chatterjee, K. N. (ed.), *Vijñaptimātratāsiddhi*, First edition (1980), Kishor Vidya Niketan, Varanasi.

37. विज्ञप्तिमात्रमेवेदमसदर्थावभासनात् ।
यद्वत् तैमिरिकस्यासत् केशोण्डुकादिदर्शनम् ॥
V. M. S. *Viṃśatikā*, 1.

38. यदि विनापि रूपाद्यर्थेन रूपादिविज्ञप्तिरुत्पद्यते न रूपाद्यर्थात्, कस्मात् क्वचिद् देश उत्पद्यते, न सर्वत्र: तत्रैव च देशे कदाचिदुत्पद्यते न सर्वदा: तद्देशकालप्रतिष्ठितानां सर्वेषां सन्तान उत्पद्यते, न केवलमेकस्य ?
V. M. S. *Viṃśatikā Vṛtti*, p.1.

39. स्वप्ने विनाप्यर्थेन क्वचिदेव देशे किञ्चिद् भ्रमरारामस्त्रीपुरुषादिकं दृश्यते न सर्वत्र । तत्रैव च देशे कदाचिद् दृश्यते, न सर्वकालम् इति सिद्धो विनाप्यर्थेन देशकालनियम: ।
V. M. S. *Viṃśatikā Vṛtti*, p.2.

40. .... असत्यर्थे कथमियं बुद्धिर्भवति प्रत्यक्षमिति?
V. M. S. *Viṃśatikā Vṛtti*, p.18.

41. प्रत्यक्षबुद्धि: स्वप्नादौ यथा विनाप्यर्थेनेति पूर्वमेव ज्ञापितम् ।
V. M. S. p.18.

42. न योऽर्थो दृश्यते तस्य प्रत्यक्षत्वं कथं मतम्।
V. M. S. *Viṃśatikā* 16 (cd).

43. यदा च सा प्रत्यक्षबुद्धिर्भवतीदं मे प्रत्यक्षमिति तदा न सोऽर्थो दृश्यते । मनोविज्ञानेनैव परिच्छेदाच्चक्षुर्विज्ञानस्य च तदा निरुद्धत्वादिति कथं तस्य प्रत्यक्षत्वमिष्टम्: विशेषेण तु क्षणिकस्य विषयस्य तदानीं निरुद्धमेव तद्रूपं रसादिकं वा।
V. M. S. *Viṃśatikā Vṛtti*, p.19.

44. नाननुभूतं मनोविज्ञानेन स्मर्यत इत्यवश्यमर्थानुभवेन भवितव्यं तच्च दर्शनमित्येवं तद्विषयस्य रूपादे: प्रत्यक्षत्वं मतम्।
V. M. S. *Viṃśatikā-Vṛtti*, p.19.

45. असिद्धमिदमनुभूतस्यार्थस्य स्मरणं भवतीति। यस्माद् — उक्तं यथा तदाभासा विज्ञप्ति:— विनाप्यर्थेन यथार्थाभासा चक्षुर्विज्ञानादिका विज्ञप्तिरुत्पद्यते तथोक्तम् — स्मरणं तत: । ततो हि विज्ञप्ते: स्मृतिसम्प्रयुक्ता तत्प्रतिभासैव रुपादिविकल्पिका मनोविज्ञप्तिरुत्पद्यत इति न स्मृत्युत्पादादर्थानुभव: सिध्यति।
V. M. S. *Viṃśatikā Vṛtti*, pp. 19-20.

46. यदि यथा स्वप्ने विज्ञप्तिरभूतार्थविषया तथा जाग्रतोऽपि स्यात्तथैव तदभावं लोक: स्वयमवगच्छेत् । न चैवं भवति । तस्मान्न स्वप्न इवार्थोपलब्धि: सर्वा निरर्थिका ।
V. M. S. *Viṃśatikā Vṛtti*, p.20.

47. स्वप्न दृग्विषयाभावं नाप्रबुद्धोऽवगच्छति॥
V. M. S. *Viṃśatikā* 17, p.21.

48. एवं वितथविकल्पाभ्यासवासनानिद्रया प्रसुप्तो लोक: स्वप्न इवाभूतमर्थं पश्यन्न प्रबुद्धस्तभावं यथावन्नावगच्छति । यदा तु तत्प्रतिपक्षलोकोत्तरनिर्विकल्पज्ञान लाभात् प्रबुद्धो भवति तदा तत्पृष्ठलब्धशुद्धलौकिकज्ञानसंमुखीभावाद्विषयाभावं यथावदवगच्छतीति समानमेतत् ।
V. M. S. *Viṃśatikā Vṛtti*, p. 21.

49. एवं बाह्यार्थाभावाद् विज्ञानमेवार्थाकारमुत्पद्यते, स्वप्नविज्ञानवद् इत्यभ्युपेयम् ।
V. M. S. *Triṃśikā Vṛtti*, p. 28.

50. न तदेकं न चानेकं विषय: परमाणुश: ।
न च ते संहता यस्मात्परमाणुर्न सिध्यति ॥
V. M. S. *Viṃśatikā*, 11, p.12.

51. यत्तद्रूपादिकमायतनं रूपादिविज्ञप्तीनां प्रत्येकं विषयः स्यात्तदेकं वा स्याद्यथावयविरूपं कल्प्यते वैशेषिकैः अनेकं वा परमाणुशः संहता वा त एव परमाणवः ।

V. M. S. Viṃśatikā Vṛtti, p.2

52. न तावदेकं विषयो भवत्यवयवेन्यऽन्यस्यावयविरूपस्य क्वचचिदप्यग्रहणात् । नाप्येकं, परमाणूनां प्रत्येकमग्रहणात् । नापि ते संहता विषयीभवन्ति । यस्मात्परमाणुरेकं द्रव्यं न सिध्यति ।

V. M. S. Viṃśatikā Vṛtti, p.12.

53. षट्केन युगपद्योगात्परमाणोः षऽंशता ।
यषण्णां समानदेशत्वात् पिण्डः स्यादणुमात्रकः ॥

V. M. S. Viṃśatikā, 12, p.13.

54. अथ य एवैकस्य परमाणोर्देशः त एष षण्णाम् । तेन सर्वेषां समानदेशत्वात् सर्वः पिण्डः परमाणुमात्रः स्यात्परस्पराव्यतिरेकादिति न कश्चित्पिण्डो दृश्यः स्यात् । नैव हि परमाणवः संयुज्यन्ते निरवयवत्पात् ।

V. M. S. Viṃśatikā Vṛtti, pp. 13-14.

55. अथ संघता अप्यन्योन्यं न संयुज्यन्ते । न तर्हि परमाणूना' निरवयवत्वातसंयोगो न सिध्यतीति वक्तव्यम् । सावयवस्यापि हि संघातस्य संयोगानभ्युपगमात् । तस्मात्परमाणुरेकं द्रव्यं न सिध्यति ।

V. M. S. Viṃśatikā Vṛtti, p.15.

56. दिग्भागभेदो यस्यास्ति तस्यैकत्वं न युज्यते ।
छायावृती कथं वा अन्यो न पिण्डश्चेन्न तस्य ते ॥

V. M. S. Viṃśatikā, 14, pp. 15-16.

English translation from Thomas A. Kochumuttom, *A Buddhist Doctrine of Experience*, Ch.V, p. 178, First edition (1982), Motilal Banarsidass.

57. यद्येकैकस्य परमाणोर्दिग्भागभेदो न स्यादादित्योदये कथमन्यत्र छाया भवत्यन्यत्रातपः । न हि तस्यान्यः प्रदेशोऽस्ति यत्रातपो न स्यात् । आवरणं च कथं भवति परमाणोः परमाण्वन्तरेण यदि दिग्भागभेदो नेष्यते । न हि कश्चिदपि परमाणोः परमाणोऽस्ति यत्रागमनादन्वेनान्यस्य प्रतिघातः स्यात् । असति च प्रतिघाते सर्वेषां समानदेशत्वासर्वः संघातः परमाणुमात्रः स्यादित्युक्तम् ।

V. M. S. Viṃśatikā Vṛtti, p.16.

58. यत्तच्चक्षुरादीनां विषयो नीलपीताधिकामिष्यते
किं तदेवं द्रव्यमथवा तदनेकमिति ।

V. M. S. Viṃśatuikā Vṛtti, p. 17.

59. एकत्वे न क्रमेणेतिर्युगपन्न ग्रहाग्रहौ ।
विच्छिन्नानेकवृत्तिश्च सूक्ष्मानीक्षा च नो भवेत् ।

V. M. S. Viṃśatikā 15, p. 17.

60. यदि यावददिच्छिन्नं नानेकं चक्षुषो विषयस्तदेकं द्रव्यं कल्प्यते पृथिव्यां क्रमेणेतिर्न स्याद्गमनमित्यर्थः। सकृत्वादक्षेपणे सर्वस्य गतत्वात् । अवोग्भागस्य स ग्रहणं परभागस्य चाग्रहणं युगपन्न स्यात् । न हि तस्यैव तदानीं ग्रहणं चाग्रहणं च युक्तम् । विच्छिन्नस्य चानेकस्य हस्त्यश्वादिकस्यैवात्र वृत्तिर्न स्याद्यत्रैव सेकं तत्रैवापरमिति कथं तयोर्विच्छेद इष्यते । कथं वा तदेकं यत्राप्तं च ताभ्यां न च प्राप्तमन्तराले तच्छून्यग्रहणात् । सूक्ष्माणां चोदकजन्तूनां स्थूलैः समानरुपाणमनीक्षणं न स्यात् । यदि लक्षणभेदादेव द्रव्यान्तरत्वं कल्पय्ते नान्यथा । तामादवश्यं परमाणुशो भेदः कल्पयितव्यः । त चैको न सिद्धति ।

V. M. S. Viṃśatikā Vṛtti, pp. 17-18.

61. तस्यासिद्धौ रूपादीनां चक्षुरादिविषयत्वमसिद्धमिति सिद्धं विज्ञप्तिमात्रं भवतीति ।

V. M. S. Viṃśatikā Vṛtti, p. 18.

62. यदन्तर्ज्ञेयरूपं तु बहिर्वदवभासते ।
सोऽर्थो विज्ञानस्यत्वात्तत्प्रत्ययतयापि च ॥

Ālambanaparīkṣa, 6.

English translation from Aiyaswami N. Sastri (ed.), *Ālambanaparīkṣā and Vṛtti (1942), The Adyar Library Series, 32.*

63. आत्मधर्मोपचारो हि विविधो यः प्रवर्तते ।
विज्ञानपरिणामेऽसौ परिणामः स च त्रिधा ॥
विपाको मननाख्यश्च विज्ञप्तिर्विषयस्य च ।
तत्रालयाख्यं विज्ञानं विपाकः सर्वबीजकम् ॥

V. M. S. Triṃśikā, 1, 2.

64. असंविदितकोपादिस्थानविज्ञप्तिकं च तत् ।
सदा स्पर्शमनस्कारवित्संज्ञाचेतनान्वितम् ॥

V. M. S. Triṃśikā, 3.

65. उपेक्षा वेदना तत्रानिवृताव्याकृतं च तद् ।
तथा स्पर्शादयः तच्च वर्तते स्रोतसौधवत् ॥

V. M. S. Triṃśikā, 4.

English translation from : Thomas A. Kochumuttom, *A Buddhist Doctrine of Experience*, Ch.IV, p.135, First dition (1982),Motilal Banarsidass.

66. तस्य व्यावृत्तिरर्हत्वे......

V. M. S. Triṃśikā, 5(a).

67. ......तदाश्रित्य प्रवर्तते ।
तदालम्बं मनोनाम विज्ञानं मननात्मकम् ।

V. M. S. Triṃśikā, 5.

68. क्लेशैश्चतुर्भिः सहितं निवृताव्याकृतैः सदा ।
आत्मदृष्टात्ममोहात्ममानात्मस्नेह संज्ञितैः ॥

V. M. S. Triṃśikā, 6.

69. यत्रजस्तन्मयैरन्यैः स्पर्शायैश्च अर्हतो न तत् ।
निरोधसमापत्तो, मार्गे लोकोत्तरे न च ॥

V. M. S. Triṃśikā, 7.

70. ......तृतीयः षड्विधस्य या ।
विषयस्योपलब्धिः ता कुशलाकुशलाद्वया ॥

V. M. S. Triṃśikā, 8.

71. विज्ञानपरिणामोऽयं विकल्पो यदिकल्पयते ।
तेन तन्नास्ति तेनेदं सर्वं विज्ञप्तिमात्रकम् ॥

V. M. S. Triṃśikā, 17, p.102.

72. दृष्टा चाभिन्नेऽप्यर्थे प्रतिपत्तृणां परस्परविरूद्धा प्रतिपत्तिः । न चैकत्य परस्परविरुद्धानेकात्मकत्वं युज्यते । तस्मात् अध्यारोपितरूपत्वाद् विकल्पस्यालम्बनम् असदिति प्रतिपत्तव्यम् ।

V. M. S. Triṃśikā Vṛtti, p.103.

73. तस्माद् विषायाभावात् सर्वं विज्ञप्तिमात्रकम् ।

V. M. S. Triṃśikā Vṛtti, p.104.

74. सर्वबीजं हि विज्ञानं परिमाणमस्तथा तथा ।
यात्यन्योन्यवशाद् येन विकल्पः स स जायते ॥
V. M. S. Triṃśikā, 18, p.105.

75. अन्योन्याधिपतित्वेन विज्ञप्तिनियमो मिथः ।
V. M. S. Viṃśatikā, 18(ab), p.21.

76. सर्वेषां हि सत्त्वानामन्योऽन्यविज्ञप्त्याधिपत्येन मिथो विज्ञप्तेर्नियमो भवति यथायोगम् । ..... अतः सन्तानानन्तरविज्ञप्तिविशेषात्सन्तानान्तरे विज्ञप्तिविशेषात्सन्तानान्तरे विज्ञप्तिविशेष उत्पद्यते नार्थविशेषात् ।
V. M. S. Viṃśatikā Vṛtti, p.22.

77. मरणं परविज्ञप्तिविशेषाद्विक्रिया यथा ।
V. M. S. Viṃśatikā, 19 (ab).

78. तथा परविज्ञप्तिविशेषाधिपत्यात्परेषां जीवितेन्द्रियविरोधिनी काचिद्विक्रियोत्पद्यते यया सभागसन्ततिविच्छेदाख्यं मरणं भवतीति वेदितव्यम् ।
V. M. S. Viṃśatikā Vṛtti, p.23.

79. तदेवं भिन्नस्यार्थस्य स्वरूपाभावेऽपि चित्तसन्तानप्रतिनियतत्वात्प्रत्येकं स्वबीजादि्भन्नार्थादिप्रतिभासं विज्ञानं प्रसूयते ।
Commentary of Sthiramati on the *Madhyāntavibhāgasūtrabhāṣya*, p.16; Vibhushekhar Bhattacarya, Tucci (ed.), *Madhyāntavibhāgasūtrabhāṣya, Part-I* (1932), *Calcutta Oriental Series*, No.24.

80. सूत्रेषु हि त्रयः स्वभावा उक्ताः — परिकल्पितः, परतन्त्रः, परिनिष्पन्नश्च ।
V. M. S.Triṃśikā Vṛtti, p.115.

त्रिविधेन विकल्पेन बालैर्भावा विकल्पिताः ।
L. S. X. 171 (ab).

81. विज्ञप्तिमात्र एव सति स्वभावत्रय व्ययस्थानात् ।
V. M. S. Triṃśikā Vṛtti pp. 115-16.

82. येन येन विकल्प्येन यद्यद् वस्तु विकल्प्यते ।
परिकल्पित एवासौ स्वभावो न स विद्यते ॥
V. M. S. Triṃśikā, 20, p.116.

83. .....परैर्हेतुप्रत्ययैस्तन्त्र्यत इति परतन्त्र उत्पाद्यत इत्यर्थः ।
V. M. S.Triṃśikā Vṛtti, p.118.

84. निष्पन्नस्तस्य पूर्वेण सदा रहितता तु या ॥
V. M. S. Triṃśikā, 21 (cd.), p.118.

85. कल्पितः परतन्त्रश्च परिनिष्पन्न एव च ।
त्रयः स्वभावाः धीराणाम् गम्भीरज्ञेयम् इष्यते ॥
Trisvabhāvanirdeśa, 1.
Mukhopadhyaya, S., *Trisvabhāvanirdeśa of Vasubandhu* (1939), *Visvabharati Series-4*, Calcutta.

86. "The *Yogācāra* is an idealist only transcendentally, in empirical matters he has no quarrel with the realist."
Chatterjee, Ashok Kumar, *The Yogācāra Idealism*, Ch.IV., p.74. Second Edition (1975), Motilal Banarsidass.

87. Dasgupta, S.N., *Indian Idealism,* Ch.V., p.137 (1962), Cambridge University Press.

88. सहोपलम्भनियमादभेदो नीलतद्धियोः ।
Sarvadarśanasaṅgraha, p.13, *Ānandāśrama Sanskrit Granthāvalī*-51, (1906).

89. ......तस्मात्स्वव्यतिरिक्तग्राह्यविरहात्तदात्मिका
बुद्धिः स्वयमेव स्वात्मरूपप्रकाशिका प्रकाशवदिति.....
Sarvadarśanasaṅgraha, p.13.

90. यश्चायं ग्राह्यग्राहकसंवित्तीनां पृथगवभातः ।
स एकस्मिंश्चन्द्रमसि द्वित्वावभास इव भ्रमः ॥
Sarvadarśanasaṅgraha, p.13.

4

Idealistic Thought in the *Yoga-Vāsiṣṭha*

THE *Yoga-Vāsiṣṭha* is considered to be a landmark in the history of Indian Philosophy. Though it is known as a *Purāṇa,* it is replete with philosophy, and is an ocean of *Vedāntic* thought. Besides, as the author of the *Yoga-Vāsiṣṭha* is very much influenced by Buddhistic Idealism, the concept of the unreality of the world is strongly emphasised by considering the world as a mere ideation of the mind; and this will be examined in the course of this chapter. As we have seen in the previous chapters, Idealistic views were already presented in the *Upaniṣads;* but it was Idealism in the general sense, which asserts the Ultimate Reality as spiritual. But after that period, Buddhism was established and naturally it affected the views of the later philosophical works. So obviously the *Yoga-Vāsiṣṭha;* under the great spell of Buddhistic Idealism denounced the reality of the world of appearance. Since the Idealistic views expressed in the *Yoga-Vāsiṣṭha* are quite complicated, a successful effort has been made to make its philosophy easy to understand by relating stories, similes, illustrations etc. The lucidity of its style does not fail to impress the reader. Many attempts have been made to ascertain the date of the *Yoga-Vāsiṣṭha.* A number of scholars have expressed their opinions about the date of the *Yoga-Vāsiṣṭha.* B. L. Atreya considers it as a pre-Śaṅkara work (5th or 6th century A.D.) and S. N. Dasgupta as contemporaneous with Gauḍapāda and Śaṅkara or a century anterior (900 A.D.). Shivaraprasada Bhattacharya places it somewhere between the 10th and the 12th century. P. C. Divanji places it in the second, third or the fourth quarter of the 10th century. V. Raghavan places it between the 11th and the 13th century, and Farquhar in the 14th century.[1] It would not be out of place to mention that references to the *Sāṃkhya, Vijñānavāda, Śūnyavāda, Vedānta* and *Nyāya* systems are also found in the *Yoga-Vāsiṣṭha*.[2]

The *Yoga-Vāsiṣṭha* contains six *prakaraṇas,* namely: (a) *vairāgya,* (b) *mumukṣu,* (c) *utpatti,* (d) *sthiti,* (e) *upaśṃa* and (f) *nirvāṇa*. This philosophical poem has about thirty-two thousand verses.

Idealistic Views Expressed in the *Yoga-Vāsiṣṭha*

The author of the *Yoga-Vāsiṣṭha* very forcefully denies the existence of the phenomenal world. Being fully influenced by Buddhist Idealism, very often he has emphasized the falsity (*mithyātva*) of the world of appearance. It is stated that as a son of a barren woman never happens to be in the sky-forest similarly the whole appearance (*dṛśya*), consisting of the world etc. is never there.[3]

It would not be wrong to state that a three-fourth part of the *Yoga-Vāsiṣṭha* reveals the type of Idealism, which negates the reality of the world. So, the views expressed differently have presented below.

The world : A Projection of the Mind

Nobody is unaware of the mind's creative power. The mind can make heaven of hell and *vice versa*. In our day-to-day life we all experience the mind's great constructive as well as destructive role.

The author of the *Yoga-Vāsiṣṭha* has taken rather a bold step in considering the worldly phenomena as projected by the mind. It is stated, "Everything unreal is spread out by the mind like the *Saṁkalpanagara* and *gandharvanagara*.[4] So the world of appearance is nothing but an imagination of the mind. Mountains, rivers, oceans, trees, sky etc. whatever we perceive, are only ideas of the mind. The phenomenal world is only a projection of the mind (*manovijruṁbhita*).[5] Whatever the mind imagines, it perceives.[6] All the things which we perceive around us, are only projections of the mind.[7] In this phenomenal world, whatever forms of things are seen are all false appearances and so when one views the world as such, the world disappears. The seed of imagination, which is sown in the field of consciousness, shoots forth as the sprout of the mind, which becomes the cause of the vast spreading arbour of the universe.[8] And the mind is the sprout of this tree in the form of the phenomenal world.[9] It is the mind, which is the producer and destroyer of this world of appearance, and so we should make efforts to know the mind.[10] The mundane world (*saṁsāra*) is within the mind as the *ghaṭākāśa* (pot-space) is within the pot. On the destruction of the mind, the *saṁsāra* does not remain just as on the destruction of the pot, there remains no *ghaṭākāśa*.[11] It is stated that as flavour remains in the objects, oil remains in the sesamum, fragrance remains in the flower, similarly the motion of the cognisables (*dṛśyadhi*) remains in the perceiver only.[12]

In short, the whole world is in the mind only. As the mind imagines it, it appears accordingly. When the mind starts vibrating, the world springs forth before it, and on the other hand, when the mind stops vibrating, there remains no world.

This shows that the attitude of the mind towards the objects and situations is mainly responsible for how one takes the situations. Hence, the mind plays an active part in the world construction. As a matter of fact, this world of appearance never existed before, nor does it exist now and will not exist in the future also.[13] But the mind is a factor, which expands the whole world of appearance. So what is there inside the mind, that springs forth before its perceiver.

Perhaps, this is the main doctrine of the *Yoga-Vāsiṣṭha* which is put forth variously by the author.

The Empirical World : Compared with the Dreaming World

Usually the unreality of the phenomenal world is compared with the unreality of the dreaming state. In the *Yoga-Vāsiṣṭha* too the world of appearance (*dṛśya prapañca*) is compared to a dream. The objects, which we perceive during the dreaming state, are results of *vāsanā* (residual impressions). So are the objects of the empirical world also. It is stated in the *Yoga-Vāsiṣṭha* that a prolonged dream known as *saṁsāra* (mundane world) has come to stay by the force of the mind.[14] As the dream is an illusion only and not a real one, similarly know it (the world) as a huge dream projected by the mind (*citta*).[15] We can find the very same idea put forth in the *Gauḍapādakārikā,* where Gauḍapāda has compared the waking state with the dreaming state.[16]

Now a question perplexing the mind is as to whose dream the world is — whether of the individual mind or of the cosmic mind. This point will be discussed later.

It is stated in the *Yoga-Vāsiṣṭha* that the universe is the dream of *prajāpati.* In the beginning, God conceived himself as the lord of creation (*Brahmā*) and then as in a dream, he saw in himself all the forms as they continue to this time.[17] The question is asked as to why the world should appear unreal to *Brahmā* and others whereas it appears real to us.[18] The answer to this is given in the next verse.[19] When *Brahmā* and others were not enlightened, the earlier creation appeared real to them as it does to us. The so-called Reality of the world persists only as long as we are in the mundane state. But the world certainly is not real.

The Theory of Relativity

In the third, viz. *Utpatti Prakaraṇa,* the theory of Relativity is propounded very clearly. Both time and space are related to the ideas of the mind. According to the state of the mind, time and space change. Sometimes a moment seems as long as one year; on the other hand, a year seems short like a moment only.

The story of Līlā explains this theory of Relativity.Queen Līlā was very eager to know how the human being could be immortal. She wanted that her husband (King Padma) should be immortal. As a result of her penance, Goddess Sarasvatī appeared before her and preached about the falsity of the world of appearance. This story is narrated as follows:

In order to make her husband (King Padma) immortal, Queen Līlā performed penance. As a result of it, Līlā gained a boon from Goddess Sarasvatī that after the death of her husband, his soul would not go out from the room. After his death, Līlā remembered Sarasvatī, who appeared before her. Because of her grace, Līlā got *yogic* power and entered into *cidākāśa*. She saw worlds within worlds and visualised her previous births and became very much confused. She could not make out clearly as to which world was true. Whether the world of her husband or the world which she herself and Goddess Sarasvatī were perceiving was true.[20] The Goddess instructed her in respect of the false character of the mundane world. A false world could not be created out of a real world. In any case, an effect different from the cause could not be created.[21] Hence both the worlds should be considered false. But according to their own time and space both the worlds are considered real. Because of *saṁskāra* (residual traces) of the past cognition a new world is created. It is stated that people performing the acts according to their *vāsanā*, get their fruits accordingly and not in any other way.[22] There is no sweetness in the sugarcane nor bitterness in the *nimba,* nor is there any heat or cold in the fire or in the moon. As one is used to things, so are they apprehended. It is the strong obsession regarding them that gives them the shape.[23] As the mind (*citta*) vibrates, things appear. The mind-vibration relation is just like the relation of sesamum and oil, flower and fragrance, fire and heat. They are just non-different. Their difference which is imagined is false.[24] This phenomenal world is nothing else but only a network of constructive imaginations, the result of the vibrations of the mind only. The phenomenal world changes according to time and space, and this depends on the ideas of the mind. As a result, one moment may seem as long as one *kalpa*. When someone is happy, a night seems short like a moment only. On the other hand, when someone is miserable, a night seems long like a *kalpa*. In the dream, a moment becomes a *kalpa* and *vice versa*.[25] King Hariścandra experienced one night to be as long as the period of twelve years.[26]

The story of King Lavaṇa illustrates the very same ideas.[27] Under the great influence of magic, King Lavaṇa experienced a hundred years as a *cāṇḍāla* within one night only.[28] This story is as follows : One day, in the Court a magician came to show the wonders of his magic to King Lavaṇa. Under the great influence of magic, the King experienced hundred years as a *cāṇḍāla* within one night only. During that period he experienced many passing scenes in one single moment. Due to magic, he felt that he was wandering in the forest. There he met a *cāṇḍāla* girl, and married her. As a *cāṇḍāla* he passed many miserable years. In his old age, because of famine he left his village with his family. To save his younger son, he decided to die so that his son could eat his flesh. But as soon as he entered into the fire, he found himself as King Lavaṇa in his own court.

Hence, the creative impulse (*spaṁda-śakti*) of the mind creates this world of appearance.

As the mind imagines the world, so it appears.[29] Everything we perceive is nothing but the mind only.[30] Because of the *saṁkalpa* (constructive imagination) of the mind, the world of appearance is created. Heaven, earth, air, sky, mountains, rivers, etc. are imagined by the *saṁkalpa* of the self like a dream.[31] Hence King Lavaṇa found the same series of events with the *cāṇḍālas* of Vindhya, as he had been impressed within his dream and the same took possession of the minds of the Vindhya people.[32] In the case of different poets of different countries, the same thoughts or expressions arising out of mental conceptions occur. In the same manner people seem to see or have or talk about the same object and are tempted to conclude that it is real.[33]

Thus common experiences of empirical events are possible, though they are as a matter of fact unreal. The false dream that King Lavaṇa had of the Vindhya people, the same dream took possession of their minds also. Hence it can be said that the common belief of the reality of things is the effect of a universal delusion. Thus in common experience, people seem to experience the very same object and thus different people have common experience.

Thus, the story of King Lavaṇa shows the possibility of

common experiences as well as emphasizes the theory of Relativity, that both time and space are completely dependent on the mind. In short, according to the ideas of the mind both time and space keep on changing.

The Concept of *Avidyā*

There is no other alternative, except *Avidyā* which could serve as a solution to the question as to how this world appears real to us. The author of the *Yoga-Vāsiṣṭha* openly considers *Avidyā* as the cause,[34] due to which this mundane world appears before us. But a question may arise as to how it (the world) appears as real? *Avidyā*, due to which the world appears as real, cannot be related to the *Ātman*, because there can be no intimate relation between two dissimilar things, and without mutual relation, there cannot be mutual experience.[35] . . . On the other hand, the relation of lac-wood (*jatukāṣṭha*) which have both similarities as well as dissimilarities, thought possible, cannot be mutually experienced. In fact, it cannot serve to explain the possibility of the relation of *Ātman* and *Avidyā* for here both *jatu* and *kāṣṭha* are just the vibration of *Avidyā*.[36] It may be argued that everything is of the nature of the Ultimate Reality. Therefore, stones etc. which are similar, are illumined by consciousness (*cit*) due to relation.[37] If all the things in the world be of the nature of pure consciousness-cum-existence, then they should be mutually manifested by force of self-illumination.[38] (Stones etc. would not require consciousness for their illumination). Dissimilar things cannot possibly be intimately related. They cannot have mutual experience on account of mutual connection.[39] A similar thing having attained sufficient unity with the existent reveals its one form even because it is one, not otherwise.[40] Again the objection may arise that wood and stone are seen to be connected with each other in a house construction, but they are not of the nature of sentiency.[41] A (non-sentient) thing is seen to be modified in the form of another thing. But sentiency cannot be so modified. The experience of taste, which arises pure and clear by means of homogeneous things (tongue and taste), is experienced by the tongue only and not *vice versa*. Relation is not possible between two different things, namely sentient and non-sentient.[42]

In answer of this objection, it is stated that the experience (of the ignorant people) arises with the notion that knowledge-knowable cannot be explained on the basis of non-difference between the sentient and non-sentient.[43] But the sentient and non-sentient being quite dissimilar cannot be one. The sentient and non-sentient if different, can never be united. Nor could the things of the nature of sentiency have any relation with sentiency for there would be no difference between the two: sentiency itself takes the form of stone, wall etc.[44] Everything (wood, stone, etc.) is of the nature of Ultimate Reality. Thus everything is *Brahman* and it is in relation to sentiency that the world appears to be filled with crores of illusions, which are false.[45] Only when we have the knowledge of difference, can the illusion of 'I'ness etc. arise; just as only when we lose sight of gold, can the illusion of bracelet etc. arise. For, the illusion of bracelet etc. is dependent for its existence on gold.[46] In reality, the illusion of the world is nothing else, but the one *Brahman*. In the relation of seen-seeing-seer, the very essence of the seer is devoid of seer-seeing-seen.[47] The eternal nature of the sentient is devoid of the waking state, dreaming state and the sleeping state. It is neither sentient nor non-sentient.[48] It is of the nature of existence, and bliss.

Hence, due to *Avidyā* the duality of sentient and non-sentient arises, and this is only an illusion. Because of ignorance only, the so-called difference appears. But in reality, all this is *Brahman* only. *Avidyā* is the creative force, due to which this world of appearance seems to be real.

In this context, a question perplexing the mind is; whose *Avidyā* is responsible? That is to say, whether the *Avidyā* of the cosmic soul or of the individual soul is responsible for the world of appearance.

The *Avidyā* of Cosmic Soul and the Individual Soul

If this world phenomenon is imagined by the *Avidyā* of an individual soul, then the doubt would arise that when an individual soul stops imagining, then this world should not be seen. But such a thing never happens. When one soul stops imagining, then the world imagined by that particular soul gets lost. But the other souls keep on observing this world of appearance, as each and every mind creates its own universe separately. On the other hand it is stated: Whenever the thought of making the world rises in the mind of *Brahmā*, the creator, he assumes an unreal body according to his own will.[49] He had the conception of the world in his own imagination. He conceived at first the luminous idea of light.[50] Then the sun sprung forth from the light.[51] Afterwards *Brahmā* produced some other bright forms. He stretched the seas, mountains and trees. It was he who created happiness and misery, birth, death, disease and decay, the passions and feelings of living beings, all consisting of the three *guṇas;* viz. *sattva, rajas,* and *tamas.*[52] By just the vibration of the mind, arose the *citta* which gave rise to the phenomenal world.[53]

Hence the reply to the doubt, as why this phenomenal world appears the same to all, could be given as follows: above these individual souls, there is the existence of the cosmic soul, which also have imagined this phenomenal world; and that is why common phenomenal experiences occur.

So the individual soul (*Vyaṣṭi jīva*) and the cosmic soul (*Samaṣṭi jīva*) both are responsible for the creation of the phenomenal world. We experience illusions in our mundane life, e.g., *rajju-sarpa,* dream etc. But these are what we may call personal illusion brought about by our respective individual imagination, e.g., 'A' perceives *sarpa* in *rajju* but 'B' does not. 'B' perceives *rajju* only. So *sarpa* appearing instead of *rajju* is a fiction of 'A's mind. Thus each and every individual is responsible for its own imaginary world.[54] The author of the *Yoga-Vāsiṣṭha* has presented an example that people, living in the northern direction do not know anything about people living in the southern direction except as their own conceptions.[55] This individually created universe dissolves into nothingness in the Great dissolution (*Mahā Pralaya*).

At the time of the new creation in the case of ignorant souls, birth and death are caused by their reminiscences of earlier birth. Memory (*smṛti*) becomes the cause of birth and death.[56]

When the soul at the end of death appears to be as if opening out internally, it is really non-awake (winking) externally. That is the stage of *Pradhāna*.[57] It is the cause of *ākāśa*. As the living principle begins to have its awareness, it is called intelligent being.[58] When it is on the point of awaking, it is known as the *mahat* element. When awake, it is called *ahaṁkāra*. And then *tanmātrā*, time, direction, etc. arise.[59] These things slightly developed and slightly awakened are known as the five sense-organs. Then only arises the intermediary (*ātivāhika*) body.[60] This has the awareness of material body by force of long standing notions, which are fastened by imagination.[61] Then arises the concept of the imagination of things on the basis of the concept of the gross body. They appear to arise eventhough they are not there. Thus the illusion of the world grows strong falsely. But like the union with the woman in the dream, though experienced it is non-existent,[62] being born as it were, (the foolish) identify themselves with the body etc. and experience the illusion of 'I' and the world.[63]

It is also stated in the *Yoga-Vāsiṣṭha* that mountains etc. which appear as real, are superimposed by *Māyā*. In the beginning of the world, *ādi prajāpati* in the manner of *svapna-puruṣa*, very clearly appeared as mountains etc. He continues to remain so.[64] The same manner of existence continues. This first vibration serves as the *bimba* for things. What is reflected from it, continues to remain even now.[65] When the wind moves in the different open spaces of the body and moves the limbs, we say a person is living.[66] In the beginning of the world, the position was the same in regard to moving things, though they were motionless. The *cidākāsa* — *Īśvara* himself dreams about the classification of sentient soul and that aspect alone is sentient. The rest is non-sentient.

The soul penetrates gross things through the intellect. The sentient entity which has identified with the intellect, through it enters the city in the form of the human body which serves as its adjunct. The soul leads the intellect superimposed by it to the eye-ball and through the perceptual psychosis becomes aware of external objects. It may be objected that the eye etc. being directly superimposed on the sentient entity and occupying the body could function without requiring the help of *buddhi* and so it is not necessary to imagine the soul as having *buddhi* as its adjunct. The answer to this is as follows : The 'eye' that is a sense-organ cannot itself appear as a sentient entity, because only by being superimposed on the *cit* a thing cannot be said to be sentient, *Buddhi* alone can be an adjunct of the soul, and thus all dealings occur through *Buddhi*.[67] And with this intellect (*buddhi*) as adjunct, the soul imagines *ākāśa* etc. and so they appear.[68] Because of ignorance about the Ultimate Truth, one believes that this world of appearance is real, but as a matter of fact, it is only an imagination.

So, the world of appearance is imagined by the cosmic soul as well as by individual soul. That is why, on the one hand the universe differs from one individual soul to another, and on the other hand each one has a common worldly experience. It is stated in the *Yoga-Vāsiṣṭha*: "As each and every soldier of the same army experiences different army in the dream according to his own *vāsanā* and believes that the army is the same, similarly individual souls experience different worlds according to their own *vāsanā* and believe that world they all experience the very same.[69]

One may say that the author of the *Yoga-Vāsiṣṭha* is reiterating that the world is an imagination of the individual soul, and constantly harping on the idea that each soul imagines its own universe and even explains how all have the same empirical experiences. This philosophical approach of the author was perhaps because of the influence of *Vijñānavāda* literature. (See, e.g., *Vijñaptimātratāsiddhi*). But being a follower of the *Vedic* school, the author of the *Yoga-Vāsiṣṭha* cannot think of giving up the Monistic thought; and therefore again and again refers to the cosmic mind as imagining the world.

It may be remarked that this theory of the unreality of the world, though it could be germinally traced in the *Upaniṣads* it did not overtly develop in the *Vedic* school till about the time of the *Yoga-Vāsiṣṭha* and Gauḍapāda, and it is quite likely that the *Vedāntic* thought in this direction was not quite ripe and mature enough for formulating a terminology suitable for idealism and yet in conformity with the *Vedāntic* thought and linguistic expression. The main source for argument in favour of Idealism was naturally *Vijñānavāda* and even *Cārvāka* literature (that propounding *Tattvopaplava*). This accounts for the profusion of Buddhist terms and thoughts in works like the *G.K.* and the *Yoga-Vāsiṣṭha;* though the authors remained strong adherents of the *Vedāntic* current of thought.

Creativity of *Māyā* : Now, coming to the point we would like to illustrate the creative power of *Māyā,* which is presented in the form of the story of Gādhi.[70]

In a country named Kośala, lived a *brāhmaṇa* named Gādhi, who was very eager to see the mysterious *Māyā* of Lord Viṣṇu. By virtue of his penance, Lord Viṣṇu appeared before him, and by God's grace Gādhi got a vision of *Māyā* — the creative power of God. It is stated in the *Yoga-Vāsiṣṭha* that *Māyā* is *Guṇamayī.* Actually it does not exist but by virtue of illusion and delusion it appears as the world of appearance. It disappears when it is examined as waves disappear in water.[71] The story of Gādhi narrates a number of interesting experiences of Gādhi. As soon as Gādhi entered into a large pond to take his bath, a miracle happened. He saw himself as a dead person in his house. Then he took rebirth as a *cāṇḍāla.* Gradually he became youthful and married a *cāṇḍāla* girl. In his old age, as he was very unhappy, he left that country and went to another country named Kīra. As chance would have it, he became a King over there; under the same 'Gavala'. Once some *cāṇḍālas* recognised him. As a result, people of that country insulted him. So he became very unhappy and decided to die. As soon as he entered into the fire, he found himself in that very same pond, which he had entered to take his bath. Thus Gādhi had the experience of the mysterious *Māyā.* By virtue of *Māyā,* he had an experience of a number of years as a *cāṇḍāla* within some moments only. Thus the phenomenal world (*Prapañca*) is a magical show presented by *Māyā.* This fictitious drama of *Māyā* is unending, and disappears only with the conquest of the mind, i.e., the imaginative faculty.[72]

After that, Gādhi met other people, who also had the very

same experience. Because of the similarity of the *saṁkalpa* (conceptual construction), similarity of time and space is brought about. Whatever Gādhi experienced, was true according to the people, whom he asked about its reality. It is clearly understood that in the world of imagination, nothing is impossible. One may pass several years within a few moments of the empirical state.

Power of *Saṁkalpa* (Conceptual Construction): To illustrate the great power of *saṁkalpa,* the author has narrated the story of a *brāhmaṇa* named Indu in the third viz. *Utpatti Prakaraṇa.*[73] In the country, named *Suvarṇajaṭa,* there lived a *brāhmaṇa* named Indu, who had no child, so he and his wife performed penance, and received God's boon that he would be the father of ten intelligent sons. After some years when Indu and his wife both died, those ten sons became miserable and wanted to have peace of mind. They imagined themselves as Brahmā and ten different worlds were created because of their *saṁkalpa.*

It is stated in the *Yoga-Vāsiṣṭha* that nothing exists except our conceptual construction (*saṁkalpa*).[74] The objects of appearance are there only as they are imagined, just in the manner of *Saṁkalpanagara* and the dream-city. Thus the whole world is but an imagination.[75]

This very same idea is put forth through the story of three unborn boys.[76] This story emphasizes the absolute unreality of the world also. It is as follows : Once a mother told a story to her child that in a city which never existed, there lived three princes. Two of them were never born and the third one never entered the womb of any mother. In the same manner, the story narrates various episodes which never took place.

As an adherent of the *Vedāntic* thought, the author of the *Yoga-Vāsiṣṭha* has emphasized that, to the learned one, all this is simply *Brahman.* There is no such thing as the mundane world (*saṁsāra*); which is a mere belief of the unintelligent.[77] On the other hand, to the ignorant, this mundane world is eternal because of the uniformity of common experiences; but after all; it is the effect of the everlasting eternal nescience (*Avidyā*), which creates or projects the false world of appearance.[78] Due to Nescience (*Avidyā*) this mundane world appears. *Māyā* is considered as identical with *Avidyā*, which is responsible for this world of appearance.[79]

It would not be out of place to mention that the problem of locus of *Avidyā* is not put forth by the author of the *Yoga-Vāsiṣṭha*. He has simply stated that due to *Avidyā* both the cosmic soul as well as the individual soul create the false appearance of the mundane world. Whether *Avidyā* resides in the cosmic soul or in the individual soul, this point is not initiated by the author. We shall see in the later chapters how and when this complex problem of locus of *Avidyā* came to be initiated and tackled.

Till here, subjectivistic views have been expressed in the *Yoga-Vāsiṣṭha*. The author has firmly emphasized that the world of appearance is completely based on the mind. That is to say, the world remains in the mind of its perceiver.

But it is also noteworthy that the author has not completely surrendered to the Subjectivistic view. He has fully justified Monistic Idealism by describing *Brahman* as the non-dual Ultimate Reality. So, now the monistic views expressed in the *Yoga-Vāsiṣṭha* will be discussed.

Monistic Idealism — Acosmism

We have seen in the previous chapters that during the *Upaniṣadic* period, germs of absolute monism could be scented. Here, in the *Yoga-Vāsiṣṭha* Monistic Idealism has developed. Abolishing the reality of the world of appearance, the author of the *Yoga-Vāsiṣṭha* has repeatedly emphasized the only Reality of the non-dual sentiency viz. *Brahman*.

It is stated that everything is *Brahman* only. Rightly speaking the world does not exist at all. *Brahman* is the whole world and remains above the world.[80] In the world, whatever appears is *Brahman* only.[81] This world of appearance is not different from *Brahman*, in the same way as a pot is not different from clay. Gold and ornaments are not different from each other. Ornaments are different shapes only and do not differ from their very essence viz. gold.[82] Similarly the phenomenal world is not different from *Brahman.* It is stated in the *Yoga-Vāsiṣṭha* that this phenomenal appearance was not created in the past, is not created at present and will not be created in the future also. The turth is that this universe is *Brahman* of the form of existence.[83] This world of appearance, which is in reality *Brahman* only, appears as having various types of forms. When we perceive any object, it appears thus: 'This is such'. The 'thatness' is real but the 'whatness' is superimposed upon it, and is only a fiction. Thus the 'thatness' always remains unchanged, on the other hand, the 'whatness' always changes.

The story of Śikhidhvaja and Cūḍālā narrated in the sixth viz. *Nirvāṇa Prakaraṇa*[84] points out that there is no substantiality in the world of appearance. The Highest Reality viz. *Brahman* is all-pervading. But because of nescience (*Avidyā*), the mind (*citta*) superimposes false appearance on *Brahman.*

In the very same *prakaraṇa,* the conversation between Ikṣvāku and Manu is narrated;[85] which simply states that all this is *Brahman. Dṛśya* is never produced here; it was not produced and will not be produced. At present also it is not existing. Only the Ultimate Sentiency exists.[86] Nothing is ever produced or destroyed here. Only *Brahman* expands itself as the appearance of the world.[87] Where nothing is produced, the question of destruction does not arise at all.[88] Here the author has propounded 'Acosmism' (*Ajātivāda*), which is found in its full bloom in the *Gauḍapādakārikā.* By narration of *Ajātivāda,* the author of the *Yoga-Vāsiṣṭha* has indicated the highest position of *Vedāntic* thought.

While emphasizing Monistic views, further it is stated very clearly that *Brahman* is the only Ultimate Reality, which is pervading everywhere. This world of appearance as such is never existent just like a barren's son or forest in firmament.[89] As a matter of fact, the *dṛśya* is a fiction or false appearance, like mirage water and two moons, which springs forth accidently (*kākatālīya*).[90]

Thus, the phenomenal world is nothing else but *Brahman* only.

Brahman, the only Reality is pervading everywhere, from atom up to universe.

Such Monistic Idealism expressed in the *Yoga-Vāsiṣṭha* shows that though the author was influenced by Buddhistic Idealism, he did not ignore *Vedāntic* thought, but rather gave it the highest position.

The actual use of the term *Dṛṣṭi-Sṛṣṭi*

As already stated, this chapter deals with the views expressed in the *Yoga-Vāsiṣṭha*; that could lead us straight in the direction of the *Dṛṣṭi-Sṛṣṭi-vāda*. Strikingly enough, we can find the actual term *Dṛṣṭi-Sṛṣṭi* used in the *Yoga-Vāsiṣṭha* though it is considered to be a later development. The subject-matter of the *Yoga-Vāsiṣṭha* is very much related to the concept, which came to be later known as *Dṛṣṭi-Sṛṣṭi-vāda*. Not only *Dṛṣṭi-Sṛṣṭi*, but the term *Sṛṣṭi-Dṛṣṭi* has also been used in the *Yoga-Vāsiṣṭha*.

This phenomenal world, which does not exist in a real sense, appears the same to different people, e.g., 'table'. In the classroom all the students perceive the table; which is the same for all. In the same manner, this world of appearance is experienced as being common to all. For this reason it is believed that as the things exist really; they appear common and real to all. The author of the *Yoga-Vāsiṣṭha* has applied the term *Sṛṣṭi-Dṛṣṭi* to explain this idea. The learned person considers the creation as similar to rain emerging from water. As rain is not different from water, this seeming phenomenal world is not different from God.[91] As the leaves and seeds of a tree are not different from the tree itself, this phenomenal world is not different from God.[92].

But this mundane world is the sparkling of the mind. Things appear when they are carved like a statue on the stone pillar, otherwise the worlds remain in the unperturbable self as waves lie in the bosom of the calm sea.[93] All the outspreading world phenomena are as the waves of the ocean. As waves are not different from the ocean, this *Sṛṣṭi* is not separate from the Self.[94] This mundane world is a sparkle of the intellect; which is manifested as external sight before our eyes.[95]

Thus the term *Sṛṣṭi-Dṛṣṭi* is used in the sense that this seeming *Sṛṣṭi* is the same for all and is looked upon as non-different from God. This would admit the creation of the phenomenal world by God. It is there and so is perceived. Thus the term *Sṛṣṭi-Dṛṣṭi* is discussed at some length.

On the other hand, the term *Dṛṣṭi-Sṛṣṭi* is used only once.[96]

As Dasgupta puts it, "It is said that all is pure and simple illusion, and that things exist only when they are perceived and dissolve into nothingness as soon as we cease to perceive them."[97] It is stated in the *Yoga-Vāsiṣṭha* that this world phenomena comes into view by virtue of just ignorance and disappears at the dawn of knowledge. Objects are seen in the substratum of the soul, as snake (*sarpa*) is seen in the substratum of the rope (*rajju*).[98] Things are seen in the same manner at the same place and time as one thinks about them.[99] As the mirage water appears due to sun light reflected on sand, so do all visible objects present themselves to the sight of the cogniser, besides which, they have no form of their own.[100]

Thus things are perceived because we have imagined them as existing. It is due to *Avidyā* that this phenomenal world appears. Rightly speaking, this mundane world exists in the perceiver's perception. As fragrance remains in the flower, oil remains in the sesamum, in the same manner, the mundane world remains in the perceiver only.[101] This view can be interpreted to mean that when one perceives, the thing appears, and in this way it can be said to have resemblance with the *Dṛṣṭi-Sṛṣṭi-vāda.*

As the term *Dṛṣṭi-Sṛṣṭi* is used only once in the *Yoga-Vāsiṣṭha* one cannot get a definite idea about the concept as thought out by the author, but one can only try to interprete it. By the term *Sṛṣṭi-Dṛṣṭi* one can understand that this *Sṛṣṭi* is common to all. It is not different for different people, as all perceive a comon world, imagined by the cosmic mind. Thus *Sṛṣṭi* should be believed as real (from the empirical point of view). This view helps the *Sṛṣṭi-Dṛṣṭi-vāda;* whereas by the term *Dṛṣṭi-Sṛṣṭi* one can understand that this seeming world appears individually to each and every individual soul, as it is stated that every individual soul creates its own separate world. But here again, there arise some complications, which are difficult to solve. Though a step ahead in the direction of the *Dṛṣṭi-Sṛṣṭi-vāda;* it is difficult to find more details that could help to comprehend the problem. In a later chapter, it has been discussed how the *Dṛṣṭi-Sṛṣṭi-vāda* tried to solve some complicated questions.

Hence, it can be assumed that in the *Yoga-Vāsiṣṭha* there is the germ, from which the *Dṛṣṭi-Sṛṣṭi-vāda* developed afterwards. Both Subjective, as well as Objective Idealism are presented in the *Yoga-Vāsiṣṭha.* As the author is highly influenced by Buddhistic Idealism, he has firmly emphasized Subjective Idealism, i.e., nothing is outside the mind; but things appear 'as if' they are outside. Earth, heaven, sky, mountains, rivers, etc., are inside the mind but appear 'as if' they are outside.[102] As leaves of the tree remain in the small sprout, in the same manner this world of appearance remains in the mind only.[103] This idea is parallel to the view of the *Vijñānavāda.* It would not be out of place to mention that it resembles Idealism of Berkeley very much; according to whom *esse est percipi.* That is to say, "to be is to be perceived"; which is similar to the *Dṛṣṭi-Sṛṣṭi-vāda.*

Thus, it can be concluded that with the help of Subjective and Monistic Idealism the author of the *Yoga-Vāsiṣṭha* has tried to solve the inconceivable mystery of this world of appearance. For this purpose, he has emphasized the concepts of *Avidyā, Māyā, Saṁkalpa, Dṛṣṭi-Sṛṣṭi* etc. Besides, the author has presented two alternatives viz. individual mind and cosmic mind as imagining the world of appearance; and has tried to solve a doubt as to how each one perceives a common world, as well as how it happens that each individual has its own separate idea about the world of appearance.

Putting forth a palpable solution, the author simply emphasizes the highest position of *Vedāntic* thought, that nothing is ever produced here. Rightly speaking all is simply *Brahman.* This world of appearance is merely an illusion, which springs forth due to constructive imagination of the mind.

In nut-shell it can be stated that while presenting a fine synthesis of Subjective Idealism and Monistic Idealism, the *Yoga-Vāsiṣṭha* has captured an outstanding place in the history of Indian Philosophy. Besides, by employing expressions which are very helpful in the direction of the *Dṛṣṭi-Sṛṣṭi-vāda,* it has made its unforgettable contribution to the *Vedāntic* thought.

References

1. Mainkar, T. G., *The Vāsiṣṭha Rāmāyaṇa — A Study,* Ch. VI, (1977), Meharchand Lachhmandas.

2. *Yv.* III.5, 6, 7, III, 96-50.
   Yv. VI(b).97-4, 5, 6.
   Yv. IV. 1-17.
   Yv. IV. 21, 24, 28, 30.
   Pansikar Wasudeva Laxman Sastri (ed.), *The Yoga-Vāsiṣṭha of Vālmiki,* Third edition (1981), Munshiram Manoharlal.

3. वन्ध्यापुत्रव्योमवने यथा न स्तः कदाचन ।
   जगदाद्यखिलं दृश्य नास्ति कदाचन ॥
   Yv. III. 11.4.

4. मनसा तन्यते सर्वमसदेवदेमाततम् ।
   यथा संकल्पनगर यथा गन्धर्वपत्तनम् ॥
   Yv. III.3.30.

5. सर्वमेव मनोमात्रभ्रान्त्युल्लासविजृम्भणम ।
   Yv. III. 67.27 (ab).

6. एवं यदेव मनः कल्पयति तदेव पश्यति ।
   Yv. III. 67.82 (ab)
   यत्र यदा यदेवासौ यथा भावयति, तत्र तदा तदेवासौ प्रपश्यति ।
   *Yv.*III.63.3

7. चितमेवेदमखिलं सर्वेणैवानुभूयते ।
   Yv. III. 96.57 (ab).

8. चित्क्षेत्रे कलना बीजं यदेतत्पततिस्फुरन् ।
   चित्ताङ्कुरं तदेतस्माद्भाविसंसारखण्डकः ॥
   Yv. VI (a). 49.33.

9. अस्य संसारवृक्षस्य मनो मूलमहाङ्कुरः
   Yv. V.9.55 (cd).

10. चित्तं कारणमर्थानां तस्मिन्सति जगत्रयम ।
    तस्मिन्क्षीणे जगत्क्षीणं तच्चिकित्स्यं प्रयत्नतः ॥
    Yv. I.16.25.

11. चितान्तरेव संसारः कुम्भान्तः कुम्भरवं यथा ।
    चित्तनाशे न संसारः कुम्भनाशे न कुम्भखम् ॥
    Yv. V. 50.14.

12. यथा रसः पदार्थेषु यथा तैलं तिलादिषु ।
कुसुमेषु यथा मोदस्तथा द्रष्टरि दृश्यधीः ॥
Yv. III.1.43.

13. तस्माद्राम जगन्नासीन्न चास्ति न भविष्यति ।
Yv. IV. 2.8 (ab).

Yv. IV. 33.18.
Yv. IV. 45.45 (ab).

14. दीर्घः स्वप्नः स्थितिं यातः संसाराख्यो मनोबलात् ।
Yv. III. 65.7 (ab).

15. यथा स्वप्नो महारम्भो भ्रान्तिरेव न वस्तुतः ।
दीर्घस्वप्नं तथैवेदं विद्धि चित्तोपपादितम् ॥
Yv. IV. 45.24.

16. G.K. II. 4, 5.

17. सर्गादौ स्वप्नपुरुषन्यायेनादि प्रजापतिः ।
यथा स्फुटं प्रकचितस्तथाद्यापि स्थिताः स्थितिः ॥
Yv. III.55.47.

18. यथास्माकं मुने स्वप्नपुरपत्तन मण्डलम् ।
तथैव पद्मजादीनां यदि देहपरिग्रहः ॥१॥
तथैवेदं च संजातं यदि सर्वमसन्मयम् ।
तस्माकं दृढतरः प्रत्ययः कथमुत्थितः ॥२॥
Yv. VI (a). 61.1, 2.

19. अस्मत्सर्गवदाभाति पूर्वसर्गः प्रजापतेः ।
आजीवप्रतिभासात्मा विद्यते न तु वास्तवः ॥
Yv. VI(a). 61.3.

20. तत्र भ्रान्तिमयः सर्गः कः स्यात्कः पारमार्थिकः ।
इति पृच्छामि वागीशाममयर्च्यौक्तमसंशयम् ॥
Yv. III.18-6.

21. कृत्रिमो कृत्रिमात्सर्गान्न कदाचन जायते ।
नहि कारणतः कार्यमुदेत्यसदृशं क्वचित् ॥
Yv. III 18.18.

22. स्वया वासनया लोको यद्यत्कर्म करोति यः ।
स तथैव तदाप्नोति नेतरस्येह कर्तृता ॥
Yv. IV 13.11.

23. न निम्बेक्षू कटुस्वादू शीतोष्णौ नन्दुपावकौ ।
यद्यथा परमाप्यस्तमुपलब्धं तथैव तत् ॥
Yv. IV.21.33.

24. यथा शौक्लयहिमे राम तिलतैललवौ यथा ।
यथा कुसुमसौगन्ध्ये तथौष्ण्यदहनौ यथा ॥
तथा राघव संश्लिष्टौ चित्तस्पन्दौ तथैव हि ।
अभिन्नौ केवलं मिथ्या भेदः कल्पित एतयोः ॥
Yv. V.78.5, 6.

25. दुःखितस्य निशा कल्पः सुखितस्येव च क्षणः ।
क्षणः स्वप्ने भवेत्कल्पः कल्पश्च भवति क्षणः ॥
Yv. III. 60.22.
26. रात्रिं द्वादशवर्षाणि हरिश्चन्द्रोऽनुभूतवान् ।
Yv. III. 60.24 (ab).
27. *Yv.* III. 104 to 109.
28. लवणो भुक्तवानायुरेकरात्र्या समाः शतम् ॥
Yv. III. 60.24 (cd).
29. *Yv.* IV. 38.7.
30. *Yv.* III. 85.4(ab).
31. द्यौः क्षमा वायुराकाशं पर्वताः सरितो दिशः ।
संकल्पचितं सर्वमेवं स्वप्नवदात्मनः ॥
Yv. III. 101.35.
32. अथवा लवणेनाशु दृष्टो यः स्वप्नविभ्रमः ।
स एव संविदं प्राप्तो विन्ध्यपुष्कसचेतसि ॥
Yv. III. 121.26.
33. यथा बहूनां सदृशं वचनं नाम मानसम्।
तथा स्वप्नेऽपि भवति कालो देशः क्रियापि च ॥
Yv. III. 121.28.
34. *Yv.* VI (a). 127-20 (ab).
35. अविद्ययात्मतत्त्वस्य संबन्धो नोपपद्यते ।
संबन्धः सदृशानां च यः स्फुटः स्वानुभूतितः ॥
Yv. III. 121.33.
36. जतुकाष्ठादिसंबन्धो यः समासमयोगतः ।
नान्योन्यानुभवायासौ तदैकस्पन्दमात्रकम् ॥
Yv. III. 121.34.
37. परमार्थमयं सर्वं यथा तेनोपलादयः ।
चिता समभिचेत्यन्ते संबन्धवशतः समाः ॥
Yv. III. 121.35.
38. यदा चिन्मात्रसन्मात्रमयाः सर्वे जगद्गताः ।
भावास्तदा विभान्त्येते मिथः स्वानुभवस्थिते: ॥
Yv. III. 121.36.
39. न संभवति संबन्धो विषमाणां निरन्तरः ।
न परस्परसंबन्धाद्विनानुभवनं मिथः ॥
Yv. III. 121.37.
40. सदंशे सदृशं वस्तु क्षणाद्गत्येकतामलम् ।
रुपमास्फारयत्येकमेकत्वादेव नान्यथा ॥
Yv. III. 121.38.
41. दारुपाषाणभेदानां न तु ह्येते चिदात्मकाः ।
पदार्थो हि पदार्थेन परिणाम्यनुभूयते ॥
Yu. III. 121.41.

42. जिह्वयैव रसास्वादः सजातीयामलोदयाः ।
ऐक्यं च विद्धि संबन्धं नास्त्यसावसमानयोः ॥
Yv. III. 121.42.

43. चिच्चेत्यमिलिता दृश्यरूपयोदेति चेतनः ।
जडं जडेन मिलितं घनं संपद्यते जडम् ।
न च चिज्जडयोरैक्यं वैलक्षण्यात्क्वचिद्भवेत् ॥
Yv. III. 121.39.

44. एकीभावं गता द्रष्ट्यदृश्यादि कुरुते भ्रमम् ।
काष्ठोपलाद्यशेषं हि परमार्थमयं यतः ॥
Yv. III. 121.44.

45. *Yv.* III. 121.46-47.

46. हेमसंवित्परित्यागे कटकादिभ्रमो यथा ।
कटकादिभ्रमो हेम्नि देशाद्देशं भवाद्भवम् ॥
Yv. III. 121.49.

47. संबन्धे दृश्यदृष्टीनां मध्ये द्रष्टुर्हि यद्वपुः ।
द्रष्टदर्शनदृश्यादिवर्जितं तदिदं परम् ॥
Yv. III. 121.53.

48. अजाग्रत्स्वप्ननिद्रस्य यते रूपं सनातनम् ।
अचेतनं चाजडं च तन्मयो भव सर्वदा ॥
Yv. III. 121.55.

49. वासनावशतो ब्रह्ममनसा कल्पितं वपुः ।
Yv. IV. 59.12 (ab).

50. ततः संकल्पयामास पूर्वे तेजो महाप्रभम् ।
Yv. IV. 59.16(ab).

51. स ततस्तेजसंस्तस्मादभ्युदेति दिवाकरः ।
Yv. IV. 59.20(ab).

52. सुखदुःखजराजन्ममरणस्वाधिबोधितम् ।
रागद्वेषमयोद्विग्नां गुणत्रयमयात्मिकाम् ॥
Yv. II. 59.28.

53. मनः स्पन्दमात्रेण चित्रं चित्तं यदुत्थितम् ।
सृष्टिर्वा भोगिनी स्फारा व्यवहारविकारिणी ॥
Yv. IV. 59.34.

54. प्रत्येकमेव यच्चित्तं तदेवंरूपशक्तिकम् ।
पृथक्प्रत्येकमुदितः प्रतिचित्तं जगद्भ्रमः ॥
Yv. III. 40.29.

55. यथोत्तराब्धिजनता दक्षिणाब्धिर्सजनं स्थितम् ।
न किंचिदपि जानाति निजसंवेदनादृते ॥
Yv. III. 55.61.

56. अन्ये त्वमिव ये जीवास्तेषां मरणजन्मसु ।
स्मृतिः कारणतामेति मोक्षाभाववशादिह ॥
Yv. III. 40.37.

57. जीवो हि मृतिमूर्च्छान्ते यदन्तः प्रोन्मिषन्निव ।
अनुन्मिषित एवास्ते तत्प्रधनमुदाहृतम् ॥
Yv. III. 40.38.

58. तद्व्योमप्रकृतिः प्रोक्ता तदव्यक्त जड़ाजड्म ।
संस्मृतेरस्मृतेश्चैव क्रम एष भवोदये ॥
Yv. III. 40.39.

59. बोधोन्मुखत्वे हि महत्तत्प्रबुद्धं यदा भवेत् ।
तदा तन्मात्रदिक्कालक्रिया भूताद्युदेति खात् ॥
Yv. III. 40.40.

60. तदेवोच्छूनमाबुद्धं भवतीन्द्रियपञ्चकम् ।
तदेव बुध्यते देहः स एषोस्यातिवाहिकः ॥
Yv. III. 40.41.

61. चिरकालप्रत्ययतः कल्पनापरिपीवरः ।
अधिभौतिकतबोधमाप्नते चैष बालवत् ॥
Yv. III. 40.42.

62. वृद्धिमित्यमयं यातो मुधैव भुवनभ्रमः ।
स्वप्नाङ्गनासङ्गसमस्त्वनुभूतोऽप्यसन्मयः ॥
Yv. III. 40.44.

63. आगन्तुकदेहाद्यात्मना आत्मवान् जात इव सन् अहमिति
जगदिति च भ्रममनुभवतीत्यर्थः ॥ — तात्पर्यप्रकाश
Yv. III. 40.46.
p.228, 3rd ed. (1981), Munshiram Manoharlal.

64. सर्गादो स्वप्नपुरुषन्यायेनादि प्रजापतिः ।
यथास्फुटं प्रकचितस्तथाद्यापि स्थिता स्थितिः ॥
Yv. III. 55.47.

65. प्रथमोऽसौ प्रतिस्पन्दः पदार्थानां हि बिम्बकम् ।
प्रतिबिम्बितमेतस्माद्यत्तदद्यापि संस्थितम् ॥
Yv. III. 55.48.

66. यन्नाम सुषिरं स्थानं देहानां तग्दतोऽनिलः ।
करोत्यङ्गपरिस्पन्दं जीवतीत्युच्यते ततः ॥
Yv. III. 55.49.

67. *Yv.* III. 55.52.

68. तथां खं खं तथा भूमिर्भूमित्वेनास्ववज्जलम् ।
यद्यथा चैतति स्वैरं तद्वेत्येव तथा वपुः ।
Yv. III. 55.53.

69. यथा सैन्यस्थानरा दिवासैन्यवासनावासिता रात्रौ स्वप्ने प्रत्येकं सैन्यं स्वस्ववासनाकल्पितं नानासैन्यं पश्यन्तोऽपि ऐक्यं मन्यते तद्वदित्यर्थः ॥
Yv. IV. 17.27.

70. *Yv.* V. 44.50.

71. एषा गुणमयी माया दुर्बोधेन दुरत्यया ।
नित्यं सत्यावबोधेन सुखेनेवातिवाह्यते ॥

असत्येव कृतारम्भा हेम्नः कटकता यथा ।
प्रतिभासविपर्यासमात्रकारणकोदया ॥
परमात्मनि वाचेयमित्थं मायानुमीयते ।
तरङ्गालीव पयसि प्रेक्षमात्र विनाशिनी ॥

Yv. VI(a). 67. 7, 8, 9.

72. रामापर्यवसानेयं माया संसृतिनामिका ।
आत्मचित्तजयेनैव क्षयमायाति नान्यथा ॥

Yv. V. 44.1.

73. *Yv.* III. 86.87.

74. संकल्पमात्रादितरद्धित्यते नेह किंचन ।

Yv. III. 101.34 (ab).

75. यावत्संकल्पितं तावद्यथा संकल्पितं तथा ।
यथा संकल्पनगरं कचतीदं जगत्तथा ।

Yv. VI(b). 184.32.

76. *Yv.* III. 101.

77. ज्ञदृष्ट्या सर्वमेवेदं ब्रह्मैवेति महामते ।
नास्ति संसार इत्येतदुपपद्यत एव च ॥

Yv. IV. 47.63.

78. अज्ञदृष्टया त्वविच्छिन्नसंसारत्वादनारतम् ।
नित्या संसारमायेयं मिथ्यापीहोपपद्यते ॥

Yv. IV. 47.64.

79. एषा ह्यविद्या कथिता मायैषा सा निगद्यते ।
परमेतत्तदज्ञानं संसारादिविषप्रदम् ॥

Yv. V. 13.89.

80. ब्रह्म सर्वमिदं विश्वं विश्वातीतं च तत्पदम् ।
वस्तुतस्तु जगन्नास्ति सर्वं ब्रह्मैव केवलम् ।

Yv. IV. 40.30.

81. यत्किंचिज्जगदद्यात्र भातीदं परमेव तत् ।

Yv. VI(b). 192.20(ab).

82. घाट घडियां पछी नामरूप जूजवां, अंते तो हेमनुं हेम होये

83. इदं नासीन्न चोत्पन्नं न चास्ति न भविष्यति ।
जगद्ब्रह्मेव सद्रुपमिदमित्थमवस्थितम् ॥

Yv. (b). 164.47.

इत्थं जीवभावं विमृज्य तथैव जगद्भावमपि विर्ष्टुमारभते - इदमिति ।
इत्थं मार्जने जगद्ब्रह्मैव भूत्वावस्थितम् । — तात्पर्यप्रकाश

Yv. VI(b). 164.7, p. 1455.

84. *Yv.* VI(a). 77.100.

85. *Yv.* VI(a). 117.118.

86. नचोत्पन्नं न चैवासीद्दृश्यं न च भविष्यति ।
वर्तमानेऽपि नैवास्ति परमेवास्त्यवेषितम् ॥

Yv. IV. 33.18.

87. न जायते न म्रियते क्वचित्किंचित्कदाचन ।
जगद्विवतरूपेण केवलं ब्रह्म जृम्भते ।
Yv. VI(a). 113.19.

88. न वृद्धिमेति नो ह्रासं यन्न किंचित्कदाचन ।
किं वा तनु भोक्तत्र कस्य का नाम खण्डना ॥
Yv. IV. 45.15.

89. वन्ध्यापुत्रव्योमवने यथा न स्तः कदाचन ।
जगदाद्यखिलं दृश्यं तथा नास्ति कदाचन ॥
Yv. III. 11.4.

90. काकतालीययोगेन संजातोऽस्ति मुधैव हि ।
मृगतृष्णाद्विवच्चन्द्रत्वमिवासत्यं च वर्धते ॥
Yv. IV. 54.7.

91. तत्वज्ञविषये राम सलिलादिव वृष्टयः ।
आयान्ति सृष्टयो देवाज्जलदादिव वृष्टयः ।
Yv. IV. 47.29.

92. व्यतिरिक्ता न सर्वेषां समस्ताः सृष्टिदृष्टयः ।
व्यतिरिक्ता द्रवाम्भोधिस्वाष्ठीलाः शाल्मलेरियव ॥
Yv. IV. 47.30.

93. निखाता दृश्यतां यान्ति स्तम्भस्थाः शालभञ्जिकाः ।
अस्मिन्नक्षोभ्य एवान्तस्तरङ्गाः सृष्टिदृष्टयः ॥
Yv. VI(b). 52.46.

94. इमा याः परिदृश्यन्ते वितताः सृष्टिदृष्टयः ।
पयसीव तरङ्गास्ते पिच्छं व्योम्नीव चात्मनि ॥
Yv. V. 5.36.

95. चिति यास्तु चमत्कारं चमत्कुर्वन्ति यतस्वतः ।
स्वचमत्कृतयोऽन्तस्थास्तदेवताः सृष्टिदृष्टयः ॥
Yv. VI (b). 92.61.

96. खाद्रिद्यूर्वीनदीश्रेण्यो दृष्टिसृष्टया पुनः पुनः ।
सैवान्येव विचित्रेयमविद्या परिवर्तते ॥
Yv. III. 114.56.

"The heavens above and the earth below, with all the ranges of hills and mountains on earth, and all the lines of its rivers and lakes, are but the dissolving views of our sight, and are seen in the same or different lights as they are represented by our ignorance."

Translation by Mitra Vihari Lala, p.357 (1978), Bhartiya Publishing House.

This translation does not seem to convey the sense property.

97. Dasgupta, S. N., *Indian Idealism*, Ch. VI, p.170 (1962), Cambridge.

98. उदेत्यज्ञानमात्रेण नश्यति ज्ञानमात्रतः ।
सन्मात्रे परिविच्छेद्या रज्ज्वामिव भुजंगधीः ॥
Yv. III 114.57.

99. यत्र यदा यदेवासौ यथा भवियति तत्र तदा तदेवासौ प्रपश्यति ।
Yv. III. 63.3.

100. मृगतृष्णातरङ्गिण्यो यथा भास्करतेजसः ।
सर्वा दृश्यदृशो द्रष्टुर्व्यतिरिक्ता न रूपतः ॥
Yv. III. 94.29.

101. यथा रसः पदार्थेषु यथा तैलं तिलादिषु ।
कुसुमेषु यथा मोदस्तथा द्रष्टरि दृश्यधीः ॥
Yv. II. 1.43.

102. द्यौः क्षमा वायुराकाशं पर्वताः सरितो दिशः ।
अन्तःकरणतत्वस्य भागा बहिरिव स्थिताः ॥
Yv. V. 56.35.

103. सत्यं पृथ्व्यादि चित्तस्थं न बहिष्ठं कदाचन ।
अङ्कुरस्थः पल्लवस्तु तस्माद्यस्मात्फलश्रियः ॥
Yv. V. 48.51.

5

Idealistic Thought in the *Gauḍapādakārikā*

IN the history of early *Advaita Vadānta*, the place of Gauḍapāda is unforgettable, for he in his *Gauḍapādakārikā*; has put forth Monistic as well as Idealistic views. Gauḍapāda, clearly negates the reality of the worldly phenomena. It has been already discussed that the concept of the unreality of the world was not known to the early *Upaniṣadic* period. It was *Vijñānavāda* school of Buddhism which systematically put forth the concept of the unreality of the external world. Influenced by Buddhistic Idealism, Gauḍapāda emphasized the unreality of the world. Unfortunately, there have been many difficulties in ascertaining Gauḍapāda's identity as well as his date.

Identity and Date of Gauḍapāda

Much has been discussed and written about the identity and date of Gauḍapāda. Tradition considers Gauḍapāda to be the 'grand preceptor' of Śaṅkarācārya. On the other hand, Walleser's opinion is very striking. According to him, there was no one like *ācārya* Gauḍapāda. The *Gauḍapādakārikā* is not the work of any *ācārya* named Gauḍapāda. But the tenets of *Advaita Vedānta* as known in the Gauḍa country are found arranged systematically in the form of the *Gauḍapādakārikā*. This view is not accepted by many. According to Prof. L. D. Barnett the name Gauḍapāda is parallel to Dramiḍācārya; and the term *pāda* is honorific.[1]

We can get some help in determining the date of Gauḍapāda from Buddhist writers. Bhāvaviveka (500-550 A.D.), Śāntarakṣita (705-762 A.D.) and Kamlaśīla seem to be aware of Gauḍapāda.[2] So Gauḍapāda must be placed before them around 500 A.D. This is disputed by many as there could be a common source for these texts. And tradition cannot be wholly ignored. Besides, there is a great resemblance of ideas as well as of terminology between the *G. K.*, and the *Yoga-Vāsiṣṭha.* Both of them seem to be influenced by Buddhistic Idealism. There is also a big question mark but priority as to which is the earlier work, the *Yv.* or the *G.K.* Thus it is very difficult to decide the actual date of Gauḍapāda.

The *Gauḍapādakārikā*

The *Gauḍapādakārikā* is based on the shortest but one of the most important *Upaniṣads.* viz. the *Māṇḍūkya Upaniṣad.* It contains four chapters namely, (1) *Āgama,* (2) *Vaitathya,* (3) *Advaita* and (4) *Alātaśānti Prakaraṇa,* having respectively 29, 38, 48 and 100 *kārikās.* There are different views about the interrelation of the four *prakaraṇas.* According to tradition, these four *prakaraṇas* are interrelated with each other. But Prof. Vidhushekhar Bhattacharya has tried to refute this view. He holds that the *G. K.* is not a single work, and the four *prakaraṇas* are not interrelated with each other. They are independent, but put together in the form of one work.[3]

Gauḍapāda is one amongst those, who has denounced the objective existence of the world. As stated before, under Buddhistic influence Gauḍapāda has rejected the Reality of the external world. He has emphasized Acosmism (*Ajātivāda*) from the ultimate standpoint. Very logically he has stated, "A thing which does not exist in the beginning and in the end, does not exist in the middle also. This entire phenomenal conglomeration is not real, though it is considered to be real."[4]

Idealistic Views in the *Gauḍapādakārikā*

The idealistic views expressed in the *Gauḍapādakārikā* which are directly concerned with the topic are discussed below.

Resemblance between the Waking State and the Dreaming State

To suggest the unreality of a thing, it is always compared with the dream. In the second, viz. *Vaitathya prakaraṇa* of the G. K. the author has presented his Idealistic view about the world by comparing the waking state with the dreaming state. Gauḍapāda has put forth logical reasons to prove the unreality of the dreaming state as well as of the waking state. All the objects, which we perceive during the dreaming state are experienced in the body, eventhough there is no ample space for them. In the dreaming state, both time and space are not regulated properly, if we view them from the point of view of the waking state. The dreamer goes to another country in a very short period of time, which is something impossible, and on waking up from the dreaming state, the dreamer does not find himself in the country he saw during the dreaming state. The author quotes in support of the *Śruti* that there is the absence of the objects of the dream.[5] In several respects the world of the waking state resembles the dream-world. The only difference prevailing between them is that, in the dream, things are experienced internally, while in the waking state, things are perceived externally. Rightly speaking, the objects of the waking as well as of the dreaming state are imagined by the mind only. During the dreaming state, the objects imagined by one with an introvert *citta* are *mithyā* (false), and whatever is seen by one with an extrovert *citta*, though appearing as real is also *mithyā*.[6] The same is the case with the objects of the waking state.

Now a question may arise that if the objects are merely imagined, then what is it that is responsible for their appearance? The answer is, the *Ātman* imagines the entire conglomeration through own *Māyā*.[7] All the external as well as internal objects are simply the imagination of the *Ātman*. The only difference is that, while the objects imagined within, exist till the mind keeps on imagining, while the objects of the external word exist relatively.[8] Their existence is *dvayakālika*. That is to say, external objects are supposed to have two moments of existence (viz. before they are perceived, and when they begin to be perceived).[9] Or they exist in relation to others which also are imagined. In other words, external objects exist till we perceive them. That is to say, they exist relatively. A flower exists till we perceive it; on the other hand, we perceive it till it exists. Some believe that the term *dvaya* signifies that both the mind and sense-organs operate in the act of perception of the objects. Thus objects of both the dreaming state and the waking state are the result of the mind's constructive imagination. As the rope is imagined as a snake due to an illusion, so the *Ātman* is imagined differently due to *Māyā*. It is said that at first the *Jīva* is imagined by the *Ātman* and then these subjective as well as objective things are imagined.[10] In the seond and the third *prakaraṇas* of the G.K. it is variously stated that the self, *Māyā* and the mind are responsible for the manifestation of this phenomenal world.[11]

Thus comparing the world with a magical illusion, the dream and the *gandharvanagara*, Gauḍapāda concludes the *Vaitathya prakaraṇa* emphasizing his Monistic and Absolutistic view.[12] He has presented the criterion of the Ultimate Reality, viz. "There is no suppression, nor is there origination, no one is in bondage, no one is desirous of emancipation. This is the highest truth."[13]

Acosmism (*Ajātivāda*)

Acosmism can be said to be the acme of *Advaita Vedānta* as propounded by Gauḍapāda. It is the central doctrine emphasized in the G. K. According to Gauḍapāda, nothing is ever born, but because of *Māyā*, the phenomenal world appears to spring forth, Gauḍapāda has compared *Ātman* with *mahākāśa*. Giving the example of *ghaṭākāśa*, he has explained how individual souls are imagined.[14] Because of the different pots, the *mahākāśa* appears in the form of *ghaṭākāśas*. Similarly *Ātman* appears in the form of individual souls through *Māyā*. Because of different *ghaṭas*, different *ghaṭākāśas* appear and when these *ghaṭas* are destroyed, the different *ghaṭākāśas* seem to be merged in the *mahākāśa*. Similarly, the Self is imagined as different *Jīvas* being conditioned or limited by the different conglomerations of the limb etc. called bodies. When these conglomerations are destroyed, these different *Jīvas* are merged in the *Ātman*.[15] As *ghaṭākāśa* is neither a modification nor a part of the *mahākāśa*, so the *Jīva* is neither a modification nor a part of the *Ātman*.[16] As dirt, smoke etc. appearing in one *ghaṭākāśa* do not appear in other *ghaṭākāśas*, similarly the happiness or the grief of one individual soul does not appear in other individual souls.[17] All the conglomerations are imagined through *Māyā* like a dream. There is no essence in their empirical existence.[18] They appear as real because of *Māyā*.

In the *Vedas* we find passages describing creation;[19] and also passages saying that the Ultimate Reality undergoes no change whatsoever. But as a matter of fact, the creation of the world in different ways is stated as a means to the attainment of the Ultimate Truth. Though a distinction between the *Ātman* and the *Jīvas* is stated, in fact there is no distinction. In order to help the people of lower intellect to attain the Supreme Truth, a distinction is stated from their point of view; so that through *upāsanā* they could gradually realise the Ultimate Truth that there is no distinction at all : The *Śruti* passages describing the creation of the world are from the empirical point of view.They are stepping stones leading to the attainment of the Ultimate Truth.[20]

All the same, it is stated very emphatically in the *Śruti* that in reality there is no origination at all. Because of *Māyā* this phenomenal appearance is created.[21] In the *Bṛhadāraṇyaka Upaniṣad* it is said that Indra through *Māyā* takes various forms. The *Vājasaneyi Saṁhitā* states that 'Though unborn he is variously born through *Māyā*.' It is stated in the *Bṛ. Up.* that there is no plurality here. The *Śruti* has condemned *Saṁbhūti* (origination), and the cause of birth is also denied.[22] The birth of an existent thing could be possible only through *Māyā*. There could not be the birth of the *Ātman* which is immortal, for whatever is born, certainly perishes.[23] And that which is non-existent could not be originated either through illusion or in reality. The son of a barren woman is not born either in illusion or is reality.[24] As in a dream, because of *Māyā*, the mind projects appearance, so in the weaking state also the mind through *Māyā* projects these external appearances, and appears variously. This world of appearance is only an illusion. Whatever appears, is created by the mind only. When the mind vibrates, the appearance is projected. On the other hand, when the mind becomes non-mind that is to say, stops vibrating or imagining, the appearance vanishes. Concluding the third *prakaraṇa*, Gauḍapāda states, "No individual souls is ever born, nor is there any possibility of it. This is the highest truth, where nothing is born."[25]

In the fourth *prakaraṇa* viz. *Alātaśānti prakaraṇa*, Gauḍapāda has put forth the doctrine of non-origination (*Ajātivāda*), refuting the theory of Causation.

Refutation of the theory of Causation

While refuting the *Satkāryavāda* of the *Sāṁkhya* system as well as the *Asatkāryavāda* of the *Nyāya-vaiśeṣika* system, Gauḍapāda has strongly emphasized that in no way origination is possible.

Now, the *Satkāryavādin* holds that the effect pre-exists in the cause in a subtle form. Against this, Gauḍapāda argues that what is already existent, cannot be born. On the other hand, the *Asatkāryavādin* believes that the effect is not pre-existent in the cause. It is completely a new thing, that is produced. Gauḍapāda has refuted this theory also. That which is non-existent, cannot come to exist in any way. The followers of both these theories dispute with each other.[26] It is very clear that an object which is existent, cannot be born, and on the other hand what is non-existent, just like a barren's son, cannot be born in any way. Disputing with each other, the holders of these theories establish non-origination.[27] That which is immortal, does not become mortal. On the other hand, what is mortal does not become immortal, because change of nature is impossible.[28]

Gauḍapāda, with the help of logical arguments negates these theories. As stated above, the *Satkāryavādin* holds that the effect pre-exists in the cause in a latent form. The cause is non-different from the effect that is produced. But if the cause is produced, then how can it be *aja* (non-born) ? It cannot remain eternal and yet be produced.[29] Gauḍapāda again argues that if the effect is identical with the cause, then the effect also becomes *aja,* and how could the cause be eternal when it is identical with the effect?[30] Śaṅkara in his commentary on the *G. K.*, states that this is not possible. One cannot cook half a hen and yet have the other half for laying eggs.[32]

On the other hand, according to *Asatkāryavādin,* the effect does not pre-exist in the cause. Gauḍapāda argues while rejecting this theory that, which is non-existent cannot be produced. A barren woman's son is not born. And if one maintains that an object is born from what is born, then there would be the fault of *anāvasthā* (infinite regress), and it would be impossible to determine the ultimate cause.[33] If it is said that the cause precedes the effect and the effect precedes the cause, then by the *bījāṅkuranyāya* it would impossible to determine whether the cause precedes the effect or the effect precedes the cause. Those who believe that the effect produces the cause, as the cause produces the effect, for them, production would be just like the birth of a father from the son.[34] For causation, they must decide the order of the cause and the effect; for if they be simultaneous, they could not be related with each other just like the two horns of an animal.[35] There is no kind of relationship between the horns of an animal, which are different from each other, and simultaneously existent. If the cause and the effect produce each other, then it would be difficult to ascertain which is the cause and which the effect. Gauḍapāda states that thus nothing is produced because there is lack of potency in the cause to produce the effect, absence of knowledge and also incompatibility of order. Thus the theory of non-origination is fully acceptable.[36] Nothing is ever produced either from itself or from another. Nothing either existent, non-existent, or both existent and non-existent is born.[37]

After refuting the *Sāṁkhya* and the *Nyāyavaiśeṣika* theory of Causation, Gauḍapāda refutes the *Vijñānavāda* also. According to the *Vijñānavādins* this phenomenal appearance is created by the mind. All the seeming external objects are nothing but the creation of the mind only. After employing the argument of the *Vijñānavādin* to refute the reality of the external world,

Gauḍapāda seems to refute the *Vijñānavāda* also. He states that neither the mind nor the *citta-dṛśya* (what is perceptible by the mind) is ever produced. He who tries to see its origination, tries to see footprints in the sky.[38] It cannot be said that the *saṁsāra* which is beginningless has an end, nor can it be said that liberation has a beginning but has no end.[39] Thus, what does not exist in the beginning and in the end, does not exist in the present also. Whatever we perceive at present, is only an imagination of the mind.[40] Because of common experience and perception, all these conglomerations appear as real. Gauḍapāda gives the example of the *Māyāhastin*. The *Māyāhastin* does not exist at all. But because of the influence of magic, it seems to be existing. Similarly because of seeming practical utility and perception we believe that all these seeming objects exist. As a matter of fact, nothing is ever born. Thus non-origination is the Ultimate Truth according to Gauḍapāda.

The example of the fire-brand (*alāta-cakra*) explains non-origination. As a moving fire-brand appears to be straight, crooked or circular, so the vibrating mind appears as perceiver and the perceptible.[41] When the fire-brand stops moving, its straight, crooked, circular appearances are no longer there. Similarliy when the mind stops vibrating, these two-fold appearances do not appear.[42] Appearances of the moving fire-brand are not produced either from the fire-brand or from another thing, and when it stops moving, they do not enter either in the fire-brand or in any other thing. This is true of the phenomenal appearances which seem to arise through the vibration of the mind.[43] The objects are not created from the mind, nor is the mind created from the objects. Thus the wise are initiated into the doctrine of non-origination.[44] Whatever appears, is a mere illusion. As long as the obsession of causation remains, the world appears when one gets over it, this world of appearance disappears.[45] All this appearance seems to be there because of nescience (*saṁvṛti*). The object, existing from the empirical point of view (*kalpita-saṁvṛtyā*), does not exist from the ultimate point of view. That which is true according to other schools of philosophy, is not true ultimately.[46] Everything is without origination. All these conglomerations are said to be born only relatively; and not as the Ultimate Reality. All this is *Māyā* only; and *Māyā* also does not exist.[47] Whatever exists as empirical reality is only an imagination. All this seeming duality is just the vibration of the *citta*. As a matter of fact, the *citta* is objectless (*Nirviṣaya*), [48] that which is known as *cit*, and called the *Ātman* in *Upaniṣads*. When the mind becomes non-mind, when it ceases to vibrate, at that time it is known as *cit*. To be strictly logical, it is not even true to uphold *ajāti* or to say that the Highest Reality is *aja* (unborn). (Thus the author denies even *ajāti* as the Ultimate Truth, because the real nature of *Ātman* cannot be ascertained by any empirical means). The term *aja* is used to refute those for whom origination is true. There is no scope for any terminology to describe the Ultimate Truth. Thus the author denies *ajāti* also as a proper description of the Ultimate Truth.[49] Gauḍapāda has attempted to put forth *Brahman* as non-dual. *Brahman*, the Ultimate Truth is non-dual, without beginning, middle and end. All this seeming duality in unborn. The Absolute is unborn, changeless (same) and fearless.

Thus the doctrine of non-origination (Acosmism) is put forth repeatedly by Gauḍapāda. The author by refuting the theory of causation, presenting the analogy of the fire-brand (*Alātacakra*) and so on emphasized Acosmism.

Now, a question may naturally arise, that if non-origination is the Ultimate Truth, how could this world of appearance be seen before us. We can find an answer to this from the *Gauḍapādakārikā*. As stated before, under the great spell of Subjective Idealism of Buddhism, Gauḍapāda has emphasized the mind's wonderful constructive power. So now, we shall see how the mind plays an active part in viewing the world of appearance.

The Mind's Constructive Role

Gauḍapāda is never tired of reiterating that the objects of perception are unreal. The value of the empirical world is not more than that of the world of the dreaming state. As the dreaming world is imagined by the mind, so the empirical world is also imagined by the mind. All the objects that appear are but the vibrations of the mind (*cittaspanditam*), and hence unreal.[50] When the mind vibrates, the objects appear before us, on the other hand, when the mind stops vibrating, that is to say, when the mind becomes non-mind, this duality does not appear at all.[51] It is stated in the *Advaita Prakaraṇa* that as in the dreaming state, the mind vibrates in the form of illusive duality due to *Māyā*, so in the waking state also the mind vibrates in the form of illusive duality.[52] This duality consisting of mutable as well as immutable objects, is nothing else but an appearance (*dṛśya*) of the mind.[53]

In short, the mind has a great role in the world-construction. Through the maxim of positive and negative assertion (*anvaya-vyatireka*), it can be said that if the mind vibrates, the world of appearance springs forth before us, on the other hand when the mind stops vibrating, the world is merged away.

Here, we can say that though Gauḍapāda has not actually used the term *Dṛṣṭi-Sṛṣṭi*, somehow, his Idealism is very close to the *Dṛṣṭi-Sṛṣṭi-vāda* as he has stated that this appearing world is a result of the vibration of the mind. Of course, it can be said that the author is not precise in explaining his view as to who imagines this phenomenal world. Whether the *Ātman* or the *Jīva*? In the *Vaitathya Prakaraṇa*, it is stated that at first the *Jīva* is imagined and then these various objects are imagined. Here, it is not clear whether the *Ātman* imagines the *Jīva* and then it itself imagines this seeming duality or at first the *Jīva* is imagined and then it imagines this seeming duality.[54] It is also not clear whether he is referring to the individual souls severally. In which case there would be as many worlds as there are *Jīvas*. So one cannot get a specific and clear idea whether this world of appearance is an imagination of the cosmic mind or of the individual mind. In the *Yoga-Vāsiṣṭha* it is stated that this worlds of appearance is imagined by the cosmic mind and also by the individual mind.[55] Thus the seed of the *Dṛṣṭi-Sṛṣṭi-vāda* which has slightly present at least in the expressions of the *Upaniṣadic* period, can be said to have sprouted forth, in the *Gauḍapādakārikā* awaiting further development.

Thus it may be surmised that somehow Gauḍapāda goes

ahead in the direction of *Dṛṣṭi-Sṛṣṭi-vāda*. The *G. K.* runs parallel to the *Dṛṣṭi-Sṛṣṭi-vāda* in declaring the empirical world as unreal as the dreaming world. Gauḍapāda has employed the similes of *Svapana, Māyā, Māyāhastin* and *gandharvanagara* to establish the unreality of the world of appearance.

The factor responsible for such an Idealistic development in the *Gauḍapādakārikā* seems to be the influence of Buddhistic Idealism. One can clearly find much similarity between Nāgārjuna's *Mādhyamika* Philosophy and the views in the *Laṅkāvatāra* on the one hand, and the views put forth in the *G. K.* on the other hand.[56] Vidhushekhara Bhattacharya has quoted passages and stanzas from Buddhist works to show how much Gauḍapāda is indebted to Buddhism. (As a matter of fact, he and even Dasgupta are apt to regard Gauḍapāda as a Buddhist).

According to Dr. Mahadevan "Gauḍapāda lived and taught in an age when *Mahāyāna* was having a great hold on the minds of people . . . Gauḍapāda adopted the logical method of expounding the *Vedānta*, as also the Buddha modes of expression and argumentation.[57] Under the Buddhistic influence, Gauḍapāda has used Buddhistic terminology in the *Alātaśānti Prakaraṇa.*" [58]

It would not be out of place to state that though Gauḍapāda is greatly influenced by the Buddhistic Idealism, he has not completely surrendered to it. He has even refuted the *Vijñānavāda*, for he does not accept a continuum of consciousness as the Ultimate Reality. He has put forth the concept of *Brahman* according to the *Upaniṣads*; and his view is firmly rooted in the *Upaniṣads.* He can be said to have explained and justified non-duality under the influence of subjectivism of the *Vijñānavāda* as well as the philosophy of the *Mādhyamikas*. It has been stated, "His Absolutism is blended with the relativism and phenomenalism of Nāgārjuna and subjectivism of the *Vijñānavādins*."[59]

In conclusion, it would be proper to quote the view of Dr. Radhakrishnan, "The *Kārikā* of Gauḍapāda is an attempt to combine in one whole the negative logic of the *Mādhyamikas* with the positive idealism of the *Upaniṣads*."[60] Hence, the *G. K.* can be considered as a subtle combination of Subjective Idealism and Monistic Idealism.

References

1. Mahadevan, T. M. P., *Gauḍapāda : A Study in Early Advaita*, Ch. I, p.5, 3rd Edition, (1960), University of Madras.
2. Bhattacharya, Vidhushekhar (ed.), *The Āgamaśāstra of Gauḍapāda. Introduction*, lxxv (1943), University of Calcutta.
3. *Ibid.*, lvii.
4. आदावन्ते च यन्नास्ति वर्तमानेऽपि तत्तथा ।
   वितथैः सदृशाः सन्तोऽवितथा इव लक्षिताः ॥
   G. K. II. 6.
5. न तत्र रथा न रथयोगा न पन्थानो भवन्ति ।
   Br. Up. IV. 3.10.
6. स्वप्नवृत्तावपि त्वतश्चेतसा कल्पितं त्वसत् ।
   बाहिश्चेतो गृहीतं सद्दृष्टं वैतथ्यमेतयोः ॥
   G. K. II.9.
7. कल्पयत्यात्मनात्मानमात्मा देवः स्वमायया ।
   स एव बुध्यते भेदानिति वेदान्तनिश्चयः ॥
   G. K. II. 12.
8. द्वयकालाश्च भेदकाला अन्योन्यपरिच्छेद्याः । यथा गोदोहनमास्ते यावदास्ते तावद्गां दोग्धि, यावग्दां दोग्धि तावदास्ते ।
   Śāṅkara Bhāṣya on the *G. K. II.* 14, p.200;
   Ten Principal Upaniṣads (1978), Motilal Banarsidass.
9. Dasgupta, S. N., *Indian Idealism*, Ch. VI, p.150, Reprinted (1962), Cambridge.
10. जीवं कल्पयते पूर्वं ततो भावान्पृथग्विधान् ।
    बाह्यानाध्यात्मिकांश्चैव यथा विद्यस्तथा स्मृतिः ॥
    G. K. II. 16.
11. *G. K.* II.12.
    मायया भिद्यते ह्येतन्नान्यथाजं कथंचन ।
    G. K. III.19(ab).
    मनोदृश्यमिदं दैवं यत्किञ्चित्र सचराचरम् ।
    मनसो ह्यमनीभावे द्वैतं नैवोपलभ्यते ॥
    G. K. III. 31.
12. स्वप्नमाये यथादृष्टे गन्धर्वनगरं यथा ।
    तथा विश्वमिदं दृष्टं वेदान्तेषु विचक्षणैः ॥
    G. K. II. 31.
13. न निरोधो न चोत्पत्तिर्न बद्धो न च साधकः ।
    न मुमुक्षुर्न वै मुक्तः इत्येषा परमार्थता ॥
    G. K. II. 32.

14. आत्मा ह्याकाशवज्जीवैर्घटाकाशैरिवोदितः ।
घटादिवच्च संघातैर्जातावेतन्निदर्शनम् ॥
G. K. III. 3.

15. *G. K.* III.4.

16. *G. K.* III.7.

17. संघाताः स्वप्नवत्सर्वे आत्ममायाविसर्जिताः।
G. K. III.10 (ab).

18. See *G. K.* III.8.

19. *Tai. Up.* 3.1.
Bṛ. Up. II. 1.10 etc.

20. मृल्लोहविस्फुलिङ्गाद्यैः सृष्टिर्या चोदितान्यथा ।
उपायः सोऽवताराय नास्ति भेदः कथञ्चन ॥
G. K. III.15.

21. नेह नानेति चाम्नायादिन्द्रो मायाभिरित्यपि ।
अजायमानो बहुधा मायया जायते तु सः ॥
G. K. III. 24.

22. सम्भूतेरपवादाच्च सम्भवः प्रतिषिध्यते ।
कोन्वेनं जनयेदिति कारणं प्रतिषिध्यते ॥
G. K. III. 25.

23. जातस्य हि ध्रुवो मृत्युः ध्रुवं जन्म मृतस्य च।
Bha. Gita. II.27(ab).

24. असतो मायया जन्म तत्वतो नैव युज्यते ।
वन्ध्यापुत्रो न तत्वेन मायया वापि जायते ॥
G. K. III. 28.

25. न कश्चिज्जायते जीवः सम्भवोऽस्य न विद्यते ।
एतत्तदुत्तमं सत्यं यत्र किञ्चिन्न जायते ॥
G. K. III. 48.

26. भूतस्य जातिमिच्छन्ति वादिनः केचिदेव हि ।
अभूतस्य धीरा विवदन्तः परस्परम् ॥
G. K. IV.3.

27. भूतं न जायते किंचिदभूतं नैव जायते ।
विवदन्तो द्वयाः ह्येवमजातिं ख्यापयन्ति तै ॥
G. K. IV.4.

28. *G. K.* IV.7.

29. *G. K.* IV.11.

30. कारणाद्यद्यनन्यत्वमतः कार्यमजं यदि ।
जायमानाद्धि वै कार्यात्कारणं ते कथं ध्रुवम् ॥
G. K. IV.12.

31. There is a great doubt prevailing whether Ādi Śaṅkara has written the commentary on the *G. K.*

32. न हि कुक्कुट्या एकदेशः पच्यते एकदेशः प्रसवाय कल्पयते ।
Śaṅkara's Com. on the *G. K.* IV.12, p.231; *Ten Principal Upaniṣads* (1978), Motilal Banarsidass.

33. *G. K.* IV-13.

34. हेतोरादि फलं येषामादि हेतुः फलस्य च ।
तथा जन्म भवेत्तेषां पुत्राज्जन्म पितुर्यथा ॥
G. K. IV.15.

35. सम्भवे हेतुफलयोरेषितव्यः क्रमस्त्वया ।
युगपत्सम्भवे यस्मादसम्बन्धो विषाणवत् ॥
G. K. IV.16.

36. अशक्तिरपरिज्ञानं क्रमकोपोऽथवा पुनः ।
एवं हि सर्वथा बुद्धेरजातिः परिदीपिता ॥
G. K. IV.19.

37. स्वतो वा परतो वापि न किञ्चिद्वस्तु जायते ।
सदसत्सदसद्वापि न किञ्चिद्वस्तु जायते ॥
G. K. IV.22.

38. तस्मान्न जायते चित्तं चित्तदृश्यं न जायते ।
तस्य पश्यन्ति ये जातिं खे वै पश्यन्ति ते पदम् ।
G. K. IV.28.

39. *G. K.* IV.30.

40. सर्वं चित्रदृश्यमवस्तुकम् ।
G. K. IV.36.

41. *G. K.* IV. 47.

42. *G. K.* IV. 48.

43. *G. K.* IV. 49-50.

44. *G. K.* IV. 54.

45. *G. K.* IV. 56.

46. योऽस्ति कल्पितसंवृत्या परमार्थेन नास्त्यसौ ।
परतन्त्राभिसंवृत्या स्यान्नास्ति परमार्थतः ॥
G. K. IV.73.

47. धर्मा य इति जायन्ते ते न तत्त्वतः ।
जन्म मायोपमं तेषां सा च माया न विद्यते ॥
G. K. IV.58.

48. चित्तस्पंदितमेवेदं ग्राह्यग्राहकवद्द्वयम् ।
चित्तं निर्विषयं नित्यमसङ्गं तेन कीर्तितम् ॥
G. K. IV. 72.

49. अजः कल्पितसंवृत्या परमार्थेन नाप्यजः ।
परतन्त्राभिनिष्पत्या संवृत्या जायते तु सः ॥
G. K. IV.74.

50. *G. K.* IV.36.

51. मनसो ह्यमनीभावे द्वैतं नैवोपलभ्यते ॥
G. K. III.31(cd).

52. *G. K.* III. 29.

53. मनोदृश्यमिदं द्वैतं यत्किञ्चित् सचराचरम् ।
G. K. III.31(ab).

54. *G. K.* II.16.

55. *Yv.* VI (a). 67.13.

56. *Laṅkāvatāra*, III.96.; *G. K.* IV.72.
M. K. XXI.13 ab; *G. K.* IV.22 ab.
M. K. XV.8 cd.; *G. K.* IV.7cd, 29 cd.

57. Mahadevan T. M. P., *Gauḍapāda : A Study in Early Advaita*. Ch.X, p.248, 3rd ed. (1960), University of Madras.

58. धर्म, संघात, प्रज्ञप्ति, संक्लेश, धर्मधातु, शुद्धलौकिक, लोकोत्तर, संवृति, परतन्त्र, परिनिष्पन्न, निर्वाण, तायिन्......etc.
G.K. III, 3, 10, 33, 34, 57, 73, 81
G.K. IV, 87, 88, 89.

59. Sinha, Jadunath, *A History of Indian Philosophy*, Vol. II, Ch. VI, p.454 (1956), Sinha Publishing House, Calcutta.

60. S. Radhakrishnan, *Indian Philosophy*, Vol.II, Ch. VIII, p.465, Seventh Impression (1962), George Allen & Unwin.

6

Idealistic Thought in the *Vivekacūḍāmaṇi*

SO far as the unreality of the world of appearance is concerned, the *Yoga-Vāsiṣṭha* and the *Gauḍapādakārikā* opine positively. That is to say, both of these works clearly declare the unreality of the world. These works may be considered as of the initial stage of a type of Idealism, which firmly challenges even the phenomenal existence of the world.

Besides the *Yoga-Vāsiṣṭha* and the *Gauḍapādakārikā,* there is another work namely the *Vivekacūḍāmaṇi,* that strikingly enough puts forth similar views. So the idealistic views propounded in the *Vivekacūḍāmaṇi* will be discussed here.

Unfortunately, there is a great doubt prevailing about the authorship of the *Vivekacūḍāmaṇi,* though traditionally this work is believed to be that of Śaṅkara. As there are hundreds of works attributed to Śaṅkara, much controversy exists about their authorship. Amongst the numerous works, the commentary on the major *Upaniṣads,* the commentary on the *Brahma-sūtras* and the *upadeśasāhasrī* are regarded as undoubtedly the works of Śaṅkara. The *Vivekacūḍamaṇi,* a *prakaraṇa grantha,* is one of those works whose authorship is doubtful. Daniel Ingalls States, "It is improbable that Śaṅkara wrote the *Vivekacūḍāmaṇi* . . ." The author of the *Vivekacūḍāmaṇi* makes an absolute equation of the waking and the dreaming states after the fashion of Gauḍapāda. Śaṅkara may likes the two to each other, but he is careful to distinguish them. Again, and most decisive of all, the *Vivekacūḍāmaṇi* accepts the classical theory of the three truth values, the existent, the non-existent and that which is *anirvacanīya,* indescribable as being either existent or non-existent. The work a day world according to the classical theory is *anirvacanīya.*[1] On the other hand, Dasgupta seems to regard the *Vivekacūḍāmaṇi* as the work of Śaṅkara.[2]

Whatever it be, here the main concern is about the philosophical views emphasized in the *Vivekacūḍāmaṇi.*

Idealistic Views in the *Vivekacūḍāmaṇi*

The *Vivekacūḍāmaṇi* is regarded as a valuable work, propounding the main tenets of *Advaita Vedānta.* It contains 581 verses in the form of a dialogue between the teacher and the pupil. The pupil asks the teacher seven questions viz.

(1) What is bondage?

(2) How does it arise?

(3) How does it continue?

(4) How is one released from it?

(5) What is the *anātman* (non-self)?

(6) What is the nature of the *paramātman* (supreme self)?

(7) How can one distinguish between the *ātman* and the *anātman*?[3]

Answering these questions, the teacher has given expression to his Absolutistic views very lucidly, presenting appropriate similes, analogies and metaphors, which certainly ensure pleasant reading and easy understanding.

That *Brahman* is the Ultimate Reality and this world of appearance is unreal (*mithyā*) is the main purport of this work.[4] The phenomenal world is brought about due to delusion (*moha*), during which, one cannot discriminate between the *Ātman* (self) and *Anātman* (non-self) and one superimposes *Anātman* on the *Ātman.* As a result, bondage is created. One can cross the gulf of delusion only by discrimination between the eternal and the non-eternal (*nityānitya-vastuviveka*), detachment from the enjoyments of fruits of this world and the other world (*ihāmutraphalabhogavirāga*), possession of six virtues (*śamādisādhanāsaṁpat*) and the desire for liberation (*mumukṣutva*).[5]

While explaining *Vedāntic* tenets, the author of the *Vivekacūḍāmaṇi* has expressed Idealistic views, which shall be examined in points.

Waking State compared with the Dreaming State

In the fashion of Gauḍapāda, the author of the *Vivekacūḍāmaṇi* has put the waking state on the same footing as the dreaming state. It is stated very clearly that in the dreaming state, not a single thing exists, but it is the mind itself, which creates the world consisting of the enjoyer etc. Similarly in the waking state, there is no difference. Hence everything is merely an expansion of the mind.[6] Further, it is stated that if the phenomenal world be real, it should appear in the state of dreamless sleep also. But it does not, so it is unreal like a dream.[7] A thing which is real, never perishes in any period of time. If the phenomenal world be real, then it should appear in every period of time. But it does not appear during the dream as well as during the dreamless sleep. So it must not be considered real. Comparing the waking state again with the dreaming state it is stated that the place, time, objects, knower etc. imagined during a dream are all unreal (*mithyā*). Similarly, the waking world is also unreal, as it is brought about by one's own *ajñāna*.[8]

This reminds us of the *Gauḍapādakārikā*, where Gauḍapāda has compared both the states — namely, the dreaming and the waking; and has concluded that there is no difference between the dreaming and the waking state; both the states are unreal.[9] On the other hand, the author of the *Vivekacūḍāmaṇi* seems to differ from the view put forth by Śaṅkara in works, which can with certainty be said to be his. On the commentary on the *Brahma-sūtra* II.2.29; Śaṅkara clearly differentiates the waking state from the dreaming state.[10]

Here, a doubt arises about the authorship whether the *Vivekacūḍāmaṇi* was composed by Śaṅkara or not. Śaṅkara distinguishes the waking state from the dreaming state, while the author of the *Vivekacūḍāmaṇi* has put both the states on the same footing.

The Concept of *Avidyā (Māyā)*

As in the *Yoga-Vāsiṣṭha* and the *Gauḍapādakārikā,* in the *Vivekacūḍāmaṇi* — *Avidyā-Māyā-Ajñāna* and mind are held responsible for the projection of the mundane world. It is stated that all these, *Māyā* and its effects, from the *mahat* up to the body are *asat* and of the nature of the *Anātman* like a mirage. Further, the author states that there is no *Avidyā* apart from the mind. The mind clearly is *Avidyā,* the cause of bondage of *saṁsāra.*[11] It is noteworthy that the *Vivekacūḍāmaṇi* regards *manas* (mind) and *Avidyā* as one and the same.

As the Ultimate Reality viz. *Brahman* pervades everywhere and everything; whatever one perceives, is *Brahman* only. But due to ignorance or false knowledge, superimposition is brought about; as a result, one superimposes this world of appearance on *Brahman.* As long as ignorance persists, such superimposition lasts. But with the dawn of knowledge of the Ultimate Reality, the superimposition vanishes. The author has presented the well- known analogy of rope-snake (*rajju-sarpa*). Due to delusion, rope is mistaken for a snake, but when the delusion disappears, the (unreal) snake also disappears. The existence of what is projected by false knowledge due to error, continues as long as the illusion lasts. The *sarpa* exists in *rajju* as long as the illusion persists. When the illusion is dispelled, the thing, which is wrongly projected does not exist at all. Similar is the case of the world-illusion.[12] When one obtains true knowledge, this phenomenal world does not appear at all, for *Brahman* alone exists in reality.

Now, to a lay man a question may occur : "If everything is *Brahman,* why does it appear as the phenomenal world?" The *Vivekacūḍāmaṇi* states that it is *Māyā,* the potency of the Supreme Lord, because of which this phenomenal world appears.

The concept of *Māyā* plays an important role in the *Advaita Vedānta*. As we have elsewhere stated that it helps to solve the mystery of the seeming existence of the world to some extent. It is stated in the *Vivekacūḍāmaṇi* that — *Māyā,* which is the potency of the Supreme Lord, called *avyakta* (unmanifest), is beginningless *Avidyā* of the nature of the three *guṇas*. It is to be inferred from its effects. This world of appearance is born from *Māyā*.[13] Here, it is noteworthy that the author of the *Vivekacūḍāmaṇi* holds *Māyā* is identical with *Avidyā*. In later chapters it can be seen that some of the Śaṅkarites consider *Māyā* as different from *Avidyā*.

Further, the *Vivekacūḍāmaṇi* explains the characteristics of *Māyā* as follows : *Māyā* is neither *sat* nor *asat*, nor *sat-asat*. It is neither different, nor non-different, nor different-non-different. It neither has parts; nor is without parts, nor is both. It is wonderful and inexplicable.[14]

Another noteworthy thing is that, the *Vivekacūḍāmaṇi* is perhaps the first work, which specifically describes *Māyā* as having two powers viz. concealing power (*āvaraṇa śakti*) and projecting power (*vikṣepa Śakti*).[15] In the *Yoga-Vāsiṣṭha* and in the *Gauḍapādakārikā* we do not find the concept of *Avidyā* or *Māyā* developed to this extent. As we are not sure about the date and the authorship of the *Vivekacūḍāmaṇi,* we cannot enter into details. Nevertheless, it can be stated that the concept of *Avidyā* (*Māyā*) is found developed in the *Vivekacūḍāmaṇi* to some extent. Besides, in the *Brahmasiddhi* the concept of *Avidyā* developed to this extent.

As *Māyā* has two types of powers, its concealing power enables it to conceal the real nature of its object; while its projecting power is responsible for the persistence of mundane life. It is stated that from *mahat* up to the gross body, everything is brought about by *Māyā* only.[16] So this world of appearance can be considered to be a display of *Māyā*.

After examining the concept of *Avidyā* (*Māyā*), we may now concentrate on the creative power of the mind, as emphasized in the *Vivekacūḍāmaṇi*.

Creative Power of the Mind

As already stated the *Vivekacūḍāmaṇi* considers the mind and *Avidyā* as one and the same. It is stated that *Avidyā* is not different from the mind. Mind itself is *Avidyā*, which is the cause of the bondage. When the mind perishes, everything perishes. On the other hand, when the mind expands itself, everything is expanded.[17] Hence it can be said that this world of appearance is nothing else but the mind's constructive network. Mind is the only seed, from which this huge tree of the mundane world has sprouted. With the aid of the maxim of positive and negative concomitance (*anvaya-vyatireka*) it can be said that when the mind starts vibrating, this world of appearance appears before its perceiver. On the other hand, when the mind stops vibrating, there remains no such construct. Thus this world is caused by the mind; and it is not there in the absence of the mind.[18] The very same idea put forth in the *Yoga-Vāsiṣṭha* as well as in the *Gauḍapādakārikā*.[19] So this mundane world (*saṁsāra)* is imagined by the mind; but it does not exist as a matter of fact.[20]

It is further stated that as clouds are brought together by the wind, and are scattered away by the wind itself, similarly bondage as well as liberation are imagined by the mind.[21] As clouds wonder here and there because of the wind, so this entire universe is projected by the mind.[22]

Here, we may state that the author of the *Vivekacūḍāmaṇi* seems to be influenced by the Subjective Idealism of *Vijñānavāda,* which asserts that this phenomenal world is in no sense real, but is a projection of the mind only. The above-mentioned view runs parallel with the Idealism of Buddhism (*Vijñānavāda*). Of course, the *Vivekacūḍāmaṇi* does not specifically state whether this phenomenal world is imagined by the cosmic mind or by the individual mind.

One thing is noteworthy that the *Vivekacūḍāmaṇi* does not throw any more light on the concept of the unreality of the world of appearance. That is to say, we do not find any development in the concept ahead of the *Yoga-Vāsiṣṭha* and the *Gauḍapādakārikā.* Problems such as whose *Avidyā* is responsible for the projection of the world, or whether the *Jīva* is the locus of *Avidyā* or the Supreme self are not found discussed. The Idealistic views, though not clearly and precisely spelt out in such *Vedāntic* works as the *Vivekacūḍāmaṇi*, are yet necessarily different from those in the Buddhist works.

Absolute-Monistic Idealism

As the main purport of the *Vivekacūḍāmaṇi* is to elucidate the *Vedāntic* tenets, naturally it believes in Absolute-Monistic Idealism. It strongly emphasizes that there is no reality except *Brahman*. This world is nothing else but *Brahman*. It is stated that the world, consisting of various forms which is experienced due to *ajñāna*, is nothing else but *Brahman* devoid of all defects of imagination.[23]

The *Vivekacūḍāmaṇi* gives the well-known analogy of clay and pot, that though the pot is an effect of the clay, it is not different from the clay, as the clay is its very essence. The pot does not exist independently of the clay. So where is the pot ? It is just a falsely imagined name.[24] Similarly this world of appearance does not exist independently of *Brahman*, as *Brahman* is the only reality pervading everything and everywhere. Quoting a statement from the scripture,* the author states that "All the universe is *Brahman*" is the supreme declaration of the scripture.[25]

The author has used the term *Ābhāsa* for this world of appearance. It is stated that this world is like the reflection (*ābhāsa*) of a city in the mirror.[26] As different things reflected in the mirror do not exist inside the mirror, but are mere *ābhāsas* (appearances), similarly the world which is unreal, is reflected in *Brahman*.

Another term used by the author to show the unreality of the world is *asatkalpa* (as good as non-existent). It is stated that this world with its manifold differences is imagined in the one Reality, and is *asatkalpa* (as good as non-existent). How could there be any difference in that differenceless Reality which is devoid of change, shape and quality?[27]

Here the term *asatkalpa* is used to show the inexplicable character of the world. This world is neither real nor unreal. That is to say, as there is only one Supreme Reality viz. *Brahman,* what is other than *Brahman,* must be considered unreal. But on the other hand, in our practical life we respond to this world of appearance, hence how could it be considered unreal? It is rather impossible to positively state that the world is unreal or real. There is no other alternative except accepting the empirical as well as the ultimate points of view, i.e., accepting the world as real from the empirical standpoint and as unreal from the ultimate standpoint.

Thus the author has not completely negated the reality of the world. Until the Ultimate Truth is realised, the world appears as real. The author admits the world as unreal only after self-realisation. It is stated that when the Ultimate Truth is realised, there exists no phenomenal world in the unchanging *Brahman,* which is the Supreme Reality, as the snake does not exist in the rope, nor water drops exist in the mirage-water in any of three periods of time.[28] This seeming duality is merely *Māyā*. The Ultimate Truth is non-duality.[29]

Here, the author obviously emphasizes Absolute Monistic Idealism, according to which the Absolute is the Ultimate Reality. The conclusion of Absolutist *Advaita Vedānta* is that the *Jīva* and the entire univese are not different from *Brahman;* they are *Brahman* only.[30] Going a step ahead, the author declares the highest position of the *Advaita Vedānta* that there is no suppression, no origination, no one is bound, no one is desirous of liberation, and no one is liberated. This is the Highest Truth.[31] We find similar views narrated in the *Mūla Madhyamakakārikā* of Nāgārjuna, except there is no reference to any Ultimate Reality. *Ajātivāda* (Acosmism) put forth in this verse is the highest *Vedāntic* position. That is to say, as all this is *Brahman,* there arises no question of another thing. If another exists, then the problems of origination, suppression, bondage, liberation would arise. But as everything is just *Brahman,* nothing else exists.

So, from the ultimate standpoint, there is no world of appearance, but *Brahman* is the only reality.

Therefore it may be stated that in the *Vivekacūḍāmaṇi* there are some expressions which can guide towards the direction of the *Dṛṣṭi-Sṛṣṭi-vāda.* In the *Vivekacūḍāmaṇi*, the acutal term *Dṛṣṭi-Sṛṣṭi* is not used, but we do find expressions which can be said to indicate an initial stage of the *Dṛṣṭi-Sṛṣṭi-vāda.* It is stated that if the phenomenal world were real, it would appear in the dreamless sleep also. But it is well-known that nothing of the mundane world appears in the dreamless sleep, hence the mundane world is only an imagination of the mind. It does not exist in reality.[32] So the mind is the cause of the world. If this mind is understood as the individual mind, it would mean that there are as many worlds as there are minds or this can be interpreted in the light of *Ekajīvavāda* — the only *Jīva* enveloped in *Ajñāna*; that is the mind imagines everything — all the *Jīvas* and the world of manifold differences.

Such expressions can be assumed as stating the doctrine of Subjective Idealism. Though the author seems eager to elucidate Absolutism, at the same time he is concerned with proving the unreality of the world; and thus invites comparison with the expression and ideas found in the *Yoga-Vāsiṣṭha* and the *Gauḍapādakārikā.* Though similar views and expressions are traced in Buddhistic works, these latter works do not admit one Absolute Reality, but admit only individual streams of consciousness.

References

1. Ingalls, H. H. Deniel, 'Study of Śaṅkarācārya', p.7, In *Annals of the Bhandarkar Oriental Research Institute*, Vol. XXXIII (1952), Poona.
2. "... no commentary however, is attributed to the *Vivekacūḍāmaṇi*, which seems, to be genuinely attributed to Śaṅkara ..."
—Dasgupta, S. N., *History of Indian Philosophy*, Vol. II. Ch. XI, p.79 (1975), Motilal Banarsidass.
3. को नाम बन्धः कथमेष आगतः
कथं प्रतिष्ठास्य कथं विमोक्षः ।
कोसावनात्मा परमः क आत्मा
तयोविवेकः कथमेतदुच्यताम् ॥
Vi. 51.
Śaṅkaranārayaṇan, P., (tr), *Vivekacūḍāmaṇi* (1979), Bhartiya Vidya Bhavan.

4. ब्रह्म सत्यं जगन्मिथ्येत्येवंरुपो विनिश्चयः ।
Vi. 20 (ab).

5. आदौ नित्यानित्यवस्तुविवेकः परिगण्यते ।
इहामुत्रफलभोगविरागस्तदनन्तरम् ।
शमादिषट्कसंपत्तिः मुमुक्षुत्वमिति स्फुटम् ।
Vi. 19.

6. स्वप्नेऽर्थशून्यं सृजाति स्वशक्तया
भोक्त्रादि विश्वं मन एव सर्वम् ।
तथैव जाग्रव्यपि नो विशेषः ।
तत्सर्वमेतन्मनसो विजृम्भणम् ॥
Vi. 172.

7. यदि सत्यं भवेद्विश्वं सुषुप्तावुपलभ्यताम् ।
यन्नोपलभ्यते किञ्चिदतोऽसत् स्वप्नवन्मृषा ॥
Vi. 236.

8. निद्राकल्पितदेशकालविषयज्ञात्रादि सर्वं यथा मिथ्या,
तद्वदिहापि जाग्रति जगत्स्वाज्ञानकार्यत्वतः ।
Vi. 254 (ab).

9. *G. K.* II. 4, 5.

10. वैधर्म्याच्च न स्वप्नादिवत् । वैधर्म्यं हि भवति स्वप्नजागरितयोः ।
Br. Sū. Śā. Bhā. II. 2.29.

11. माया मायाकार्यं सर्वं महदादिदेहपर्यन्तम् ।
असदिदमनात्मत्वं विद्धि त्वं मरुमरीचिकाकल्पम् ।
Vi. 125.

न ह्यस्त्यविद्या मनसोऽतिरिक्ता मनो ह्यविधां भवबन्धहेतुः ।
Vi. 171 (ab).

12. यावद् भ्रान्तिस्तावदेवास्य सत्ता
मिथ्या ज्ञानोज्जृम्भितस्य प्रमादात् ।
रज्जवां सर्पो भ्रान्तिकालीन एव
भ्रान्तेर्नाशे नैव सर्पोऽस्ति तद्वत् ॥
Vi. 199.

यत्र भ्रान्त्या कल्पितं तद्विवेके
तनुन्मात्रं नैव तस्माद्विभिन्नम् ।
भ्रान्तैनाशै भ्रान्तिदृष्टाहितत्वं
रज्जुस्तस्माद्विश्वमात्मस्वरुपम् ॥
Vi. 388.

13. अव्यक्तनाम्नी परमेशशक्तिः अनाधविद्या त्रिगुणामिका परा ।
कार्यानुमेया सुधियैव माया, यया जगत्सर्वमिदं प्रसूयते ॥
Vi. 110.

14. सन्नाप्यसन्नाप्युभयात्मिका नो
भिन्नाप्यभिन्नाप्युभयात्मिका नो ।

साङ्गाप्यनङ्गाप्युभयात्मिका नो
महाद्भुताऽनिर्वचनीयरूपा ॥
Vi. 111.

15. एषाऽऽवृत्तिर्नाम तमोगुणस्य शक्तिर्यया वस्त्ववभासतेऽन्यथा ।
सैषा निदानं पुरूषस्य संसृते: विक्षेपशक्ते: प्रसरस्य हेतु: ॥
Vi. 115.

16. माया मायाकार्यं सर्वं महदादिदेहपर्यन्तम् ।
Vi. 125 (ab).

17. न ह्यस्त्वविद्या मनसोऽतिरिक्ता
मनो ह्यविद्या भवबन्धहेतु: ।
तस्मिन् विनष्टे सकलं विनष्टं
विजृम्भितेऽस्मिन् सकलं विजृम्भते ॥
Vi. 171.

18. चित्तमूलो विकल्पोऽयं चित्ताभावे न कश्चन ।
Vi. 408 (ab).

19. चित्तान्तरेव संसार: कुम्भान्त: कुम्भरवं यथा ।
चित्तनाशे न संसार: कुम्भनाशे न कुम्भरवम् ॥
Yv. V.50.14.

मनसो ह्यमनीभावे द्वैतं नैबोपलभ्यते।
G. K. III. 31 (cd).

20. अतो मन: कल्पित एव पुंस:
संसार एतस्य न वस्तुतोऽस्ति ॥
Vi. 173 (cd).

21. वायुना नीयते मेघ: पुनस्तेनैव लीयते ।
मनसा कल्प्यते बन्ध: मोक्षस्तेनैव कल्पते ॥
Vi. 174.

22. *Vi.* 182.

23. यदिदं सकलं विश्वं नानारूपं प्रतीतमज्ञानात् ।
तत्सर्वं ब्रह्मैव प्रत्यस्ताशेषभावनादोषम् ॥
Vi. 229.

24. मृत्कार्यभूतोऽपि मृदो न भिन्न: कुम्भोऽस्ति सर्वत्र तु मृत्स्वरूपात् ।
न कुम्भरूपं पृथगस्ति कुम्भ: कुतो मृषाकल्पितनाममात्र: ॥
Vi. 230.

ब्रह्मैवेदं विश्वमिदं वशिष्ठम् ।
Mund. Up. II. 2.11

25. ब्रह्मैवेदं विश्वमित्येव वाणी
श्रौती ब्रूतेऽथवैनिष्ठा वरिष्ठा ।
Vi. 233 (ab).

26. यत्रैष जगदाभास: दर्पणान्त: पुरे यथा ।
Vi. 292 (ab).

27. असत्कल्पो विकल्पोऽयं विश्वमित्येकवस्तुनि ।
निर्विकारे निराकारे निर्विशेषे भिदा कुतः ॥
Vi. 400.

28. नह्यस्ति विश्वं परतत्वबोधात्
सदात्मनि ब्रह्मणि निर्विकल्पे ।
कालत्रये नाप्यहिरीक्षितो गुणे
नह्यम्बुबिन्दुः मृगतृष्णिकायाम् ।
Vi. 405.

29. मायामात्रमिदं द्वैतम् अद्वैतं परमार्थतः ।
Vi. 406 (ab).
G. K. I.17(cd)

30. वेदान्तसिद्धान्त निरुक्तिरेषा ब्रह्मैव जीवः सकलं जगच्च ।
Vi. 479 (ab).

31. न निरोधो न चोत्पत्तिः न बद्धो न च साधकः ।
नं मुमुक्षुः न वै मुक्तः इत्येषा परमार्थता ॥
Vi. 575.

32. सुषुप्तिकाले मनसि प्रलीने नैवास्ति किंचित् सकलप्रसिद्धेः ।
अतो मनः कल्पित एव पुंसः संसार एतस्य न वस्तुतोऽस्ति ॥
Vi. 173.

7

Idealistic Thought in the *Brahma-Sūtra-Śāṅkara-bhāṣya*

THE *Brahma-sūtra* does not contain any specific expression that can lead us towards the concept of the unreality of the phenomenal world. Bādarāyaṇa, the author of the *Brahma-sūtra* does not seem to be admitting the unreality of the phenomenal world. But Gauḍapāda, who flourished after Bādarāyaṇa, being influenced by the full-fledged Buddhistic Idealism, admitted the unreality of the phenomenal world. After Gauḍapāda, his disciple's disciple Śaṅkara emphasized that everything except *Brahman* is unreal.

The Early *Vedic* thought of monism is said to have reached its zenith in the Absolutist philosophy of Śaṅkara. The most noteworthy and distinctive characteristic of his philosophy is the synthesis of Realism and Idealism. Exoterically Śaṅkara seems to be a Realist, but esoterically he proves himself a great Idealist. From the pragmatic point of view Śaṅkara admits the Objective Reality of this phenomenal world. While from the transcendental standpoint he considers everything also except *Brahman* as unreal. Thus it would be rendering injustice to Śaṅkara to consider him either as just a Realist or as just an Idealist. Of course, he is more of an Idealist, rather Absolutist, than a Realist, as he puts forth the non-dual *Brahman*-devoid of difference as the sole Ultimate Reality. Śaṅkara's philosophy can be summed up in one sentence as follows : "*Brahman* is the only Reality, while this phenomenal world (*jagat*) is unreal (*mithyā*); *Jīva* is non-different from *Brahman*."[1] From this, it seems that the very purport of his philosophy is to relegate this world of appearance to unreality (*mithyātva*), and to accept non-dual sentiency viz. *Brahman* as the Supreme Reality.

As Śaṅkara has employed both the empirical as well as the ultimate standpoints to reveal his philosophy, it is necessary to examine his Realistic views before one tries to peep into his Absolutism. So these passages which show Śaṅkara as a Realist will be discussed first.

Śaṅkara as a Realist

As Śaṅkara considers the worldly dealings as real from the empirical point of view, one can easily say that he does not reject the Objective Reality of this world of appearance.

Some points are presented here which openly show Śaṅkara's attempts to prove the Objective Reality of the worldly phenomena from the empirical standpoint.

(i) In the introductory passage of his commentary on the *Brahma-sūtra*, Śaṅkara states that our day-to-day life is merely based on the subject-object relationship. In the empirical world, all living beings impose the nautre and attributes of the subject (the self) on the object (sense-organs, body) and *vice versa*. Thus interrelating the nature and attributes of each other, one thinks 'I am this', 'This is mine', etc. Such type of behaviour is common to all.[2] And in this respect beasts, men and gods are alike.[3] Superimposition (*adhyāsa*) which is considered false from the ultimate point of view, is considered very natural from the empirical point of view. Without superimposition no worldly dealing could be possible. People superimpose the attributes of the body and the sense-organs on the self viz. 'I am fat', 'I am thin', 'I am dumb', 'I am deaf', etc.[4]

The entire complex of worldly dealings is considered as true, as long as the knowledge of *Brahman* being the self of all has not arisen.[5] Śaṅkara has repeated many a time, ".We accept that before true knowledge springs forth, the soul is implicated in the transmigratory state, and that this state constitutes the sphere of the operation of perception and so on . . ."[6]

It is true, that until one has gained true knowledge, one cannot believe this world of appearance to be unreal (*mithyā*). It is not proper to consider this world as unreal while experiencing it every moment. The man, who is captured by delusion, does not understand that he is perceiving a thing, which is not existing as a matter of fact. During the period of delusion, every action of his is considered meaningful. Suppose, man perceives a mirage in a desert. As he is under the influence of delusion, the sight of mirage, running after it etc. are considered to be full of meaning. Only when he realises that it is not water, does he conclude that what he perceived was not real.

Śaṅkara does not condemn the phenomenal world as absolutely non-existent like a hare's horn. It is neither absolutely real, nor is it absolutely unreal. Śaṅkara admits *anirvacanīya-khyāti,* as it is not possible to describe the world of appearance. There is no other alternative except accepting the nature of the world as inexplicable. A well-known example of it is of *rajju-sarpa.* In dim light, one knows a rope as a snake, so the snake that appears instead of rope is neither real nor unreal. It is not real because when one realises that it is a rope and not a snake, the snake disappears. On the other hand, it is not unreal as it was the object of knowledge and created fear in its perceiver.

Similarly, this world of appearance is neither real, nor unreal and hence it is inexplicable. As the world appears during its perception and as it fulfils common usages, it is real. But from the ultimate point of view, it is not real, as nothing else than *Brahman* can be real. Thus, on the strength of *anirvacanīya-khyāti.* Śaṅkara emphasizes that during empirical dealings the world of appearance has got Objective Reality.

(ii) Śaṅkara has described all knowledge including *Brahmavidyā* as *vastutantra.*[7] That is to say, knowledge is dependent on the existing thing, and on means of knowledge and not on any man or action. *Brahman* is self-existent. It does not depend on something else for its existence. Śaṅkara has stated that, as in perception knowledge depends on the objects of the perception, similarly *Brahmajñāna* depends on *Brahman* itself.[8]

(iii) Śaṅkara considers perception valid from the empirical point of view. Through the testimony of perception one can prove the validity of the external world. Various objects such as house, tree, mountain, river, table etc. are proved to be existing by perception.

While refuting the view of *Vijñānavādins,* that consciousness itself appears as if it were outside, Śaṅkara states that the external objects do exist. According to the *Vijñānavāda,* the external world does not exist at all. Various objects are seen 'as if' they exist outside. So there is the absence of external objects. This should be regarded lika a dream. As a dream, mirage, *gandharvanagara* etc. are perceived without there being external objects, so are pillar etc. perceived during the waking state, for there is no difference in their being knowledge,[9] so there is no difference between the objects appearing during the dreaming state as well as during the waking state. It is the consciousness that appears as if it were external.

Śaṅkara rejects this view,[10] and emphasizes that external objects do exist. In respect of an already existing thing we do not have the experience. "It is as if it were existing", "It looks like existing". Śaṅkara cites the example that no one says that Viṣṇumitra appears like the son of a barren woman.[11] A thing which is already existing, is not experienced as though it looks like existing. A man perceiving a rose, does not say that this rose looks like existing. It is absolutely foolish to say like this. Hence in accordance with our direct experience we must admit that the object of perception appears to us as something external, not like something existing.[12] It has an identity distinct from its knowledge as it is the object of knowledge and has played its part in the rise of knowledge. Śaṅkara is never tired of repeating that, it is not possible to determine the non-existence of the external objective world, for we experience it.[13] Śaṅkara while presenting the example of our practical life says that a man, who has already eaten food and is satisfied, cannot say that he has not eaten the food, and is not satisfied.[14]

Thus Śaṅkara rejects Subjective Idealism (*Vijñānavāda*) with full force and emphasizes the Objective Reality of the phenomenal world very clearly. Here, it would not be out of place to mention that Śaṅkara firmly holds that the knowledge and the object to be known are different from each other.[15] While refuting Subjective Idealism, Śaṅkara has stated that for the same reason (i.e., because the distinction of thing and idea is given in consciousness) the invariable concomitance of idea and thing has to be considered as proving only that the thing constitutes the means of the idea and not that the two are identical.[16]

This openly shows that Śaṅkara would not have supported the *Dṛṣṭi-Sṛṣṭi-vāda;* which holds that *Sṛṣṭi* is identical with the *Dṛṣṭi.* This shall be examined later in detail.

(iv) Śaṅkara has commented upon the process of creation which is discussed in the third *pāda* (quarter) of the second *adhyāya.* Bādarāyaṇa has presented the process of creation according to the scriptures. Remaining faithful to the *Vedic* text Śaṅkara has commented upon the order of creation. From the empirical point of view he has accepted creation, as he has admitted the Objective Reality of this world of appearance.

Śaṅkara has discussed about the origination, sustenence and dissolution of the world. Five elements, namely *ākāśa* (ether), *vāyu* (air), *teja* (light), *āp* (water) and *pṛthivī* (earth) are produced from the Ultimate Reality. It is stated that it is proved by the scriptures that from *Brahman* this phenomenal world is originated in the order of ether etc.[17] Refuting the *pūrvapakṣa.* Śaṅkara on the strength of scriptural authenticity proves that the ether is an effect of *Brahman.*[18]

Thus the five elements are originated from *Brahman* and similarly the intellect and mind are also originated from it. There is no specific order, whether the elements are originated first or the intellect and mind, for it is stated that there is no difference between the sense-organs and the elements. If the organs are of the nature of the elements, their production and dissolution occur on account of those of the elements.[19] It is immaterial whether the organs are produced first or the elements.[20] Now, at the time of dissolution, all the elements are dissolved in the reverse order. That is to say, the earth dissolves into the water, the water merges into the fire, the fire into the air. In this order a subtle element dissolves into a more subtle cause and ultimately everything merges into the most subtle cause viz. *Brahman*.[21]

A doubt may arise that when everything merges into *Brahman* at the time of dissolution, how could everything emerge again at the time of the new creation. The *Veda* has got its answer. It is declared that no contradiction arises about the name and form in the new world. Śaṅkara has emphasized the sameness of names and forms that take place in the new aeon. Śaṅkara cites the example of man who rises from sleep, continues the same dealings as he indulged in previous to his sleep. Admitting the authenticity of the word of the *Veda*, Śaṅkara states that, therefore the phenomenal world is the same in all the *kalpas* and as the Lords are able to continue their previous forms of existence, they manifest themselves in each new creation, individuals bearing the same names and forms as the individuals of the preceding creations, and owing to this equality of names and forms, the admitted periodical renovations of the world in the form of general *pralayas* and general creation do not conflict with the authoritativeness of the word of the *Veda*.[22]

Thus Śaṅkara has without any hesitation discussed the process of creation and dissolution and has also admitted that after dissolution, according to the previous order, the phenomenal world again emerges.

(v) Śaṅkara emphasizes all kinds of worldly dealings during a mundane state. It seems that Śaṅkara fully supports the classification of *varṇa, āśrama* etc.[23] This shows that during the empirical existence, all types of worldly dealings are in their proper place. Actions performed in daily life are not meaningless. Even a stick in one's hand can make a cow run away from that person. Śaṅkara accepts qualifications for *Vedic* study, importance of action, morality etc. from the empirical point of view.

Śaṅkara does not reject action (*karma*) especially selfless action, which can indirectly lead one towards *Brahman*. In the fourth *pāda* of the third *adhyāya*, it is established that actions, which are co-operative to knowledge; can lead, though indirectly, towards the origination of the knowledge.[24] The utility of selfless action is accepted inasmuch as it helps to purify the mind. It by erasing *rajas* and *tamas* and by enhancing the force of *sattva* gives rise to the desire to know *Brahman*.

Further, Śaṅkara states that by performing actions one goes by the *pitṛyāna* path to the *Candraloka* and after enjoying the fruits of one's deeds, has to be born again to experience the fruits of *prārabdha karmas*.[25] On one hand, actions lead one towards *pitṛyāna* path, on the other hand, by virtue of the knowledge of *Brahman* — namely *Saguṇa Brahman*, one goes by the *Devayāna* path to *Brahmaloka* and at the time of dissolution, merges into *Brahman* and thus attains the Ultimate Goal. This whole process is explained at length in the fourth *pāda* of the fourth *adhyāya*. Śaṅkara states that one who meditates and has the knowledge of *Brahman* — namely of *Saguṇa Brahman*, goes by the *Devayāna* path and stays in the *Brahmaloka*, where he enjoys extraordinary powers (except that of creating, maintaining and dissolving the world).[26] And at the time of final dissolution, this soul merges in *Brahman* and at the time of a new creation, it does not come back again in this world. On the other hand, one who has realised *Nirguṇa Brahman* does not go anywhere; as he has realised the true nature. It is stated that there is absence of departure for the knower of *Brahman*.[27] When one realises one's own nature, he has not to go anywhere else. As a matter of fact, *Jīva* is *Brahman* only, but due to the veil of *Avidyā* (ignorance), its true nature is concealed. When it is removed, it realises that it is nothing else but *Brahman*.

Then there is the other path for those, who have not performed good actions or have not known *Saguṇa Brahman*. It is stated that, those who have not got the right of the *Devayāna* through knowledge, nor of the *pitṛyāna* through actions, for those there is a third path on which they repeatedly return to the existence of small animals.[28]

In short, Śaṅkara admits the usefulness of action and accepts that by performing actions, one is able to gain its result accordingly.

(vi) From the lower point of view Śaṅkara accepts the necessity of the worship of God (*Īśvara*) viz. *Saguṇa Brahman*. Due to ignorance, *Brahman* is worshipped as *Īśvara*. From the lower point of view, worship of God is considered as a step for making *Brahman* enter into the intellect. Worship of *Saguṇa Brahman* leads towards the path, that takes the soul to the Ultimate Goal.

In the commentary on the *Brahma-sūtra* II.1-14; Śaṅkara has pointed out that from the empirical point of view, omniscience, omnipresence etc. are admitted as characteristics of *Īśvara*. It is stated that the Lord's being a lord, his omniscience, his omnipresence etc. all depend on the limitation due to the adjuncts whose nature is Nescience.[29] And the illusive power, viz. *Māyā* of the omniscient Lord, is the germ of *Prapañca*. Thus, Śaṅkara fully supports the view that the world phenomenon is created by the omniscient Lord. Of course, from the empirical point of view. Accordingly Śaṅkara has stated that all *Vedānta* texts declare that the Lord (*Īśvara*) is the only cause of all creation.[30] And according to the actions of the souls, *Īśvara* assigns fruits, *Īśvara* is the one common cause of the creation of gods, men etc.[31] God's position is described by giving the analogy *parjanya* (rain).[32] The peculiar potentialities in the respective seeds are the causes in respect of the creation of the different rice, barley, etc.; even when rain is the common cause of their production, so, the differences between the classes of beings are due to the different merits of the individual souls, even when God is the common cause of creation.[33]

Thus *Īśvara* is considered as the sole cause of the things of enjoyment of the soul in the transmigratory state. From the lower point of view, Śaṅkara has established the place of *Īśvara* and has considered Him as the cause of the creation; and as the giver of the fruits of the actions, that have been performed. The souls, who worship *Saguṇa Brahman* viz. God, are entitled to the *Devayāna* path and after their stay and enjoyment, gain the *Brahmaloka*.

(vii) As Śaṅkara has admitted the Objective Reality of the phenomenal world, he can be said to have accepted its *Vyāvahārika Sattā*. Śaṅkara has not banished this phenomenal world as absolutely unreal like a sky flower. Until the dawn of knowledge, the Objective Reality of the world of appearance is admitted. In his commentary on the first *Sūtra*, Śaṅkara has stated that everyone is conscious of his being. No one thinks, 'I am not existing.'[34] Śaṅkara accepts that before the dawn of knowledge, there is the transmigratory state and the operation of perception etc.[35]

Hence, all worldly and *Vedic* dealings have got *Vyāvahārika Sattā* before the attainment of knowledge.

The above-mentioned points clearly establish Śaṅkara as a Realist from the empirical angle. But if these points are considered from the ultimate standpoint, we find Śaṅkara as an Absolutist.

Since Śaṅkara has commented on the *Sūtras* of Bādarāyaṇa, which reveal nothing else but Realism, naturally the commentary on these *Sūtras* seems to be supporting Realism at first sight. But esoterically Śaṅkara has put forth his belief supporting Absolutism. At many places he has stated that the reality of the world is accepted from the empirical point of view, but ultimately it is rejected with full force. To remain faithful to every letter of the *Upaniṣads* and the *Sūtras* he has admitted the empirical standpoint over and above his esoteric view. Though he could not restrain himself from revealing his own belief about the unreality of this phenomenal world, even when he was discussing passage pertaining to creation or the like.

Śaṅkara as an Absolutist

Śaṅkara has never missed any opportunity to indicate that everything else except *Brahman* is unreal (*mithyā*). At many places at the end of *bhāṣya*, Śaṅkara has mentioned that the view should be taken from the empirical standpoint and not from the ultimate standpoint.[36]

(i) *Adhyāsa* is *Mithyā*

In the introductory passage, Śaṅkara has admitted the phenomenal world as real, as it fulfils practical usages. Now these worldly dealings are based on superimposition (*adhyāsa*). And superimposition by its nature is misguiding. It presents attributes of something in some other places.

Śaṅkara states that the only root cause responsible for this superimposition is Nescience or ignorance (*avidyā* or *mithyājñāna*). Hence superimposition must be considered as false (*mithyā*).[37] So all the worldly dealings based on superimposition must be considered as false. That is to say, superimposition is due to Nescience, which is responsible for this world phenomenon, which (the world) does not exist independently of *Brahman*. So due to superimposition, people consider worldly dealings as real, but they are false as a matter of fact. Under the spell of superimposition one cannot discriminate between the true and the false. As a result one is misguided. Take the example of silver and mother of pearl. In the bright sun-light a person cannot judge properly that the mother of pearl is shining due to sun-light and he takes it to be silver. Similarly in the empirical world, ignorant people cannot judge properly and as a result this world of appearance is superimposed on the non-dual *Brahman*.

(ii) The Concept of *Avidyā*

The doctrine of *Avidyā* is the only solution by which the riddle of this world of appearance can be solved. In Śaṅkara *Vedānta*, the concept of *Avidyā* can be considered to be its very foundation stone.

Śaṅkara has reiterated now and then that this world of appearance of seeming duality has sprung forth due to *Avidyā* only. Śaṅkara states that the only purport of the scriptures is to demolish duality imagined by *Avidyā*.[38] In his commentary on the *Tai.Up*. It is stated that the main goal of *Vedānta* is to bring an end to difference imagined by *Avidyā*, by the knowledge of the Absolute non-dual *Brahman*.[39]

This seeming duality is projected by false knowledge (*mithyājñāna vijṛmbhitaṁ*).[40] Śaṅkara states that as due to a defect in the eyes, one moon appears as many, so this multiplicity of name and form is brought about by nescience and should be dissolved by knowledge.[41] Further, it is stated that this transmigratory state is imagined by *Avidyā*.[42]

In short, Śaṅkara admits everything as brought about by virtue of *Avidyā*. Transmigration, this seeming multiplicity of name and form, creation (*Sṛṣṭi*), *Jīva*, *Īśvara*, scriptures everything is imagined by *Avidyā*. Each and everything apart from *Brahman* comes under the realm of *Avidyā* and hence is false (*mithyā*).

Next, it is briefly dealt with the above-mentioned, which are considered false under the realm of *Avidyā*.

Creation : As it has been already stated that from the empirical point of view Śaṅkara has admitted the Objective Reality of this world (*jagat*), and has also discussed its creation according to the scriptures.

But from the ultimate standpoint Śaṅkara has rejected creation (*Sṛṣṭi*) as false (*mithyā*); and has stated that *Sṛṣṭi* is projected by *Avidyā*. In his commentary on the *Brahma-sūtra* II.1-33 following Bādarāyaṇa, he says that there is no purpose behind this creation. It is merely a play. As in the empirical world, a king or his minister acts and wanders without any purpose just for fun, so is the cause with creation.[43] Further, it is stated that as respiration occurs very naturally, without depending on any extraneous purpose, similarly the activity of creation is performed by God naturally as a play.[44]

Thus creation is compared with a play. And play is always without any ulterior intention except that of pleasure. But at the end of his commentary on the *Brahma-sūtra* II.1-33 Śaṅkara has stated that the scriptural passages describing creation are not true from the ultimate standpoint; for these worldly dealings of name and form are projected by nescience (*Avidyā*).[45] For it should not be forgotten that the main purport of scriptures is to indicate non-duality.[46]

The *Upaniṣads* speak of the emergence of the world from *Brahman* not because it is their purport to indicate the reality of the creation. Their only intention behind statements describing creation is to state and emphasize the oneness and non-duality of *Brahman* and that nothing exists apart from *Brahman*.

Vācaspati, commenting on Śaṅkara's commentary on the *Brahma-sūtra* II.1-33; has emphasized this point, that *Sṛṣṭi* is not real (*pārmārthikī*), so no intention behind it is required. Furthermore, it has taken place due to beginningless *Avidyā*. And *Avidyā* is active by its very nature. So it does not require any intention. Vācaspati has cited analogies of the illusion of two moon, firey circle and *gandharvanagara*; such illusions have no intention behind them; and has put *Sṛṣṭi* on the same footing as the illusion of two moons, firey circle, *gandharvanagara*.[47]

The commentary of Śaṅkara on the *Brahma-sūtra* II.1-14 throws some light on this concept of creation. Śaṅkara has presented his view as supported by the *Chā. Up.*[48] that this seeming duality is brought about by speech.

Here, it would not be out of place to mention that Śaṅkara has also discussed about the examples of the clay and pot, water and ripples, which might lead one to support the theory of transformation (*pariṇāmavāda*). But this is not acceptable. In the commentary on the *Brahma-sūtra* II.1-14 Śaṅkara has discussed this point very clearly. In the *Chā. Up.* it is stated that by knowing the clay, its effects namely pot, etc. are known; as they are modifications brought about by speech and only the clay is real. Commenting on this Śaṅkara has stated that the pot, dish etc. which are the effects of clay are made out of clay and so are not different from clay, but are clay only. Difference is brought by speech. As a matter of fact, there is no difference, but the clay alone is there. From this analogy, the absence of the entire body of effect, independently from *Brahman* is understood.[49] It is stated that the distinction of enjoyers and enjoyables appearing in this manifold world is not real from the ultimate point of view; because it is to be understood that the effect, consisting of ether and so on, is non-different from its cause, namely *Brahman*. The effect does not exist apart from its cause. This *prapañca* consisting of enjoyables and enjoyer does not exist independently of *Brahman*.[50] The statement of the *Chā. Up.* that the difference in the manifold world is brought about by the speech (*vācārambhaṇaṁ*) indicates the unreality of all the effects.[51] Śaṅkara has asserted that manifoldness is projected by *mithyājñāna* (wrong knowledge).[52]

Śaṅkara regards this *prapañca* as unreal from the ultimate standpoint. His only concentration is centered on proving non-duality, that is to say the oneness of this world of appearance with *Brahman*. A doubt has been raised that oneness and manyness could both be real. As a tree is considered one but it is manifold if viewed as branches etc. So the Sea is one in itself but manifold as waves, foam etc. And clay is one but manifold if viewed with regard to the jars and dishes made of it. Śaṅkara puts aside this view by stating that the expression 'as clay they are real' asserts that the cause only is real while the expression 'having its origin in speech' declares the unreality of all the effects.[53] Thus examples of clay, water etc. are not to be understood as favouring the theory of transformation. Their purport is to show that name and form are modifications, i.e., appearances of *Brahman*, and have no reality apart from *Brahman*, which is the sole reality. As the existence of the snake in the rope of any period of time is merely *Māyā*, similarly, the appearance of the manifold world at any period of time. viz. origination, sustentation and destruction is just unreal.[54] The manifold world appears to be real only as long as *Avidyā* is there. Rightly speaking, it does not exist at any period of time, as nothing exists except *Brahman*.

One thing is noteworthy here that Śaṅkara has not used the analogy of the firey circle (*alāta cakra*) for establishing the unreal character of this world of appearance. On the other hand, in the *Gauḍapādakārikā*, Gauḍapāda has presented the analogy of firey circle to emphasize the unreality of the world and to establish *Ajātivāda*.[55] The only possible reason for not presenting such an analogy could be that Śaṅkara wanted to emphasize the Objective Reality of the world of appearance from the empirical point of view. According to Śaṅkara it is not possible to totally denounce the Objective Reality of the world to admit the world as real independently of *Brahman*. This notion is mentioned as *anirvacanīya-khyāti*, as we have seen already.

Śaṅkara solves the puzzle of the description of the phenomenal world, rather of its creation, by the theory of *Adhyāropa-Apavāda* (superimposition and negation). A well-known analogy is that of the Arundhati star. The star of Arundhati is too small to perceive. So one points out the nearer star and then shows that it is not the star of Arundhati, but the other smaller one is the star of Arundhati. Similarly at first the creation is imposed and then it is negated.

As it has been stated before that since Śaṅkara admits the Objective Reality of the phenomenal world, he has not used any term that shows the absolute unreality of the world. In the *Vivekacūḍāmaṇi* the term *asatkalpa* is used,[56] but there is a difference of opinion about its authorship.[57]

Vedic and Worldly Dealings Relegated to the Realm of *Avidyā*

Śaṅkara admits *Vedic* and worldly dealings as meaningful from the empirical point of view. But from the ultimate standpoint they are said to be fully within the realm of *Avidyā*. Again and again, Śaṅkara has said that before the dawn of knowledge both the type of dealings are possible, but after self-realisation there can be no dealing based on duality.

Śaṅkara states that the embodiedness of the self is caused by wrong conception.[58] And all kinds of worldly dealings are also performed by a wrong conception. Therefore the transmigratory state does not remain. as before after self-realisation.[59] Furthermore he states that the *Śruti* passage[60] speaks of the absence of dealings of the type of perception etc. after the dawn of knowledge.[61] He does not hesitate to say that even scriptures fall within the realm of *Avidyā* as even they are based on the concept of duality.[62]

Jīva :'The *Jīva* (individual soul) is non-different from *Brahman*. But due to ignorance it experiences differentiation from *Brahman*. It is stated that Jīvahood is caused by *Avidyā*;[63] and it is dependent on its limiting adjunct (*upādhi*) viz. *buddhi*.[64] Furthermore, it is stated that the relation of an individual soul with its limiting adjunct (*buddhi*) is due to wrong knowledge (*mithyājñāna*).[65] As long as its (individual soul's) connection with the *buddhi*, its limiting adjunct lasts, so long the individual soul remains as experiencing transmigration.[66] Thus, limited by *buddhi* and other adjuncts due to nescience, an individual soul feels separation from the Supreme Self viz. *Brahman*. As soon as its connection with *Buddhi* etc. ceases, it is non-different from *Brahman*.

It is stated in the commentary on the *Brahma-sūtra* II.3-46, that just as the light of the sun or the moon which pervades the entire space becomes straight or bent as it were when the limiting adjunct with which it is in contact, such as finger or the stick, is straight or bent, but does not really become so; and just as the ether, although imagined to move as it were when jars are being moved, does not really move, and as the sun does not tremble, although its image trembles when you shake the cup filled with water in which the sun's light is reflected; so the Lord also is not affected by pain, although pain can be felt by that aspect of him which is called the individual soul, as presented by nescience, and limited by the *buddhi* and other adjuncts.[67]

The *Brahma-sūtra* II.3-50 declares that the *Jīva* is an *ābhāsa* (appearance). The *ācāryas* have explained this *Sūtra* differently. So it is difficult to say what Bādarāyaṇa must have meant by the term *ābhāsa*. Śaṅkara has stated that the *Jīva* is a reflection of the Supreme Self, the individual soul is to be considered a mere appearance of the highest self, like the reflection of the sun in the water . . . .[68]

But Śaṅkara has not specifically accepted either the theory of Appearance (*Ābhāsavāda*) or the theory of Reflection (*Pratibiṁbavāda*) for explaining how *Brahman* can appear like the *Jīva*, and for explaining the empirical experiences of different individual souls.

But later, on the basis of the explanation of Śaṅkara, his followers interpreted it in both the ways. As it is stated that *ābhāsa* is due to *Avidyā,* it can be assumed that Śaṅkara might have meant that the *Jīva* is a reflection of a sentiency in *Avidyā.* In the commentary on the *Chā. Up.* Śaṅkara has stated that the *Jīva* is a reflection of God, brought about by the relation of man is perceived in the mirror and as the sun is reflected in the water.[69] So it can be said that he favours the *Pratibiṁbavāda.* On the other hand, analogies indicating the Appearance theory (*Ābhāsavāda*) and the Limiting theory (*Avacchedavāda*) are also found. It is stated that the lord differs from the soul which is the product of *Avidyā,* in the same way as the real magician standing on the ground differs from the illusive magician holding a sword and climbing up in the sky by means of a rope, or as the free unlimited ether differs from the ether of a jar which is determined by its limiting adjunct.[70]

So it cannot be stated with certitude that Śaṅkara favours either the theory of Reflection or of Appearance or of Limiting theory.

Īśvara (Saguṇa Brahman) : According to Śaṅkara, *Īśvara* (*Saguṇa Brahman*) is not the Ultimate Reality, as it is also imagined by *Avidyā.*

From the lower point of view, *Īśvara* is believed to be the ruler of all the living beings. God is a casual agent in all activities as we know from the scriptures.[71]

But from the higher point of view, the reality of *Īśvara* like that of the *Jīva* is rejected. It is stated in his commentary on the *Brahma-sūtra* II.1-14 that the Lord's being a lord, his omniscience, his omnipotence, etc. all depend on the limitation due to the adjuncts whose self is Nescience, in reality none of these qualities belong to the Self whose true nature is cleared by right knowledge, from all adjuncts whatsoever.[72]

Some *Śruti* passages describe *Brahman* as having attributes,[73] on the other hand some others as without having any attributes.[74] This is so because from the lower point of view, *Saguṇa Brahman,* that is, *Brahman* having attributes is to be worshipped as the Almighty Lord (*Īśvara*). But that also comes under the realm of *Avidyā.*

From the ultimate standpoint, *Brahman* is devoid of attributes, for according to the scriptures *Brahman* is to be ascertained only as devoid of attributes and not as having attributes.[75]

Thus, according to Śaṅkara's philosophy both the *Jīva* and *Īśvara* are imagined by *Avidyā*. Now, a question may arise that if the *Jīva* and *Īśvara* are both imagined by *Avidyā*, then what about this world of appearance? It is also imagined. But by whom? By the *Jīva* or by the Supreme Self? Who is the creator of this world of appearance?

Creator of the world of appearance : From the ultimate standpoint, this world of apearance is negated. But before the dawn of knowledge, its Objective Reality is admitted.

Since the creation is denounced from the ultimate point of view, it must be falsely imagined. But by whom? Could the world be constructed by *Brahman* who is eternally free from all imagination and is self-sufficient? The *Upaniṣads* repeatedly declare that these five elements *viz.*, earth, water, light, air and sky are brought about by *Brahman*. On the other hand it could be said that this phenomenal world is falsely imposed as there is only non-duality. Then who is the one responsible for such a superimposition ? Is it imagined by God or by the *Jīvas* or by just one principal *Jīva* to whom others are subservient. Or is there only one *Jīva* and everything is imagined by it?

We cannot get any answer to such question from Śaṅkara's thought. Only while discussing about the dreaming state, it is stated that the *Jīva* imagines the dreaming creation. Śaṅkara has quoted a statement from the *Bṛhadāraṇyaka Upaniṣad (Bṛ. Up.)* and has admitted that the dreaming world is a construction of the *Jīva*.[76] The *Bṛ. Up.* does not clearly state that the dreaming world is created by the *Jīva*. Nevertheless, its context indicates that it is the *Jīva*, who creates the dream world. It is stated that, there are no chariots, no spans, no roads. But he projects from himself chariots, spans, roads. . . .For he is a creator.[77] Thus quoting the *Brahma-sūtra* Śaṅkara declares that the *Jīva* is the creator of the dreaming world. But ultimately the *Jīva* is nothing else but *Brahman*. So who is the creator ? The question remains almost unsolved, even for a dream. Nevertheless Śaṅkara seems to regard the *Jīva* as projecting the dream-creation.

It seems that this problem of creation and its creator was immaterial for Śaṅkara, rather for all Idealistic philosophy. Śaṅkara's main concern was to establish the non-dual *Brahman* as the Ultimate Reality and everything else as unreal. Once this point is established, the question of giving a plausible explanation for the world of appearance and its diversity arises. We find no clear hint in respect of this from the writings of Śaṅkara. Afterwards, Śaṅkara's followers framed theories for the explanation of the world of appearance and the multiplicities of the *Jīvas*, which has been discussed in later chapters.

It would not be out of place to mention that Gauḍapāda has also not clearly stated as to who is responsible for the creation. He has stated that at first the *Jīva* is imagined and then this phenomenal world is imagined.[78] But by whom ? Whether it is imagined by the Supreme Self or by an individual soul ? This point is not clearly mentioned. It seems that it was immaterial for Gauḍapāda also as he emphasized the theory of non-origination (*ajātivāda*).

While discussing about the dreaming and the waking state, Gauḍapāda has compared them and has put them on the same footing. On the other hand, Śaṅkara clearly distinguished both the states while refuting Subjective Idealism.[79] In the dreaming state, an individual soul creates the things by imagination, which again vanish away while waking. On the other hand, in the waking state, one perceives things which are actually there before its perceiver and do not vanish away. Śaṅkara has stated that the things of the dreaming state are negated by the waking state, "I wrongly thought that I had a meeting with a great man, no such meeting took place, but my mind was dulled by slumber, and so the false idea arose " . . . but the thing viz. pillar etc. of which we are conscious in the waking state are never negated in any state.[80] Further on, while the dreaming state is a reminiscence, the waking state is an experience.[81]

Śaṅkara thus seems to hold that the dreaming world is

constructed by the *Jīva*; but the objective world is a construction of God. While discussing the *Devayāna* path and the position of the soul on its way towards liberation; Śaṅkara has stated that the soul enjoys all the powers except of the creation of the world; which proves that the objective world is created by God.[82]

Hence it can be stated that both individual superimposition as well as cosmic superimposition play an important role in the world construction. It can be stated in later terminology that the dreaming state is a production of an individual superimposition (*vyaṣṭi Avidyā*) and the waking state is a production of cosmic superimposition (*samaṣṭi Avidyā*).

Locus (*Āśraya*) of *Avidyā* : Whether Śaṅkara regards the *Jīva* as the locus (*āśraya*) of *Avidyā*. or *Brahman* as the locus is the main query. In the *Brahma-sūtra Śāṅkara Bhāṣya* we do not find this point emphasized clearly. Śaṅkara has not specifically stated whether the *Jīva* or *Brahman* is the locus of *Avidyā*. It seems that Śaṅkara is not much worried about the problem of *Avidyā*. This problem has been taken up by Maṇḍana Miśra and later Śaṅkarites. Nevertheless, Śaṅkara considers *Avidyā* to be a cosmic power responsible for this objective world as well as for the individual souls; for without *Avidyā* playing its part multiplicity could not have been experienced.

At one or two places Śaṅkara has touched this problem. In this commentary on the *Brahma-sūtra* IV.1-3 Śaṅkara has imagined a questioner asking, "To whom does *Avidyā* belong?" Śaṅkara replies, "It belongs to you all, who are asking such a question." The questioner replies that the scriptures declare that the individual self is identical with the Supreme self. Śaṅkara says, "Then you are enlightened. Ignorance does not belong to anyone."[83]

Śaṅkara seems to consider *Brahman* as the locus of *Avidyā*. It cannot be said that *Brahman* which is knowledge in itself, is opposed to *Avidyā*, as *Avidyā* itself is illuminated by *Brahman*. And *Avidyā* is opposed to right knowledge but not to *Brahman* of the nature of pure knowledge or sentiency. Hence *Avidyā* acts owing to its illumination by *Brahman*.

Now another question may arise that if *Avidyā* is illuminated by *Brahman,* then whether it is its power or its very nature or something else. In the *Brahmasiddhi* this very same inquiry is put forth.[84]

But Śaṅkara is not interested in discussing such questions, for as a matter of fact, *Avidyā* does not exist at all. According to Śaṅkara, *Avidyā* is unreal, for otherwise it could not be destroyed by knowledge.

Nevertheless, Śaṅkara has at times indicated that *Brahman* is the locus of *Avidyā.* In his commentary on the *Brahma-sūtra* I.4-3; he has stated that casual potentiality is of the nature of nescience, it is, rightly denoted by the term 'undeveloped'; it has the highest lord for its substratum . . .[85] Thus Śaṅkara seems to hold *Brahman* as the locus of *Avidyā.*

As stated already, when *Avidyā* itself is admitted as unreal, there was no need for discussing whether *Brahman* or the *Jīva* is the locus of *Avidyā.* After Śaṅkara, his followers started a serious inquiry into this as they felt that for communication with rival thinkers a rational and exact theory would have to be put forth in respect of such problems.

This problem of locus and object of *Avidyā* aroused much thinking amongst the Śaṅkarites. Some hold *Brahman* as the locus of *Avidyā* and through it the theory of *Sṛṣṭi-Dṛṣṭi* developed. On the other hand, the *Dṛṣṭi-Sṛṣṭi-vāda* evolved gradually when Śaṅkara's followers put forth the problem of the locus of *Avidyā* and especially when they regarded the *Jīva* as the locus of *Avidyā* and even cancelled the God-entity.

Summing up, one may conclude that it is Absolute Idealism that is revealed in Śaṅkara's philosophical writings.

Śaṅkara seems to be against Subjective Idealism, which strongly denounces the Objective Reality of this world of appearance. On the other hand Śaṅkara's philosophy puts forth Absolutism, which admits only *Brahman* as the eternal, unchanging, sentient Ultimate Reality. Since everything is *Brahman;* that is to say, since *Brahman* pervades everywhere, there remains nothing to negate. Of course, Śaṅkara holds everything unreal (*mithyā*), independently of *Brahman*.

Thus, one does not find any expression, that could clearly support the *Dṛṣṭi-Sṛṣṭi-vāda*. Of course, we may find hints, which indicate that Śaṅkara would have supported the *Sṛṣṭi-Dṛṣṭi-vāda* if he was asked to pin-point the issue.

References

1. ब्रह्म सत्यं जगन्मिथ्या, जीवो ब्रह्मैव नापरः ।
   Br. Sū. Śā. VI.20
2. तथाप्यन्योन्यस्मिन्नन्योन्यात्मकतामन्योन्यधर्मांश्चाध्यस्येतरेतराविवेकेनात्यन्तविविक्तयोधर्मधर्मिणोर्मिथ्या ज्ञाननिमित्तः सत्यानृते मिथुनीकृत्य 'अहमिदं' ''ममेदमिति' नैसर्गिकोऽयं लोकव्यवहारः ।
   Br. Sū. Śā. Bhā. I.1.1.
   Thibaut, George, *The Vedānta Sūtras*, Reprinted (1962), Motilal Banarsidass.
3. पश्वादिभिश्चाविशेषात् ।
   Br. Sū. Śā. Bhā. I.1.1.
4. तथा देहधर्मान् - स्थूलोऽहं, कृशोऽहं . . .
   तथेन्द्रियधर्मान् - मूकः . . .बधिरः
   Br. Sū. Śā. Bhā. I.1.1.
5. तस्मात्प्राग्ब्रह्मात्मताप्रतिबोधादुपपन्नः सर्वो लौकिको वैदिकश्च व्यवहारः ।
   Br. Sū. Śā. Bhā. I.1.1.
6. प्राक्प्रबोधात्संसारित्वाभ्युपगमात् : तद्विषयत्वाच्च प्रत्यक्षादिव्यवहारस्य . . .
   Br. Sū. Śā. Bhā. IV.1.3.
7. तत्रैवं सति ब्रह्मज्ञानमपि वस्तुतन्त्रमेव, भूतवस्तुविषयत्वात् ।
   Br. Sū. Śā. Bhā. I.1.2.
8. प्रत्यक्षादिप्रमाणविषयवस्तुज्ञानवद्वस्तुतन्त्रा ।
   Br. Sū. Śā. Bhā. I.1.4.
9. स्वप्नादिवच्चेदं द्रष्टव्यम् । यथा हि स्वप्नमायामरीच्युदकगन्धर्वनगरादिप्रत्यया विनैव बाह्येनार्थेन ग्राह्यग्राहकाकारा भवन्ति, एवं जागरितगोचरा अपि स्तम्भादिप्रत्यया भवितुमर्हन्तीत्यवगम्यते, प्रत्ययत्वाविशेषात् ।
   Br. Sū. Śā. Bhā. II.2.28.
10. *Br. Sū. Śā. Bhā.* on II.2.28.
11. न हि विष्णुमित्रो वन्ध्यापुत्रवदवभाति इति कश्चिदाचक्षीत ।
    Br. Sū. Śā. Bhā. II. 2.28.
12. तस्माद्यथानुभवं तत्त्वमभ्युपगच्छद्भिर्बहिरेवावभासत इति
    युक्तमभ्युपगन्तुं न तु बहिवदवभासत इति ।
    Br. Sū. Śā. Bhā. II. 2.28.
13. न खल्वभावो बाह्यस्यार्थस्याध्यवसातुं शक्यते ।
    कस्मात् १ उपलब्धैः ।
    Br. Sū. Śā. Bhā. II. 2.28.

14. यथा हि कश्चिद्भुञ्जानो भुजिसाध्यायां तृप्तौ स्वयमनुभूयमानायामेवं ब्रूयान्नाहं भुञ्जे न वा वा तृप्यामीति . . . ।

Br. Sū. Śā. Bhā. II. 2.28.

15. According to the *Sahopalaṁbhaniyama* of *Yogācāra* Buddhism (Subjective Idealism) both the knowledge and the object to be known are identical.

16. अत एव सहोपलम्भनियमोऽपि प्रत्ययविषययोरूपायोपेयभावहेतुको ना भेदहेतुक इत्यभ्युपगन्तव्यम् ।

Br. Sū. Śā. Bhā. II. 2.28.

English Translation by George Thibaut : *The Vedānta Sūtras*, Part-I, p. 422. Reprinted (1962), Motilal Banarsidass.

17. अत: श्रुतिप्रामाण्यादेकस्माद्ब्रह्मण आकाशादिमहाभूतोत्पतिक्रमेण जगज्जातमिति निश्चीयते ।

Br. Sū. Śā. Bhā. II.3.7.

18. तस्मादब्रह्मकार्यं वियदिति सिद्धम् ।

Br. Sū. Śā. Bhā. II.3.7.

19. . . .अविशेषात् । यदि तावद्भौतिकानि करणानि, ततो भूतोत्पत्तिप्रलयाभ्यामेवैषामुत्पत्तिप्रलयौ भवति इति. . . ।

Br. Sū. Śā. Bhā. II.3.15.

20. प्रथमं करणान्युत्पद्यन्ते चरमं भूतानि, प्रथमं वा भूतानुत्पद्यन्ते चरमं करणानीति ।

Br. Sū. Śā. Bhā. II.3.15.

21. एवं क्रमेण सूक्ष्मं सूक्ष्मतरं चानन्तरमनन्तरं कारणमपीत्य सर्वे कार्यजातं परमकारणं परमसूक्ष्मं च ब्रह्माप्येतीति वेदितव्यम् ।

Br. Sū. Śā. Bhā. II.3.14.

22. समाननामरूपत्वाच्चवृत्तावपि महासर्गमहाप्रलयलक्षणायां जगतोऽभ्युपगम्यमानायां न कश्चिच्छ्ब्दप्रामाण्यादिविरोध:

Br. Sū. Śā. Bhā. I.3.30.

English Translation from George Thibaut ; *The Vedānta Sūtra*, Part-I, p.-215, Reprinted (1962), Motilal Banarsidass.

23. शास्त्राण्यात्मनि वर्णाश्रमिवयोऽवस्थादिविशेषाध्यासमाश्रित्य प्रवर्तन्ते ।

Br. Sū. Śā. Bhā. I.1.1.

24. तस्माद्यज्ञादीन्याश्रमकर्माणि च भवन्ति विद्यासहकारीणि चेति निश्चितम् ।

Br. Sū. Śā. Bhā. III.4.35.

25. इष्टादिकारिणां धूमादिना वर्त्मना चन्द्रमण्डलमधिरुढानां भुक्तभोगानां तत: प्रत्यवरोह आम्नायते –

Br. Sū. Śā. Bhā. III.1.8.

26. जगदुत्पत्यादिव्यापारं वर्जयित्वाऽन्यदणिमाद्यात्मकमैश्वर्य मुक्तानां भुवितुमर्हति, . . .

Br. Sū. Śā. Bhā. IV.4.17.

27. तस्मादभाव: परब्रह्मविदो गत्युत्क्रान्त्यो:

Br. Sū. Śā. Bhā. IV.2.14.

28. ये न विद्यासाधनेन देवयाने पथ्याधिकृता:, नापि कर्मणा पितृयाणे, तेषामेष क्षुद्रजन्तुलक्षणोऽसकृदावर्ती तृतीय: पन्था भवतीति ।

Br. Sū. Śā. Bhā. III.1.17.

29. तदेवमविद्यात्मकोपाधिपरिच्छेदापेक्षमेवेश्वरस्येश्वरत्वं सर्वज्ञत्वं सर्वशक्तित्वं च, . . .

Br Sū. Śā. Bhā. II.1.14.

30. सर्ववेदान्तेषु चेश्वरहेतुका एव सृष्टयो व्यपदिश्यन्ते ।
Br. Sū. Śā. Bhā..

31. एवमीश्वरो देवमनुष्यादिसृष्टौ साधारणं कारणं भवति ।
Br. Sū. Śā. Bhā. II.1.34.

32. ईश्वरस्तु पर्जन्यवद्द्रष्टव्यः ।
Br. Sū. Śā. Bhā. II.1.34.

33. यथा हि पर्जन्यो व्रीहियवादिसृष्टो साधारणं कारणं भवति व्रीहियवादिवैषम्ये तुतु तद्बीजगतान्येवा साधारणानि सामर्थ्यानि कारणानि भवन्ति . . .
Br. Sū. Śā. Bhā. II.1.34.

34. सर्वो ह्यात्मास्त्रित्वं प्रत्येति, न नाहमस्मीति ।
Br. Sū. Śā. Bhā. I.1-1.

35. प्राक्प्रबोधात्संसारित्वाभ्युपगमात्, तद्विषयत्वाच्च प्रत्यक्षादिव्यवहारस्य, . . .
Br. Sū. Śā. Bhā. IV.1.3.

36. *Br. Sū. Śā. Bhā.* II.1.14, II.1.12, II.1.33.

37. ऽध्यासो मिथ्येति भवितुं युक्तम् ।
Br. Sū. Śā. Bhā. I.1.1.

38. अविद्याकल्पितभेदनिवृत्तिपरत्वाच्छास्त्रस्य ।
Br. Sū. Śā. Bhā. I.1.14.

39. प्रयोजनं चास्या ब्रह्मविद्याया अविद्या निवृत्तिः ततश्चात्यंतिकः संसाराभावः ।
Ten Principal Upaniṣads with Śāṅkara-Bhāṣya, p.281, (1978), Motilal Banarasidass.

40. मिथ्याज्ञानविजृम्भितं च नानात्वम् ।
Br. Sū. Śā. Bhā. II.1.14.

41. एकस्मिश्चन्द्रे तिमिरकृतानेकचन्द्रप्रपञ्चवदविद्याकृतो ब्रह्मणि नामरूपप्रपञ्चो विद्यया प्रविलापयितव्य इति ।
Br. Sū. Śā. Bhā. III.2.21.

42. अतोऽविद्याकल्पितसंसारित्व . . .
Br. Sū. Śā. Bhā. I.1.4.

43. यथा लोके कस्यचिदाप्तैषणस्य राज्ञो राजामात्यस्य वा व्यतिरिक्तं किंचित्प्रयोजनमनभिसंधाय केवलं लीलारूपा प्रवृत्तयः क्रीडाविहारेषु भवन्ति; . . .
Br. Sū. Śā. Bhā. II.1.33

44. यथा चोच्छ्वासप्रश्वासावयोऽनभिसंधाय बाह्यं किंचित्प्रयोजनं स्वभावादेव संभवन्ति, एवमीश्वरस्याव्यसनपेक्ष्य किंचित्प्रयोजनान्तरं स्वभावादेव केवलं लीलारूपा प्रवृत्तिर्भविष्यति ।
Br. Sū. Śā. Bhā. II.1.33.

45. न चेयं परमार्थविषया सृष्टिश्रुतिः, अविद्याकल्पितनामरूपव्यवहारगोचरत्वात्
Br. Sū. Śā. Bhā. II. 1.33.

46. ब्रह्मात्मभावप्रतिपादनपरत्वाच्चेत्येतदपि नैव विस्मर्तव्यम् ।
Br. Sū. Śā. Bhā. II.1.33.

47. अपि न नेयं पारमार्थिकी सृष्टिर्येनानुयुज्येत प्रयोजनम्, अपि त्वनाद्यविद्यानिबन्धना । अविद्या च स्वभावत एव कार्योन्मुखी न प्रयोजनमपेक्षते । न हि द्विचन्द्रालातचक्रगन्धर्वनगरादिविभ्रमाः समुद्दिष्टप्रयोजना भवन्ति ।
Bhāmati on *Br. Sū. Śā. Bhā.* II.1.33.

48. यथा सोम्येकेन मृत्पिण्डेन सर्वं मृन्मयं विज्ञातं स्याद्वाचारम्भणं विकारो नामधेयं मृत्तिकेत्येव सत्यम् ।
Chā. Up. VI.1.1.

49. ब्रह्मव्यतिरेकेण कार्यजातस्याभाव इति गम्यते ।
Br. Sū. Śā. Bhā. II.1.4.

50. एवमस्य भोग्यभोक्त्रादिप्रपञ्चजातस्य ब्रह्मव्यतिरेकेणाभाव इति द्रष्टव्यम् ।
Br. Sū. Śā. Bhā. II.1.14.

51. वाचारम्भणशब्देन च विकारजातस्यानृतत्वाभिधानात् . . .
Br. Sū. Śā. Bhā. II.1.14.

52. मिथ्याज्ञानविजृम्भितं च नानात्वम् ।
Br. Sū. Śā. Bhā. II.1.14.

53. 'मृत्तिकेत्येव सत्यम्' इति प्रकृतिमात्रस्य दृष्टान्ते सत्यत्वावधारणात् वाचारम्भणशब्देन च विकारजातस्यानृतत्वाभिधानात् . . .
Br. Sū. Śā. Bhā. II.1.14.

54. मायामात्रं ह्येतद्यत्परमात्मनोऽवस्थात्रयात्मनावभासनं रज्ज्वा इव सर्पादिभावेनेति ।
Br. Sū. Śā. Bhā. II.1.9.

55. G. K. IV. 47-50.

56. असत्कल्पो विकल्पोऽयं विश्वमित्येकवस्तुनि।
Vivekacūḍāmaṇi 400 (ab).

57. "It is improbable that Śaṅkara wrote the *Vi . . .*"
Deniel, M. Ingalls, 'A Study of Śaṅkarācārya', In *Annals of the Bhandarkar, Oriental Research Institute,* Vol. XXXIII, p.7 (1952), Poona.

58. तस्मान्मिथ्याप्रत्ययनिमित्तत्वाशरीरत्वस्य . . .
Br. Sū. Śā. Bhā, I.1.4.

59. . . . तस्मान्नावगतब्रह्मात्मभावस्य यथापूर्वं संसारित्वम्।
Br. Sū. Śā. Bhā. I.1.4

60. 'यत्र त्वस्य सर्वमात्मैवाभूतत्केन कं पश्येत्'
Bṛ. Up. II.4.14.

61. प्रबोधे प्रत्यक्षाद्यभावं दर्शयति ।
Br. Sū. Śā. Bhā. IV.1.3.

62. वेदा अवेदाः। बृ. ४, ३, २२। इति वचनादिष्यत एवास्माभिः श्रुतेरप्यभावः प्रबोधे ।
Br. Sū. Śā. Bhā. IV.1.3

63. अविद्यानिमित्तजीवभाव . . .
Br. Sū. Śā. Bhā. II.3.46

64. उपाधितन्त्रो हि जीव इत्युक्तम् ।
Br. Sū. Śā. Bhā. II.3.49.

65. अपि च मिथ्याज्ञानपुरःसरो यमात्मनो बुद्ध्युपाधिसंबन्धः ।
Br. Sū. Śā. Bhā. II.3.30.

66. यावदेयं चायं बुद्ध्युपाधिसंबन्धस्तावज्जीवस्य जीवत्वं संसारित्वं च ।
Br. Sū. Śā. Bhā. II.3.30.

67. यथा चाकाशो घटादिषु गच्छत्सु गच्छन्निव विभाव्यमानोऽपि न परमार्थतो गच्छति, यथा चोदशरावादिकम्पनात्तद्गते सूर्यप्रतिबिम्बे कम्पमानेऽपि न तद्वान्सूर्यः कम्पते, एवमविद्याप्रत्युपस्थापिते बुद्ध्याद्युपहिते जीवाख्येंऽशे दुःखायमानेऽपि न तद्वानीश्वरो दुःखायते ।
Br. Sū. Śā. Bhā. II.3.46.

68. आभास एव च

Br. Sū. II.3.50.

69. जीवो हि नाम देवताया आभासमात्रम् । बुद्ध्यादिभूतमात्रासंसर्गजनितः, आदर्शे इव प्रविष्टः पुरुष प्रतिबिम्बां जलादिष्विव च सूर्यादीनाम् ।
Ten Principal Upaniṣads with Śaṅkara Bhṣya, p. 513 (1978) Motilal Banarsidass.

70. यथा मायाविनश्चर्मखड्गधरात्सूत्रेणाकाशमधिरोहतः स एव मायावी परमार्थरूपो भूमिष्ठोऽन्यः । यथा वा घटाकाशादुपाधिपरिच्छिन्नादनुपाधि परिच्छिन्न आकाशोऽन्यः ।

Br. Sū. Śā. Bhā. I.1.17.

71. सर्ववेदान्तेषु चेश्वरहेतुका एव सृष्टयो व्यपदिश्यन्ते ।

Br. Sū. Śā. Bhā. III.2.41.

72. तदेवमविद्यात्मकोपाधिपरिच्छेदोपेक्षमेवेश्वरस्येश्वरत्वं सर्वज्ञत्वं सर्वशक्तित्वं च, न परमार्थतो विद्यायाउपास्तसर्वोपाधिस्वरूप आत्मनीशित्रीशितव्य सर्वज्ञत्वादिव्यवहार उपपद्यते ।

Br. Sū. Śā. Bhā. II.1.14.

73. सर्वकर्मा सर्वकामः सर्वगन्धः सर्वरसः ।

Chā. Up. III. 14.2.

74. नेति नेति

Br. Up. III. 3.6.

अस्थूलमनणुः

Br. Up. II. 8.8.

75. रूपाद्याकाररहितमेव ब्रह्मावधारयितव्यं न रूपादिमत् ।

Br. Sū. Śā. Bhā. III.2.14.

76. जीव एवायं कामानां निर्माता संकीर्त्यते। 'स्वयं विहृत्य स्वयं निनिर्मायि स्वेन भासा ज्योतिषा प्रस्वपिति'। बृ. ४, ३, ९ । इति
जीवव्यापार श्रवणात् ।

Br. Sū. Śā. Bhā. III.2.4.

77. *Bṛ. Up.* IV.3.10.
English Translation by Hume Robert Ernest.
The Thirteen Principal Upaniṣads; p.134, fifth impression (1962), Oxford University Press.

78. जीवं कल्पयते पूर्वं ततो भावान्पृथग्विधान् ।

G. K. II. 16(ab).

79. न स्वप्नादिप्रत्ययवज्जाग्रत्प्रत्यया भवितुमर्हन्ति ।
. . . वैधर्म्यं हि भवति स्वप्नजागरितयोः ।

Br. Sū. Śā. Bhā. II.2.29.

80. बाध्यते हि स्वप्नोपलब्धं वस्तु प्रतिबुद्धस्य मिथ्या मयोपलब्धो महाजनसमागमो इति, न ह्यस्ति मम महाजनसमागमो निद्राग्लानं तु मे मनो बभूव तेनेषा भ्रान्तिरूद्बभूवेति । . . . नैवं जागरितोपलब्धं वस्तु स्तम्भादिकं कस्यांचिदव्यवस्थायां बाध्यते ।

Br. Sū. Śā. Bhā. II.2.29.

81. अपि च स्मृतिरेषा यत्स्वप्नदर्शनम् । उपलब्धि जागरितदर्शनम् ।

Br. Sū. Śā. Bhā. II.2.29.

82. जगदुत्पत्त्यादिव्यापारं वर्जयित्वाऽन्यदणिमाद्यात्मकमैश्वर्यं मुक्तानां भवितुमर्हति, जगद्व्यापारस्तु नित्यसिद्धस्यैवेश्वरस्य ।

Br. Sū. Śā. Bhā. IV.4.17.

83. कस्य पुनरयमप्रबोधं इति चेत्, यत्त्वं पृच्छसि तस्य त इति वदामः । नन्वहमीश्वर एवोक्तः श्रुत्या, यद्येवं प्रतिबुद्धोऽसि, नास्ति कस्यचिदप्रबोधः ।

Br. Sū. Śā. Bhā. IV.1.3.

84. नाविद्या ब्रह्मणः स्वभावः, नार्थान्तरम्, नात्यन्तमसती, नापि सती

Brahmasiddhi - Brahma Kāṇḍa. p.9.

85. अविद्यात्मिका हि बीजशक्तिरव्यक्तशब्दनिर्देश्या परमेश्वराश्रया मयामयी महासुप्तिः . . .

Br. Sū. Śā. Bhā. I.4.3.

English translation by Thibaut George, *The Vedānta Sūtras,* Part-1, p. 243, (1962), Motilal Banarsidass.

8

Idealistic Thought in the *Brahmasiddhi*

IN the previous chapter it has been stated that according to Śaṅkara, this world of appearance is false (*mithyā*) independently of the non-dual sentient principle, viz. *Brahman*. Nevertheless, Śaṅkara admits the Objective Reality of the world of appearance. But from the transcendental point of view, according to Śaṅkara the phenomenal world is projected through *Avidyā* (*avidyāpratupasthāpita*). Thus, *Avidyā* is regarded as the root-cause of this world of appearance. Besides, it is noteworthy that for Śaṅkara, even *Avidyā* does not exist from the ultimate standpoint.

After Śaṅkara, the topic of the locus (*āśraya*) of *Avidyā* became a moot problem for the Śaṅkarites. Different views prevail amongst the Śaṅkarites regarding the locus of *Avidyā*. Maṇḍana and Vācaspati hold that the *Jīva* is the locus of *Avidyā* and *Brahman* is the object of *Avidyā*. On the other hand Sureśvara, Sarvajñātman, Prakāśātman and others are of the opinion that *Brahman* is both the locus and the object of *Avidyā*.

The belief that the *Jīva* is the locus of *Avidyā*, would imply the subjectivistic point of view in the sense that then the *Avidyā* residing in the *Jīva* could be responsible for the projection of this world of appearance. This could lead to Subjective Idealism.

The main purport of this chater is to examine Maṇḍana Miśra's idealistic views, which positively guide us towards the development of the *Dṛṣṭi-Sṛṣṭi-vāda*. But before entering into more details, Maṇḍana's identity is briefly mentioned here.

Maṇḍana Miśra

The name of Maṇḍana Miśra comes to our mind as a bold and revolutionary philosopher. Maṇḍana's contribution to both *Mīmāṁsā* and *Vedānta* is noteworthy.

The identification of Maṇḍana with Sureśvara has been a topic of much discussion. Much has been assumed about the early life of Maṇḍana. It is believed that Maṇḍana was a disciple of Kumārila, before he was converted to the *Vedāntic* fold as Sureśvara. According to some, Maṇḍana was a contemporary of Śaṅkara. On the other hand some regard Maṇḍana as a pupil of Śaṅkara. Professor Hiriyanna has expressed a doubt about the equation of Maṇḍana and Sureśvara.[1] On the other hand, R.Balasubramaniam suggests that perhaps Maṇḍana wrote the *Brahmasiddhi* setting forth a non-Śaṅkara brand of *Advaita,* then became converted by Śaṅkara, took the name of Sureśvara and wrote the Śaṅkaran *Advaita* works commonly attributed to Sureśvara.[2] These seem to be only assumptions about Maṇḍana, which do not seem to be trustworthy after the study of the works attributed to Maṇḍana and Sureśvara. On the contrary their views differ and it seems that both Maṇḍana and Sureśvara were different personalities. A very noticeable point that distinguishes Maṇḍana from Sureśvara is that, Maṇḍana admits the *Jīva* as the locus of *Avidyā;* while Sureśvara holds that *Brahman* is the locus of *Avidyā.* This proves that both could not have been one and the same.

Maṇḍana wrote the *Brahmasiddhi,* which has gained a prominent place in *Vedāntic* literature. It contains four chapters, viz. (i) *Brahmakāṇḍa,* (ii) *Tarkakāṇḍa,* (iii) *Niyogakāṇḍa* and (iv) *Siddhikāṇḍa.* The main purpose of this work is to show that this seeming duality is projected by *Avidyā* and hence it is without any essence of its own. This work is remarkable in the sense that Maṇḍana has expressed some revolutionary views differing from Śaṅkara. For instance:

(i) Taking rather a bold step, Maṇḍana has stated that the

Jīva is the locus of *Avidyā*. This view of Maṇḍana is fairly independent, and has opened a new vista in *Vedāntic* thought.

(ii) Differing from Śaṅkara, Maṇḍana emphasized the *Sphoṭa* doctrine.

(iii) Further on, Maṇḍana elucidates the doctrine of *Prasaṁkhyāna*. According to Maṇḍana, *Mahāvākyas* such as *Tat-tvam-asi* teach the identity of *Brahman* with *Ātman*. But such knowledge is indirect. So before the actual realisation of *Brahman*, one has to perform meditation; and after that only one is able to get liberation.

(iv) Going against Śaṅkara, Maṇḍana accepts the importance of action (*karma*) even after the purification of the mind.

Idealistic Views Expressed in the *Brahmasiddhi*

It may be mentioned that as Maṇḍana has some distinctive views, we have assigned a separate chapter to the *Brahmasiddhi*. Topics like Negation of duality, Negation of creation, Locus of *Avidyā*-types and nature of *Avidyā* etc. clearly signify Idealism. But which type of Idealism ? That will be examined in the later part of this chapter.

Negation of Duality: Maṇḍana, like Śaṅkara negates the seeming duality of name and form from the transcendental standpoint. Quoting the Śruti passages Maṇḍana has shown that this seeming duality has occurred merely due to Nescience, far from the ultimate standpoint, there is non-duality.

In the very first chapter of the *Brahmasiddhi* viz. *Brahmakāṇḍa*, presenting the *Naiyāyika* realist as the *Pūrvapakṣin*, Maṇḍana has refuted the opponent's views and has established the doctrine of non-duality through *Śruti*-passages.

According to the *Pūrvapakṣin*, duality is real and so the *Śruti* passages negating duality are to be understood in a secondary sense. The reasons presented by the *Pūrvapakṣin* are as follows:

(i) There is difference of enjoyment in different people.
(ii) The difference between the transmigrating and the liberated could be possible only if there is a plurality of souls.
(iii) The organ of sight must have an object different from itself, because it is contradictory for it to function on itself, and further the perceiver is known in relation to the perceptible object (*dṛśya*).
(iv) We perceive objects as possessing different characteristics related to pleasure, pain and delusion. These seeming objects are classified as being of the diverse nature of pleasure, pain and delusion, or we see them as having the classifications viz. word, form, colour, taste, etc.

And hence the *Śruti*, declaring non-duality viz. 'All this is but the self' should be understood as figurative as signifying that they are meant for the self.[3]

Answering the above-mentioned arguments, the *Siddhāntin* states that the *Śruti* passages are primarily intended to declare non-duality. This knowledge of diverse forms (*nānārūpāvagamo*) is based on *Māyā*, as declared by the *Śruti*, so how could it be said that the *Śruti* passage is to be figuratively understood ? *Nānātva* (manyness) is repeatedly negated by the *Śruti*. The *Śruti* even emphasizes the falsity of the perception of duality (difference); and tells us that there is perception as it were of duality only due to illusion. The word *Iva* used in the *Śruti* passage shows that there is absence of difference and hence the *Śruti* passages do not speak of *ekatva* (oneness) in the figurative sense.[4]

We may see how the *Siddhāntin* refutes the *Pūrvapakṣin*.

(i) While refuting the first reason put forth by the *Pūrvapakṣin* the *Siddhāntin* states that the ordered difference (*vyavasthā*) of enjoyments is a merely imagined one; and hence it is without any essence of its own.[5] The argument put forth by the *Pūrvapakṣin* does not seem to be a sound one for the ordered difference of enjoyment can even be due to difference which is imagined. For example, though the Self whether it be omnipresent or of the size of the body or atomic — is one, yet we see difference of experience (enjoyment or suffering), viz. "There is pain in my foot." "There is pain in my head"; and this is based on difference, which is imagined.[6] Further, though there is absence of difference, we see difference of colour or configuration (*saṁsthāna*) in the various reflections of a face on the different surfaces of stone, sword, mirror etc.[7] Though the original is one and the same, its reflections on various surfaces differ in colour or shape. Similarly, though there is absence of difference, it is experienced.

(ii) The difference between the transmigrating and the liberated is also not plausible. The *Siddhāntin* presents the same explanation to refute the argument of the *Pūrvapakṣin*. As the same self-experiences happiness or pain are in different parts of the body, so it could be known as bounding at one place and as liberated at another place.[8] The very same face is seen as dirty on the surface of a dirty mirror and it appears clean on a clean-surfaced mirror.[9] Besides, imagined differences can produce real effects; for example, death occurs due to imaginary snake-bite and illumination is possible from a reflected Sun.[10]

Here, the *Siddhāntin* wants to assert that, though this duality is an imagined one, it can fulfil practical dealings. Ultimately all these practical dealings of the phenomenal world are imagined ones. But as they are fulfilled, one is tempted to consider this duality as real.

(iii) According to the *Pūrvapaskṣin* the seer is assumed in relation to the seen; and therefore, the difference between the seen and its seer is proved. And the seen are many due to differences of pleasure etc. This view of the *Pūrvpakṣin* is negated as being not true.[11] The *Siddhāntin* has emphasized that the seer (*dṛṣṭṛ*) is not different from the seen (*dṛśya*), because there is no contradiction in congnition's functioning on itself, as it is self-luminous, as in the case of a lamp, and in the case of knowledge being both means and fruit.[12] The seer of the nature of sentiency is either thus transformed or appears differently.[13] And if duality be admitted, since things of different natures could not be related to each other, the relation of seer and seen could not be possible.[14] The self, which is non-dual, appears as such (as both seer and seen) either due to transformation or appearance as on the surface of the mirror.[15] As the reflection on the surface of the mirror is not different from its original; so the seen is not different from the seer. And the *Śruti* itself declaring that everything is known on the self being known, emphasizes that the seen is non-different from the seer.[16]

Thus Maṇḍana regards the seen (*dṛśya*) as identical with the seer. This could indicate Subjective point of view. When maṇḍana holds that this seeming duality is non-different from its perceiver; we could get a passing glimpse of subjectivism, which was later on developed by Prakāśānanda in the *Vedānta-Siddhānta-Muktāvalī*; in the form of the *Dṛṣṭi-Sṛṣṭi-vāda.* In this respect, Maṇḍana should be considered as an initiator of the *Dṛṣṭi-Sṛṣṭi-vāda* of the *Vedānta* school.

Thus, Maṇḍana has repeatedly stated that the seeming duality is merely an imagined one. As a matter of fact, in the realm of non-duality, there is no scope for duality. In the *Tarkakāṇḍa,* Maṇḍana has said that there is no 'difference' from the ultimate standpoint, as it is simply a display of biginningless *Avaidyā.*[17]

Negation of Creation (*Sṛṣṭi*): Since Maṇḍana has elucidated that th seen (*dṛśya*) is projected by *Avidyā,* this creation must be considered as false.

If the thing were existent, the question of its origin would arise, but when the thing itself is false; the question regarding its origination does not arise at all.

Those, who consider *Avidyā* as the material cause of the world of appearance, hold that as *Avidyā* is beginningless and purposeless, there is no scope for any prupose for the creation of difference.[18]

It may be argued that without having any prupose, even a fool does not act, so there must be some purpose behind the creation. So the purpose of *Brahman* for creation must be mentioned. But creation could not have taken place for doing favour to the *Jīvas;* as the *Jīvas* are totally absent before the creation. And even after the creation, no one experiences grace; but all seem to suffer. Again, the supreme self has not created the world for self-enjoyment as it is self-content.

Since creation is based on *Avidyā,* there remains no scope for the query regarding the purpose of the creation, as *Avidyā* does not require any motive for its action.[19]

As there are the *Śruti* passages which speak of creation, it may seem that the creation is real. But esoterically the *Śruti* passages deny creation. The main purport of the *Śruti* passages is not to show the reality of creation, but to emphasize non-duality. It is stated in the *Brahmasiddhi* that the description of creation given by the *Śruti* passages is nor for the sake of describing creation.[20] From the beginning up to the end, the *Śruti* passages are in consonance with each other as far as their purport of putting forth non-duality is concerned.

Maṇḍana like Śaṅkara has stated that the effect is identical with its cause and the one alone is real.[21] The question of duality does not arise, as everything is non-different from the non-dual Ultimate Reality. To prove this, examples of pot etc. are given. The various shapes of clay, viz. pot etc. are not different from the caly; in other words, they are nothing but the clay.[22]

It may be argued that causality in its primary sense is propounded here.[23] So the answer is given that the passage describing creation is not to be understood in its primary sense; and the theory of Causality is not propounded; but it is stated only as a means to the understanding of the concept of oneness. That is to say, the Highest Reality is one and without a second. The repeated statements of the *Śruti* are meant to negate difference,[24] so it is not possible to state that there is oneness in its nature of cause and plurality in the state of effect. The cause alone is in fact real. Elsewhere all difference is said to be known through *Māyā.* The negation of difference is positively stated. Further, difference and non-difference being contradictory cannot stay together.

Maṇḍana has presented the analogies of reflection, word and

dream-creation to make it clear that creation is not real. Reflections are produced from the originals (*bimba*), but they do not exist in reality. Similarly, words arising from letters are not real. The same is the case with dreams. So the statement that *ākāśa* etc. are produced from *Brahman* does not mean that the creation is real. And the *Śruti* itself declares that the effects are brought about by speech.

In Śaṅkhapāṇi's commentary on the *Brahmasiddhi* it is emphasized that though there is the creation of a chariot etc. in the dream, it is not regarded as real. It is the same with the creation of the elements ether, air etc. The statement of creation is only meant to propound unity.[25]

Thus, creation is not considered real by the author of this work. As has been stated above, *Avidyā* is regarded responsible for the display of the manifold world. But is *Samaṣṭi Avidyā* responsible for the creation or *Vyaṣṭi Avidyā* ? Such a question has remained unanswered in the *Brahmasiddhi*. Nevertheless, Maṇḍana has mentioned *Jīva* as the locus of *Avidyā*. This could indicate that *Avidyā*, residing in the *Jīva* is responsible for creation. But Maṇḍana has not specifically said so.

Next is the concept of *Avidyā* as it is put forth in the *Brahmasiddhi*.

The Concept of *Avidyā*: *Kevalādvaita Vedānta* simply propounds the Absolutist philosophy that everything is *Brahman*. Each and every thing other than *Brahman* is unreal, though we all seem to experience the duality consisting of name and form. We are so much absorbed in the so-called reality of the world of appearance, that we do not dare to consider it is a fiction.

So the question may arise as to which force restrains us from admitting this world of appearance as unreal. The only possible answer to this is that it is *Avidyā* (nescience), which is responsible for bringing about the wonderful display of the world of appearance; and which impels us to consider it as the real one.

We have stated in the previous chapter that according to

Śaṅkara, even *Avidyā* is unreal from the ultimate standpoint. Since Śaṅkara seems to have concentrated on emphasizing *Brahman* as the Ultimate Reality; he has not presented the concept of *Avidyā* in all its aspects and from different point of views, so as to put forth a thoroughly consistent explanation in all the details.

After Śaṅkara, the concept of *Avidyā* was developed by the Śaṅkarites. Amongst the followers of Śaṅkara, Maṇḍana is the first one, who has discussed this concept at some length. In the *Brahmakāṇḍa*; as well as in the *Niyogakāṇḍa* we find a discussion regarding the locus and types of *Avidyā*.

In the *Brahmakāṇḍa* it is stated that *Avidyā* is neither the very nature of *Brahman* nor is it another thing. It is neither absolutely unreal, not real. For this reason only, it is called *Avidyā, Māyā,* false appearance.[26] If it was the very nature of *Brahman* or if it was a different thing, then it would be ultimately real (*paramārtha*) and not *Avidyā*. If it were absolutely unreal like a skyflower, it would not be a factor subserving practical dealings. Hence it is known as inexplicable (*anirvacanīya*).[27] Refuting the views of the *Śūnyanvādins* and the *Yogācārins,* Maṇḍana has proved the inexplicable nature of *Avidyā*.

According to the *Śūnyavādin,* things are existent as they are seen.There have been no *Avidyā* if it were existent as it is seen. It would not be *Avidyā* but rather like a sky flower. Now, in the view of the *Viajñānavādin,* consciousness alone exists. If knowledge is existent, as it appears, then the object cannot be denied as there is no denial of the shape of the knowable viz. blue, yellow etc. as appearing outside. In the view of those who uphold the reality of external objects. If what appears is unreal or non-exisent, its appearance could not be explained as real, it would be just appearance; and the conception "its appearance" also would be just an erroneous one. Therefore *Avidyā* is neither real nor unreal.[28]

It might be argued that *Avidyā* is illusion. If the knowable were to exist as it appears (or is known) it would not be an illusion; but would be right knowledge, and if the knowable were not to exist, its cognition would not be explained (i.e., would not be possible). Therefore, it (knowable) cannot be rightly said to be existent, for it can be said to be non-existent.[29]

Locus of *Avidyā* :As stated in the previous chapter, Śaṅkara would have regarded *Brahman* as the locus of *Avidyā*. But he seems to be not much worried about this problem. After Śaṅkara, the main query about the locus of *Avidyā* became a moot point amongst the Śaṅkarites.

Now amongst the Śaṅkarites, Maṇḍana has boldly declared the *Jīva* as the locus of *Avidyā*. Such a view could imply that *Avidyā*, residing in the *Jīva* is responsible for the projection of this world of appearance. This would lead to Subjective Idealism, that this manifold world is imagined by the individual mind.

In the *Brahmakāṇḍa* the author has imagined the *Pūrvapakṣin* as asking as to whom *Avidyā* belongs. It could be rightly mentioned here that this very same style of expression is found in the commentary of Śaṅkara on the *Brahma-sūtra* IV.1.3. In answer to the *Pūrvapakṣin*, Maṇḍana has positively stated that *Avidyā* belongs to the *Jīvas*.[30] It is also noteworthy that Maṇḍana seems to be against the single-soul theory, as he uses the term *Jīva* in plural.

It may be objected that the *Jīvas* are not different from *Brahman*. As the *Jīva* is non-different from *Brahman*, it would not be rational to regard *Jīvas* as the locus of *Avidyā*. The reply to this objection is that this is true from the ultimate standpoint, but by virtue of constructive imagination, the *Jīvas* are different from *Brahman*.[31] Another question is asked as to whose imagination (*kalpanā*) separates them. It could not be *Brahman*'s, as it is knowledge (*Vidyā*) itself, and hence it is devoid of false imagination. It may be argued that such imagination could not be of the *Jīvas* also; as before the functioning of imagination there was the absence of the *Jīvas*; and thus the fault of mutual-dependence would be unavoidable. The difference of the *Jīva* from *Brahman* is dependent on imagination and imagination is subsistent in the *Jīva*.[32] Such a doubt is dispelled by the *Siddhāntin* by saying that such a fault of mutual dependence would not arise as both the *Jīva* and *Avidyā* are beginningless.[33] Another objection is raised that as the *Jīvas*, being identical with *Brahman*, are pure by nature; *Avidyā* could not belong to the *Jīvas*.[34] Giving the example of the original and its reflection, the *Siddhāntin* refutes this argument of the *Pūrvapakṣin*. Though the *Jīvas* are pure by nature, they appear impure due to illusion, just as the reflection appears impure on the impure surface of the sword.[35] Regarding the destruction of *Avidyā* in the case of one who has become one with *Brahman*, it may be argued that even if a thing is natural, it could be destroyed on the rising of a concept which is different, but *Avidyā* is beginningless, innate and causeless, so it could not be destroyed. Further, it cannot be said that *Vidyā*, which is the very nature of *Ātman*, could be the destroyer of *Avidyā*, because there is absence of contradiction between the two viz. *Vidyā* and *Avidyā* as they stay together. And if there were contradiction, since this nature of *Ātman* is always there, there would be eternal absence of *Avidyā* and the world would be eternally emancipated.[36] And the other *Vidyā* produced by 'hearing' etc. too cannot be regarded as the destroyer of *Avidyā*.

The *Siddhantin*'s answer to this is that it is the *Jīvas* which are defiled by *Avidyā* and not *Brahman*, which is always pure, eternal self-luminous and unproduced otherwise *Avidyā* would not be destroyed even in the case of the one which has become one with *Brahman*.[37] Further, if *Avidyā* belonged to *Brahman*, *Brahman* itself would be the transmigrant and the liberated; and when it is released; all would be released at once. So it would mean that due to the perception of difference, *Brahman* becomes the transmigrant and due to the knowledge of non-duality, it is emancipated and thus all would be emancipated simultaneously.[38] Therefore it is better to believe that due to *Avidyā*, the *Jīvas* become the transmigrants and due to knowledge they are released.[39] Moreover, it is stated that *Avidyā* is natural and *Vidyā* is adventitious for the *Jīvas*. *Avidyā*, natural to the *Jīvas* is dissolved only by knowledge, which is produced.[40] Though the *Jīvas* are non-different from *Brahman*, the ordered arrangement of *Vidyā* and *Avidyā* is possible as in the case of the original and its reflection.[41] That is to say, as eventhough, the original is pure, its reflection over the surface of a sword etc. appears to be impure. Similarly, though *Brahman* is knowledge itself, *Jīvas* can be said to have *Avidyā*.

Hence it can be said that since in Maṇḍana's opinion *Avidyā* resides in the *Jīvas*, he can be said to have subjectivistic outlook. Of course, he has not fully discussed how *Avidyā* residing in the *Jīvas* projects duality. Nevertheless, Maṇḍana can be considered to be a pioneer of the concept that *Avidyā* resides in the *Jīva*.

Type of *Avidyā* : Giving some more details about *Avidyā*, Maṇḍana has classified *Avidyā* into two types. It is stated in the *Niyogakāṇḍa* that *Avidyā* is two-fold: (i) one which conceals the illumination, and (ii) which projects it wrongly.[42] Maṇḍana further states that *Avidyā*, which has got projecting power, is present in both the waking and the dreaming states; while the other with concealing power, is present in deep sleep and is characterised by dissolution.[43]

Non-apprehension (*agrahaṇa*) and misapprehension (*anyathāgrahaṇa*) are two aspects of *Avidyā*, which are related as cause and effect.[44] Concealing *Avidyā* is identical with non-apprehension, while projecting *Avidyā* is identical with misapprehension. The former is the cause and the latter is its effect. That is to say, at first the true nature of a thing is concealed; and then a false appearance is projected. Thus the two powers are related as cause and effect. Non-apprehension and misapprehension are both found in the dreaming as well as in the waking state; while non-apprehension which is known as cause, is found in the deep sleep.[45]

It may be noted that in the *Gauḍapādakārikā*, Gauḍapāda has put forth these aspects of *Avidyā*.[46] So Maṇḍana is indebted to *Gauḍapāda* in this respect. Maṇḍana's effort to specifically describe the nature of *Avidyā* is praiseworthy. This could be detected in Śaṅkara's writings too, but not in such clear terms.

While Summing up it may be stated :

(i) Maṇḍana seems to consider *Avidyā* as identical with *Māyā*, as he has used the terms *Māyā* as a synonym of *Avidyā*.[47]

(ii) Maṇḍana does not seem to consider the world as merely a void (*śūnya*), as it is of the nature of *Brahman* and thus has substantiality.[48] This clearly shows that Maṇḍana accepts the Objective Reality of the world of appearance and does not consider it absolutely unreal.

(iii) Like Śaṅkara, Maṇḍana holds the mundane world and its dealings to be unreal from the ultimate standpoint. While refuting the *Yogācāra* view; Maṇḍana has said that both transmigration and emancipation are imaginary from the ultimate point of view.[49] This suggests that Maṇḍana seems to accept them as real from the empirical point of view.

(iv) Maṇḍana has not shown the systematic process of the creation. Of course, he admits that *prapañca* is caused by *Avidyā*. But he has not mentioned whether it is created by *Īśvara* or by the *Avidyā* of the *Jīva*. Further, Maṇḍana has not made it clear whether *Avidyā* residing in the *Jīva* creates the world separately or as common for all. Nevertheless, Maṇḍana seems to be an Absolutist accepting that everything other than *Brahman* is non-existent.[50]

Hence, in a nutshell it can be said that we can find Absolutistic views tinctured with Subjectivism, in the *Brahmasiddhi*. A clear-cut doctrine of pure Subjective Idealism is not propounded by Maṇḍana. Still he has paved the way to the Subjective type of Idealism by putting forth the *Jīvas* as the locus of *Avidyā*. As Dr.S.S. Hasurkar states, "Maṇḍana can thus be legitimately held as the originator of the *Jiivāśrita-avidyā-vāda*, that unique aspect of the post-Śaṅkara career of the doctrine of *Māyā* with his emphatic stand over the problem of locus of *Avidyā*, and his deep Subjectivism, he can be said to be indirectly responsible for the subtle *Dṛṣṭi-Sṛṣṭi-vāda*. . ."[51]

Hence, an inkling of the *Dṛṣṭi-Sṛṣṭi-vāda* is provided by Maṇḍana, as he has promoted the *Jīvāśrita-ayidyā-vāda*. In short, by pointing out a new direction with his independent thinking, Maṇḍana has attained a prominent place in *Vedāntic* thought.

References

1. Sastri, Kuppuswami, (ed.), *Brahmasiddhi,* Introduction, p. xxv, (1937), Madras Government Press.
2. Potter Karl H., (ed.), *Encyelopedia of Indian Philosophies,*Vol.III; Ch.III; p. 347, (1981), Motilal Banarsidass.
3. अत्र केचित्—भोगव्यवस्थानात्, मुक्तसंसारिविभागोपपत्तेश्च, दृक्छक्तेचार्थवत्दात् स्वात्मनि वृत्तिविरोधात्, दृश्येन च द्रष्टनुमानात्, दृश्यस्य च सुखदु:खभेहमेदवच्छब्दादिविभागोपलबधे:, एकत्वश्रुति: जातिदेशकालविभागाभावनिमित्तोपचारान्मन्यन्ते, 'आत्मैवेदं सर्वम्' इति च तादर्थ्यनिमित्तोपचारात् ।

   Bra. Sid. I, p.6.

   Brahmasiddhi,(1937), Madras Government Press.
4. तान् प्रत्युच्यते—एकमिति । . . . नानारूपावगमो मायानिबन्धनो दर्शित: . . . तथा व्यक्तो नानात्वनिषेध: नेह नानास्ति किंचन इति . . . नानात्वदर्शननिन्दा च मृत्यो: स मृत्युमाप्नोति इति, . . . भेददर्शनस्य चाभाव: भेदृष्टिरिव भ्रमात् - य इह नानेव पश्यति इति. . . इवशब्देन प्रकाशितो नोपचरित एकत्वेऽवकल्पते ।

   Bra. Sid I, p.6.
5. कल्पितादपि भेदाद्भोगव्यवस्था सिद्धेरसारमेतत् ।

   Bra. Sid. I, p.7.
6. तथाहि—एकस्मिन्नप्यात्मनि सर्वगते शरीरपरिमाणेऽणुपरिमाणे वा कल्पितभेदनिबन्धना भोगव्यवस्था दृश्यते - पादे मे वेदना, शिरसि मे वेदना - इति ।

   Bra. Sid. I, p.7.
7. तथा मणिकृपाणदर्पणादिषु मुखादीनां वर्णसंस्थान भेदव्यवस्थानमुपलभ्यते भेदाभावेऽपि ।

   Bra. Sid. I, p.7.
8. एकोऽप्यात्मा प्रदेशै: सुखदु:खादिभिर्युज्यमान: तत्र बद्ध इव इतरत्र मुक्त इव च गम्यते;

   Bra. Sid. I, p.7.
9. यथा मलीमसे दर्पणतले मलीमसं मुखं विशुद्धे विशुद्धं दर्पणरहितं च गम्यमानं तदुपाधिदोषासंपृक्तम् ।

   Bra. Sid. I, p.7.
10. कल्पितोऽपि चाहिदंशो मरणकार्याय कल्पते, प्रतिसूर्यकश्च प्रकाशकार्याय ।

    Bra. Sid. I, p.7.
11. यदपि दृश्येनैव द्रष्टुरनुमानादृष्टृदृश्ययोर्भेद:, दृश्यस्य च सुखादिथेदोपलब्धेनानात्वमिति, तदप्यसत् . . .

    Bra. Sid. I, p.7.
12. न च स्वात्मनि वृत्तिविरोध:, प्रदीपवत् प्रमाणफलवच्चेत्युक्तम् ।

    Bra. Sid. I, p.7.
13. द्रष्टुरेव चिदात्मनरस्तथातथा विपरिणामद्विवर्तनाद्वा ।

    Bra. Sid. I, p.7.
14. नानात्वे तु विविक्तस्वभावयोरसंसृष्टपरस्परस्वरुपयोरसंबद्धयो: कीदृशो द्रष्टृदृश्यभाव:

    Bra. Sid. I, pp.7-8.
15. तत्त्वेकस्येवात्मनस्तथा तथा विपरिणामाद्विवर्तनाद्वा दर्पणतल इवात्मन:

    Bra. Sid. I, p.8.

16. एवं च द्रष्टुरव्यतिरेको दृश्यस्याम्नायते आत्मनि विज्ञाते सर्वमिदं विज्ञातं भवति इति ।
Bra. Sid. I, p.8.

17. वयमप्येतदेव ब्रूमः — न भेदो भावतोऽस्ति, अनाधविद्याविलसितमेतदिति ।
Bra. Sid. I, p.48.

18. तथा चोक्तमविद्योपादानभेदवादिभिः — 'अनादिरप्रयोजना चाविद्या' इति; तत्रानादि९ त्वान्नेनतारेतराश्रयत्वदोषः, अप्रयोजनत्वान्न भेदप्रपञ्चसर्गप्रयोजनपर्यनुयोगावकाशः ।
Bra. Sid. I, p.10.

19. यदेके पर्यनुयुञ्जते — 'प्रयोजनमनुद्दिश्य न मन्दोऽपि प्रवर्तते' इति, तत्र परस्य ब्रह्मणः प्रपञ्चसर्गप्रयोजनं वाच्यम्; न तावत् परानुग्रहः, प्राक् सर्गादनुग्राह्याणामभावात्, दुःखोत्तरत्वाच्च सर्गस्य; नात्मार्थक्रीडादिः, आप्तकामत्वादिति — तस्य अविद्यानिबन्धने सर्गे नवकाशः, न ह्यविद्या प्रयोजनमपेक्ष्य प्रवर्तते . . .
Bra. Sid. I, p.10.

20. सर्गश्रुतयोऽपि न सर्गपराः . . .
Bra. Sid. III, p.124.

21. कारणाव्यतिरेकाच्च कार्यस्य सदेकमेवेदम् . . .
Bra. Sid. III, p.125.

22. मृद्रुपेण हि घटादयो नैकत्वमतिक्रामन्ति ।
Bra. Sid. III, p.125.

23. नन्वेवं मुख्य एव कार्यकारणभाव उक्तः स्यात् ।
Bra. Sid. III, p.125.

24. नैतत्, एकत्वावतारोपायमात्रत्वात्, न खल्लवत्र कार्यकारणभाव एव प्रतिपाद्यः . . . इन्द्रो मायाभिः इति भेदस्य मायागम्यत्व श्रुतेः, साक्षाच्च भेदाभावस्य श्रवणात् — नेह नानास्ति किंचन इति . . .,
Bra. Sid. III, p.125.

25. किंच स्वप्नेऽपि सृष्टिश्रुतिरस्ति; न च तावता तत्र रथादीनां सत्यत्वम् । तद्वेदषापि भूतसृष्टिर्भविष्यति, आत्मैकत्वप्रतिपत्तिपरत्यादित्याह —
Commentary on the *Bra.Sid.* III, p.255.

26. अत्रोच्यते — नाविद्या ब्रह्मणः स्वभावः, नाथन्तिरम्, नात्यन्तमसती, नापि सती, एवमेवेयमविद्या माया मिथ्यावभास इत्युच्यते ।
Bra. Sid. I, p.9.

27. अत्यन्तासत्वे स्वपुष्पसदृशी न व्यवहाराङ्गम्; तस्मादनिर्वचनीया ।
Bra. Sid. I, p.9.

28. अवभासमानेऽसति तलवभासोऽपि सत्यतो दुर्निरूपः, अवभासमात्रं तु स्यात्, तदवभास इत्यपि भ्रान्तिरेव । तस्मान्नाविद्या सती, नाप्यसतीति ।
Bra. Sid. I, p.9.

29. अविद्या विभ्रमः, यथावभासं च वेद्यसद्भावे न विभ्रमः, किंतु सम्यज्ज्ञानम्, असति चावगमोऽनुपपन्नः। तस्मान्न परमार्थतः सत्वेन निरुच्यते, नाप्यसत्वेन . . . .
Bra. Sid. II, p.60.

30. यत्तु कस्याविद्येति; जीवानामिति ब्रूमः ।
Bra. Sid. I, p.10.

31. ननु न जीवा ब्रह्मणो भिद्यन्ते . . . सत्यं परमार्थतः, कल्पनया तु भिद्यन्ते ।
Bra. Sid. I, p.10.

32. नापि जीवानाम्, कल्पनायाः प्राक् तदभावात्, इतरेतराश्रयप्रसङ्गात्कल्पनाधीनो हि जीवविभागः, जीवाश्रया कल्पनेति ।
Bra. Sid. I, p.10.

33. तत्रानादित्वान्नेतरेतराश्रयत्वदोषः
Bra. Sid. I, p.10.

34. ननु जीवा अपि ब्रह्मतत्त्वाव्यतिरेकाद्विशुद्धस्वभावाः, तत् कथं तेष्वविद्यावकाशः
Bra. Sid. I, p.11.

35. न च तावद्बिम्बादवदातात् प्रतिबिम्बं कृपाणादिषु भिन्नम्, अथ च तत्र श्यामतादिरशुद्धिरवकाशं लभते । . . . समानमेतज्जीवानामप्यशुद्धि विभ्रमः . . .
Bra. Sid. I, p.11.

36. न खल्वात्मस्वभाव एव विद्या अविद्यानिवर्तिका, अविद्यायास्तया सह वृतेरविरोधात्, विरोधे वा नित्यनिवृत्तेर्नित्यमुक्तं जगत् स्यात् ।
Bra. Sid. I, p.11.

37. अत्रोच्यते — उक्तमेतज्जीवानामविद्याकलुषितत्वम्, न ब्राह्मणः, तद्धि सदा विशुद्धनित्य-प्रकाशमनागन्तुकार्यम्; अन्यथा ब्रह्मभूयं गतस्याविनाविद्या निवर्तेत; तत्रानिर्मोक्षः ।
Bra. Sid. I, p.12.

38. अथ ब्रह्मैव संसरति ब्रह्मैव मुच्यते, एक मुक्तो सर्वमुक्तिप्रसङ्गः, यतो भेददर्शनिन ब्रह्मैव संसरति, अभेददर्शनिन च मुच्यते, . . .
Bra. Sid. I, p.12.

39. तस्मादविद्यया जीवाः संसारिणः, विद्यया मुच्यन्ते।
Bra. Sid. I, p.12.

40. अविद्यैव हि नैसर्गिकी, तस्या आगन्तुकया विद्यया प्रलयः।
Bra. Sid. I, p.12.

41. अव्यतिरेकेऽपि च ब्रह्मणो जीवानां बिम्बप्रतिबिम्बवद्विद्याविद्या व्यवस्था व्याख्याता
Bra. Sid. I, p.12.

42. अथ मतम् — द्विप्रकारेयमविद्या, प्रकाशस्याच्छादिका विक्षेपिका च ।
Bra. Sid. III, p.149.

43. स्वप्नजागरितयोर्विक्षेपिका, सुषुप्त आच्छादिका लयलक्षणा ।
Bra. Sid. III, p.149.

44. तस्मादग्रहणविपर्ययग्रहणे द्वे अविद्ये कार्यकारणभावेनावस्थिते;
Bra. Sid. III, pp.149-50.

45. स्वप्नजागरितयोरुभे, कारणभूताग्रहणलक्षणा सुषुप्त इत्यविद्याप्रविभाग उपपद्यते ।
Bra. Sid., p.150.

46. अन्यथा गृह्णतः स्वप्नो निद्रा तत्त्वमजानतः ।
G. K. I, 15 (ab).

47. एवमेवेयमविद्या माया मिथ्यावभास इत्युच्यते ।
Bra. Sid. I, p.9.

48. सर्वं तु ब्रह्मात्मकम्, ब्रह्मरूपेण रूपवत्, न तु शून्यमेव . . .
Bra. Sid. I,p.20.

49. उक्तमेतत् - कल्पितविषयावेव संसारमोक्षो, न परस्मिन् परार्थे ।
Bra. Sid. I, p.15.

50. . . . ब्रह्मणो व्यतिरेकेण प्रत्येतव्यस्याभावत् . . .
Bra. Sid. IV, p.157.

51. Hasurkar, S.S., *Vācaspati Miśra on Advaita Vedānta*, ch. III, p.113, 1958, Mithila Institute, Darbhanga.

9

Sṛṣṭi-Dṛṣṭi-Vāda

HOW could the world which we all experience at each and every moment be unreal? We all have one and the same experience of this world. We see the same sky, rivers, houses etc. The surroundings, which we perceive at present, are the very same as we perceive the next day also. Hence, we do not dare to consider the world as unreal, being obsessed with its reality. But this is what a layman thinks about the world. According to the highest *Vedāntic* position, the world is unreal independent of the Ultimate Reality viz. *Brahman.*

In the previous chapters it has been seen that the *Yoga-Vāsiṣṭha,* the *Gauḍapādakārika,* the *Vivekacūḍāmaṇi* etc. place the common world of experience (empirical world) on the same footing as the dream-world; and boldly consider it as just unreal. On the other hand, Śaṅkara, not strictly following in the foot-steps of Gauḍapāda emphasizes the waking world as different from the dream-world. Śaṅkara regards each action as meaningful before the dawn of knowledge. Similarly, he accepts the phenomenal reality of the world; and does not condemn the world as absolutely unreal and as emphemeral as a dream. Of course, from the transcendental standpoint Śaṅkara accepts the world as unreal, as *Brahman* is the only reality. Hence, Śaṅkara's transcendental standpoint reveals him as an Absolutist rather than as a mere Idealist.[1] No doubt, he is an Idealist, so far as he considers the Ultimate Reality as pure consciousness. But since he recognises the unapprehended existence (*Ajñāta-Sattā*) of the world, his name could be said to lead us towards, the *Sṛṣṭi-Dṛṣṭi-vāda.*[2] Of course, Śaṅkara has not specifically discussed the points which could establish him as a *Sṛṣṭi-Dṛṣṭi-vāda.* Nevertheless, it could be said that he would have accepted the *Sṛṣṭi-Dṛṣṭi-vāda,* if pointedly asked to show his leaning.

After Śaṅkara, we have seen the views of Maṇḍana Miśra; which can be said to have an inclination towards *Dṛṣṭi-Sṛṣṭi-vāda.* Now, in this chapter the views of those Śaṅkarites, who favour the *Sṛṣṭi-Dṛṣṭi vāda,* have been discussed as it is also important to have a general idea about the rival theory of the *Dṛṣṭi-Sṛṣṭi-vāda.*

Regarding the views of the Śaṅkarites, the *Siddhāntaleśasaṁgraha* is very helpful, as it contains the views of the Śaṅkarites regardihng the material cause (*Upādāna Kāraṇa*) of the world, the locus of *Avidyā* etc. Here, it would be important to make it clear that regarding the views of the Śaṅkarites, the order mentioned in the *Siddhāntaleśasaṁgraha* has been followed, and not the actual chronological order. Moreover, in this connection, the material cause of the world, the locus of *Avidyā,* oneness and manyness of the *Jīva* as well as of *Avidyā* have been discussed here and then the exposition of the *Sṛṣṭi-Dṛṣṭi-vāda.*

The Material Cause of the World

So far as the theory of *Sṛṣṭi-Dṛṣṭi* is concerned, an inquiry related to the creator of the world first arises. Who is the creator of the world? This question has given rise to many perplexing problems, and as a result different theories have been formulated.

"God has created this world, and God is the material cause of the world" — this is the common response to the above-mentioned question. The world, which is commonly experienced by all, which does not change or get lost after its perception, has got an unapprehended existence (*Ajñāta Sattā*), how could it be created by any other than God? The Realist considers the world to be existing independently of the Sentient Principle. On the other hand, the *Sṛṣṭi-Dṛṣṭi-vādin* holds that the world exists independently of its perception, but not independently of the Ultimate Reality. The world is created by the Ultimate Reality (conditioned by *Avidyā*) out of itself. It has got *Ajñāta-Sattā*, which exists even when not perceived. It is our common experience that houses, trees, roads, shops etc. do not disappear, after we go away from that area. The class room which we leave does not vanish. Hence, the things of the world have phenomenal reality. This is what the *Sṛṣṭi-Dṛṣṭi-vāda* emphasizes.

Most of the Śaṅkarites consider *Brahman* as the material cause of the world, following the foot-mark of Śaṅkara, or rather the *Upaniṣads.* Śaṅkara strictly holds *Brahman* (conditioned by *Avidyā*) as the material cause (*Upādāna Kāraṇa*) as well as the efficient cause (*Nimitta Kāraṇa*) of the world. As Śaṅkara and his followers regard *Brahman* as the material cause of the world, they do not consider the world as illusory, but accept it as real of course, from the common-sense point of view.

As stated in the *Siddhāntaleśasaṁgraha,* according to some, who follow the view of the *Saṁkṣepaśārīraka,* pure *Brahman* is the material cause of the world. They base their view on the *sūtra Janmādyasya yataḥ.*[3]

Those who follow the *Vivaraṇa* School of *Prakāśātman,* hold that *Brahman,* qualified by omniscience, etc. being associated with *Māyā,* i.e., God is the material cause, as the scripture mentions that qualified *Brahman* is the cause of the world.[4]

Now, some of the Śaṅkarites consider *Avidyā* as different from *Māyā*. According to them, *Avidyā* is related to the *Jīva;* while *Māyā* is associated with *Brahman.* So the task of creation is distributed between God and the *Jīvas.* These Śaṅkarites declare that ether etc. are the products of *Māyā,* supported in God. Here, God is the material cause (*Upādāna Kāraṇa*) of the five elements, on the other hand, the internal organ, etc. are created through *Avidyā* of the *Jīva,* which is their *Upādāna*. Thus, both God and the *Jīva* are regarded as the material cause.

Some believe that God is the *Upādāna* of the ether etc. by virtue of His *Māyā,* whereas the internal organ etc. are due to

Avidyā residing in the *Jīva*, and the *Jīva* is their *Upādāna*.[5]

On the other hand, some *Advaitins* do not differentiate *Māyā* from *Avidyā*, but consider them as non-different. Some amongst these, hold that though God is the *Upādāna* of the ether etc. it is the *Jīva*; which is the *Upādāna* of the internal organ, etc., as they are known as identical with the *Jīva*.

Here, it would not be out of place to mention the view of Vidyāraṇya, as in his works, namely the *Pañcadaśī* and the *Vivaraṇaprameyasaṁgraha*, we find contradictory statements regarding *Avidyā* and *Māyā*.[6] On the one hand, Vidyāraṇya very clearly draws a distinction between *Avidyā* and *Māyā* in the *Pañcadaśī* stating that *Avidyā* is the *prakṛti*, in which the impure *sattva* is dominant, while *Māyā* is the *prakṛti*, in which the pure *sattva* is dominant. Consciousness, reflected in *Māyā* is known as omniscient God, while consciousness reflected in *Avidyā* is called the *Jīva*.[7] On the other hand, in his *Vivaraṇaprameyasaṁgraha*, he does not differentiate between *Avidyā* and *Māyā*, but regards them as identical.[8]

Hence, one cannot ascertain the specific view of Vidyāraṇya about the material cause. One can only assume that he considers God as the *Upādāna* of the five elements, while he regards the *Jīva* as the *Upādāna* of the internal organ, etc. Mahadevan says in *The Philosophy of Advaita*, "According to Bhāratītīrtha, *Īśvara* and the *Jīva* are the joint creators of the world. But there is this difference. While the Lord is the principal author, the *Jīva* is only a subsidiary parent."[9]

Besides this, one finds another view mentioned in the *Siddhāntaleśasaṁgraha*, according to which *Brahman* is the material cause of the whole phenomenal world. In its support, a *Śruti* — "From this, vital air, mind, all the sense-organs are originated" — is quoted. On the other hand, the *Jīva* is regarded as the material cause of the illusory phenomena and of the dream world.[10]

According to *Padārthatattvanirṇayakāra*, both *Brahman* and *Māyā* are the material causes of the world, as the scripture describes both of them to be the material cause. Here, it should be noted that *Brahman* is regarded as the material cause in the sense that it is the cuase of the effect being projected on it, while *Avidyā* is the cause in the sense that it is modified in the form of the effect. That is to say, *Brahman* is the *Vivartopādāna Kāraṇa* as *rajju* is of *sarpa,* while *Avidyā* is the *Pariṇāmīupādāna Kāraṇa,* the one, that is modified in the form of the world.

Sarvajñātman holds that only *Brahman* is the material cause of the world, while *Māyā* is the intermediary cause (*Dvāra Kāraṇa*), as immutable (*kūṭastha*) *Brahman* itself cannot be the cause.[11] Here, *Māyā* does not play an outstanding role in the creation of the world; though not the cause it persists in the effect as the *dvāra*-intermediary.

Vācaspati Miśra opines that *Brahman,* in the form of *Vivartopādāna*; being an object through *Māyā,* residing in the *Jīva* is the material cause of the world; so *Māyā* is only a subordinate cause and not an intermediary cause.[12] That is to say, in Vācaspati's view, *Brahman* which is made its object by *Māyā* having its locus in the *Jīva* is itself the *Upādāna* inasmuch as it appears in the form of the manifold phenomena, which is non-sentient and so *Māyā* is but a *Sahakārī Kāraṇa* (subordinate cause). *Māyā* is not an intermediary cause which persists in the effect.[13]

Here, it is noteworthy, that though Vācaspati regards *Brahman* as the material cause of the world; yet he considers the *Jīva* as the locus of *Avidyā* — a view which carried to the logical extreme could result in *Dṛṣṭi-Sṛṣṭi-vāda.* This point has been discussed at length later on.

The above-mentioned are some of the different views put forth by the Śaṅkarites about the material cause of the world. As stated before, since *Brahman* is the material cause of the world, it (the world) is considered as real till *Avidyā* is eradicated. The Śaṅkarites consider the world as unreal only if viewed as independent of its very cause. The world is not in any case illusory like a sky flower or dream. It has got phenomenal reality, as it fulfills our practical usages, and it is the common object of the worldly experience of all. This is what the

Sṛṣṭi-Dṛṣṭi-vādin holds.

As already seen, since the *Sṛṣṭi-Dṛṣṭi-vāda* holds *Brahman* as the material cause of the world-creation, (and this explains why all experience the same worldly objects) the *Jīva* has no role to play so far as the creation of the world is concerned. Thus, it is not the *Jīva,* who creates the world, but God.

In this context, a question arises whether *Brahman* is the locus of *Avidyā* or the *Jīva.*

Locus (*Āśraya*) of *Avidyā*

As it has been already stated that Śaṅkara, does not seem much bothered about the problem regarding the locus of *Avidyā.* But after Śaṅkara, this problem received much attention from the Śaṅkarites. It is also noteworthy that all the Śaṅkarites are not unanimous about the locus of *Avidyā.* A difference of opinion prevails amongst the Śaṅkarites in respect of it.

It seems that those who support the *Sṛṣṭi-Dṛṣṭi-vāda* regard *Brahman* as the locus of *Avidyā.*

Here, it is briefly mentioned about those Śaṅkarites, who regard *Brahman* as the locus of *Avidyā.*

Amongst the earliest Śaṅkarites, Maṇḍana Miśra boldly regards the *Jīva* as the locus of *Avidyā.* Such a revolutionary thinking of his thus paved the way for the *Dṛṣṭi-Sṛṣṭi-vāda.*

But Sureśvara, strictly following Śaṅkara opines that *Brahman* is the locus as well as the object of *Avidyā.* In the *Naiṣkarmyasiddhi* Sureśvara states, "Now ignorance must be ignorance of someone about something, it must have a conscious locus and a content that it conceals. We have shown that only two categories exit self and not-self. the not-self cannot be the locus of *ajñāna,* for it is itself *ajñāna,* if it were the locus the arising of it in itself would not be an event of any significance, and worse, there could be no obtaining of knowledge, ignorance is also the cause of the not-self, and it is absurd to suppose that the cause can exist only as supported by its effect. The same arguments show that the not-self cannot be the content of ignorance either. So the locus and content of ignorance must be the self."[14]

Unlike Sureśvara, Padmapāda has not specifically mentioned his view. Nevertheless, it seems that according to him, the *Jīva* is the locus and *Brahman* is the object of *Avidyā*. It is stated, "*Avidyā* concealing the illumination which is the very nature of *Brahman*, is imagined in the *Jīva*, otherwise if it were from the highest point of view of that nature, its awareness also would be eternally established and so the instruction about their identity would be superfluous.[15]

Vācaspati Miśra, following Maṇḍana Miśra, regarded the *Jīva* as the locus of *Avidyā*. Nevertheless, he regarded God in the *Upādāna* of the world inasmuch as it is the object of *Avidyā* which has its locus in the *Jīva*.

Sarvajñātman Muni consideres pure consciousness as the locus and object of *Avidyā*. The *Saṁkṣepaśārīraka* declares, "Undifferenced, absolute sentiency is the locus and object of Nescience. For that which proceeds from previously existing nescience, cannot become either locus or object of nescience."[16]

Vidyāraṇya also considers pure consciousness as the locus of *Avidyā*.[17] In the *Vivaraṇaprameyasaṁgraha* this point is discussed at some length in the first *varṇaka* of the firt *Sūtra*, Vidyāraṇya has tried to refute all the doubts put forth against the view that consciousness is the locus of *Avidyā*.

It may be doubted as to how *Avidyā* could reside in consciousness itself. But this is not proper, for the nature of *Avidyā* itself is established through witness-consciousness.[18] Furthermore, *Avidyā* does not require a locus different from its object as it is inactive like the pot etc.[19] *Avidyā* conceals the thing, in which it resides, as it is 'concealing' by its very virtue like darkness.[20] It is our daily experience that darkness resides in the very room, which it makes its object and conceals. Moreover, While accepting *Brahman* as the locus of *Avidyā*, no loss occurs to its attribute of omniscience. In this context, it would be essential to make it clear that according to Vidyāraṇya, reflection of sentiency in the pure of *sattva* of *prakṛti* is known as

God; while reflection of sentiency in the impure *sattva* of *prakṛti* is called the *Jīva*. So eventhough there is unity between the prototype and its reflection, as the fairness of the prototype is not lost even when the reflection on the mirror is darkened through the impurity of the mirror. Similarly, it can be said that the attributes of omniscience, etc. in God would remain unaffected even when *Avidyā* resides in the *Jīva*.[21]

Thus, without being affected, *Brahman* becomes the locus of *Avidyā*, and creates the world.

Now, another query is whether *Ekajīvavāda* or *Anekajīvavāda* could affect the *Sṛṣṭi-Dṛṣṭi-vāda*. For this, both the views will be examined as they are described in the *Siddhāntaleśasaṁgraha*.

Ekajīvavāda

In the *Siddhāntaleśasaṁgraha* it is stated that according to the holders of *Ekajīvavāda*, there is only one *Jīva*, and hence only one body is animate, while the rest are inanimate like the bodies seen in a dream. The world is imagined by the *Ajñāna* or nescience of that one *Jīva*. All kinds of practical dealings take place as in a dream, until the *Ajñāna* of the *Jīva* lasts. Further, as there is only one *Jīva*, there arises no question about the respective individual bondages and liberations. Liberation of *Śuka* etc. is also an imagined one like the liberation of a man that takes place in the dream. In short, all the types of doubts should be put aside by the analogy of a dream.[22]

This is *Ekajīvavāda*, which denounces all the dealings of the world and puts them on the same footing as a dream, considering them as merely illusory.

Now, some of the Śaṅkarites, not preferring this view, favour *Saviśeṣa-anekaśarīra ekajīvavāda*. Those who hold this *vāda* believe that the *Jīva* is not the creator of the world, but it is God, who creates the world. Though God is self-content, he creates the world as merely a play. *Hiraṇyagarbha*, which is the reflection of *Brahman* in *Māyā* is the main soul, while the other *Jīvas* being its reflections are just appearances.[23]

On the other hand, some Śaṅkarites, finding fault with the above-mentioned view, prefer *Aviśeṣa anekaśarīra ekajīvavāda.* They believe that there is no deciding factor as to which *Hiraṇyagarbha* could be considered the main soul from the *Hiraṇyagarbhas* in the different *kalpas*. So it is better to hold that one *Jīva* resides in all the bodies.

Here, a doubt may arise that if one soul resides in all the bodies, it must have experiences of pain, sorrow and happiness of all the bodies. But this is never seen. All the bodies have their separate pain, sorrow etc. As an answer to this it is stated that we find that there is no rememberance of the pleasures etc. of another birth so here also since the bodies are different there will not be the experience or rememberance of all the pleasures, pains etc.[24]

The above-mentioned are two offshoots of *Ekajīvavāda.* It seems that the *Ekajīvavāda* aims at being the highest *Vedāntic* position. As *Brahman* is the only one sentiency, there is no other sentient principle. So *Brahman* itself due to *Avidyā* becomes the *Jīva,* and imagines God, world and all its dealinges, like a dream. Thus, everything is considered to be simply illusion.

Now, this concept seems to be identical with the *Dṛṣṭi-Sṛṣṭi-vāda,* which has been discussed in the next chapter. In the *Siddhāntabindu,* Madhusūdana Sarasvatī has considered *Ekajīvavāda* and the *Dṛṣṭi-Sṛṣṭi-vāda* as one and the same.[25] It would be noteworthy here that Divanji, while commenting on this has stated, "The three theories above set forth are propounded by the followers of Śaṅkarācārya who differed from him in some minor particulars. His own theory is known as the *Ekajīvavāda* or *Dṛṣṭi-Sṛṣṭi-vāda.*"[26] However, one would not like to agree with this that Śaṅkara favours or prefers *Dṛṣṭi-Sṛṣṭi-vāda.*

Now, we may see whether *Anekajīvavāda* is connected with the *Sṛṣṭi-Dṛṣṭi-vāda* or not.

Anekajīvavāda

Preferring the common-sense point of view, most of the Śaṅkaraites hold *Anekajīvavāda,* and emphasize that because of the manyness of the *Jīvas*, the system of bondage and liberation becomes possible, as each *Jīva* has its pleasure or pain in accordance with its own *karma*. On holding *Ekajīvavāda*, the empirical experience would be contradicted. We do not experience that the world disappears at the very moment of the liberation of one *Jīva*. To avoid this problem, it is proper to recognise the manyness of the *Jīvas*.

Thus, concentrating mainly on the system of bondage and liberation, the Śaṅkarites favour *Anekajīvavāda*.

We experience manyness of the *Jīvas* in our practical life. Moreover, we all experience the very same objective world consisting of earth, sky, water, trees etc. In this context a question may arise as to how we all experience one common phenomenal world? Is this possible due to common nescience (*Avidyā*)? If common nescience is believed, then what about the separate experiences regarding the very same thing.

Answers to such questions are mentioned in the *Siddhāntaleśasaṁgraha* in all its different ramifications—such as (1) *Brahmāśrita-eka-Avidyā-vāda*, (2) *Anekajīvāśrita-eka-Avidyā-vāda*, and (3) *Anekajīvāśrita-anka-Avidyā-vāda*.

Brahmāśrita-eka-Avidyā-vāda

Some *Advaitins* among the upholders of the manyness of the *jīvas* believe that, though *Ajñāna* whose locus and object is *Brahman* is one, and its destruction itself is liberation, still, since its projecting aspect or power continues in the *jīvanmukti* also; it can be seen that *Ajñāna* has aspects; and in that adjunct in which knowledge of *Brahman* is produced, it would be destroyed in one aspect, while in the rest, other aspects of *Ajñāna* would continue.[27]

Thus, to make the system of bondage and liberation plausible, here *Avidyā* is believed to have numerous aspects.

Some Śaṅkarites, following the *Naiyāyika* view state that in the *vṛtti* (occurrence) of the absence of a pot on the ground, the absence of pot's connection is responsible, so here the mind is responsible for the subsistence of *Ajñāna* in sentiency. That is to say, *Ajñāna* subsists in different sentiency locations by virtue of that adjunct, viz. mind; but when on the rise of *Brahman* realisation, the mind is destroyed, *Ajñāna* is no longer associated with that sentiency location, but it continues to be associated with other sentiency — locations.

Aneka-jīvāśrita-eka-Avidyā-vāda

Some Śaṅkarites believe that the one *Ajñāna* does not reside in the pure sentiency, but in the *Jīva* making *Brahman* its object.

Now, *Ajñāna* resides in the *Jīvas* as *Jāti* resides in *Vyakti*. So when an individual dies, *Jāti* still persists in the other individuals. Thus, only in the case of that particular individual it (*Jāti*) is lost. Similarly, *Ajñāna* leaves the *Jīva*, in which knowledge arises; while it resides in the rest of the *Jīvas*, in whom there is still *Ajñāna*.[28]

Anekajivāśrita-aneka-Avidyā-vāda

Some *Advaitins* hold that *Ajñāna* differs from one *Jīva* to another *Jīva*. That is to say, each and every *Jīva* has its own separate *Ajñāna*. When *Ajñāna* residing in one *Jīva* is destroyed, it gets liberation, while for the rest of the *Jīvas* bondage still continues.[29] Vācaspati Miśra's name is noteworthy here. He says, "We *Vedāntins* do not say that there is one *Avidyā* like one *pradhāna* in all *Jīvas*, so that we should be charged with this fault. *Avidyā* is different in each *Jīva*, so only the *Avidyā* of that *Jīva* in whose case *Vidyā* has arisen will be dispelled and not of other *Jīvas*, and so there is not the contingency of their being the eradication of the entire *saṁsāra*.[30]

Here, a question perplexing the mind is, "If each *Jīva* has its own *Avidyā*, what about the world, which is commonly experienced by all of us?" We all perceive the same houses, the same trees, the same river around us. Thus, it could not be said with certitude as to whose *Ajñāna* has created the world, which is commonly experienced by all.

In order to avoid such a difficult problem, the holders of this view state that as cloth is made up from several threads, similarly, the world is created jointly by everyone's *Avidyā*. Now, when the *Avidya* of one *Jīva* is destroyed, and it gets liberation, the world (*prapañca*) for it vanishes. But the position of the world for the rest of the *Jīvas* becomes just like cloth and threads. That is to say, when a thread of a cloth is destroyed; the cloth made up from those threads is destroyed. But immediately the rest of the threads create a new cloth. Similarly, the *Avidyās* of the rest of the *Jīvas* create the common world jointly.[31] According to Appaya Dikṣit, the commonness of experience can be explained by the fact of the *adhiṣṭhāna* being one. Several men may have the simultaneous illusion of silver (in the mother of pearl) when silver is brought about by the *Avidyās* of the several erring persons. If the error of one of these is dispelled, and the error in the case of the others continues then another silver is brought about by the *Avidyās* of all the other persons and thus the commonness of the illusion is possible. This same explanation applies to the world phenomena, where *Brahman* is the Ultimate Reality common to all.[32]

Hence, though each *Jīva* has got its own *Avidyā*, the common world experience becomes possible.

Besides, there is another view, which holds that the world consisting of earth, air, sky etc. is as a matter of fact separate for each and every *Jīva;* just like *Apekṣābuddhi* [33] as described in the *Nyāya* system. That is to say, when the illusion of silver in the mother of pearl occurs to a number of people, they have the notion, viz. "The silver which you have perceived, that I also perceived." Just like this, a common experience seems to occur in the case of the perception of the world — "That world which you see, the very same one is perceived by me." But actually each one perceives the world, created by his own *Avidyā*. The world illusion is different for each creature.[34]

It would not be out of place to mention that though Vācaspati Miśra regards the *Jīva* as the locus of *Avidyā*, and *Avidyā* as numerous, he does not seem to hold that each *Jīva* creates its own world, as we do not find it specifically stated by him. The world-appearance has its *adhiṣṭhāna Brahman* which is the object of *Avidyās* of the *Jīvas* and the *Avidyās* jointly bring about the world-appearance which therefore is common to all. Moreover, in his *Bhāmati* (II.2.28) he states that all appearances are indescribable entities and not mere mental ideas. The external objects have *Ajñāta Sattā,* and are existent even when they are not perceived as they have empirical existence and are brought about by the beginningless *Avidyā-Śaktis* of all. Thus, Vācaspati Miśra did not support *Dṛṣṭi-Sṛṣṭi-vāda* though he regarded the *Jīvas* as the locus of *Avidyās* and though he accepted that each *Jīva* has its own *Avidyā.*

The above-mentioned are the views expresed by the Śaṅkarites about oneness and manyness of *Avidyā.* Amongst these views, *Brahmāśrita-Avidyā-vāda* can be said to be connected with the *Sṛṣṭi-Dṛṣṭi-vāda,* while *Jīvāśrita-Avidyā-vāda* seems to be connected with the *Dṛṣṭi-Sṛṣṭi-vāda.*

The *Sṛṣṭi-Dṛṣṭi-vāda* considers *Avidyā* as residing in *Brahman,* and hence, the world created by God is real (from the common-sense point of view) and exists even when not perceived. Moreover, so far as oneness (*Ekajīvavāda*) and manyness (*Anekajīvavāda*) is concerned, the *Sṛṣṭi-Dṛṣṭi-vāda* seems to be favouring the manyness of the *Jīvas* with God as the Supreme Lord as it is in consistency with the empirical reality of the world and the individual pleasures, etc. and bondage and realisation of the respective *Jīvas.*

Now, the *Sṛṣṭi-Dṛṣṭi-vāda,* as put forth in the *Siddhāntaleśasaṁgraha* shall be dealt with.

The *Sṛṣṭi-Dṛṣṭi-vāda*

As already stated, the *Sṛṣṭi-Dṛṣṭi-vāda* is a rival theory of the *Dṛṣṭi-Sṛṣṭi-vāda,* it (*Sṛṣṭi-Dṛṣṭi-vāda*) firmly asserts the empirial reality of the world. For this reason only, *Sṛṣṭi-Dṛṣṭi-vāda* seems to be more appealing than the *Dṛṣṭi-Sṛṣṭi-vāda.*

In the *Siddhāntaleśasaṁgraha* it is stated, "The Śaṅkarites who do not favour the *Dṛṣṭi-Sṛṣṭi-vāda,* prefer the *Sṛṣṭi-Dṛṣṭ-vāda.*[35]

In opposition to the *Dṛṣṭi-Sṛṣṭi-vāda,* the *Sṛṣṭi-Dṛṣṭi-vāda* propounds that the world is created by God as narrated in the scriptures. So the world exists, even when not perceived. In short, it has got the unapprehended existence (*Ajñānta Sattā*). Object are known through the means of knowledge, so they are not illusory in the sense the *Dṛṣṭi-Sṛṣṭi-vāda* holds them to be illusory.[36]

That is to say, in no way is the world illusory like the silver seen in the mother of pearl, as it is known and experienced by all worldly beings with the help of the means of knowledge. Food satisfies our hunger, so how could it be considered illusory? Clothes protect our bodies, so how could they be regarded as illusory? While living and satisfying our daily usages we cannot dare to consider the empirical world as illusory like a dream.

Nevertheless, one thing is obsvious that the *Advaitins*, recognising the *Sṛṣṭi-Dṛṣṭi-vāda,* though they do not denounce the phenomenal reality of the world, yet do not affirm its Ultimate Reality either.

A doubt is put forth in the *Siddhāntaleśasaṁgraha,* "If the world is not believed to be an imagined one, then the world, which is known through the scriptures, and through the other means of knowledge would be a real one.[37]

Setting aside this doubt, it is stated that though the world consisting of ether etc. does not exist simultaneously with its conception, yet since it is destroyed or it vanishes with the rise of right knowledge alone, and as it is inexplicable, and not existing in three periods of time, it is unreal.[38]

This clearly reveals the difference betweenthe *Dṛṣṭi-Sṛṣṭi-vāda* and the *Sṛṣṭi-Dṛṣṭi-vāda.* On the one hand, the *Dṛṣṭi-Sṛṣṭi-vāda* does not believe in the Phenomenal Reality. While the *Sṛṣṭi-Dṛṣṭi-vāda* clearly affirms the Phenomenal Reality of this world.[39] Of course, the world is unreal (*mithyā*) from the ultimate standpoint. But in no way could its Phenomenal Reality be denied.

In short, few points may be mentioned, which would give a clear idea of the *Sṛṣṭi-Dṛṣṭi-vāda.*

(i) *Brahman* is considered to be material cause

(*Upādāna Kāraṇa*) of the world.

(ii) *Avidyā* is believed to be located in *Brahman*.

(iii) The world, created by God is not utterly illusory, but has Phenomenal Reality.

(iv) The world has got the unapprehended existence (*Ajñāta Sattā*). That is to say, it exists, even when not perceived.

Thus, in this chapter a brief exposition of the *Sṛṣṭi-Dṛṣṭi-vāda* has been given, as it is necessary to have an idea of the rival theory before one proceeds to discuss the *Dṛṣṭi-Sṛṣṭi-vāda*.

It is noteworthy that the *Sṛṣṭi-Dṛṣṭi-vāda* in comparison with the *Dṛṣṭi-Sṛṣṭi-vāda* satisfies the minds of ordinary people with a *Vedāntic* bent of mind more. Obviously, no one would dare to consider the world as unreal and illusory while it lasts as it satisfies and fulfils the common usages and dealings. Our daily experiences compel us to regard the world as real.

As we have seen, since most of the Śaṅkarites propound the *Sṛṣṭi-Dṛṣṭi-vāda*, it has not been criticized like the *Dṛṣṭi-Sṛṣṭi-vāda*.

But if one think deeply from the ultimte standpoint, it is the *Dṛṣṭi-Sṛṣṭi-vāda*, which seems to be more faithful to the *Vedāntic* position then the *Sṛṣṭi-Dṛṣṭi vāda*. That is why the *Dṛṣṭi-Sṛṣṭi-vāda* is considered the main doctrine of the *Vedāntic* thought.[40]

References

1. "But Śaṅkara's *Advaita* is not idealism in the usually accepted epistemological sense of the word : there is a world, not projected by our thought, that is independent of our thinking and will not go away just by our thinking it away. The world is 'false', not in the sense of being a figment of our imagination, but in the sense that it is not real — the only real ultimately being *nirguṇa Brahman*."
   — Potter, Kari H., (ed), *Encyclopedia of Indian Philosophies*, Vol.III, Part-I, Ch.5, p.81 (1981), Motilal Banarsidass.
2. *Sṛṣṭi-Dṛṣṭi-Vāda* is a rival theory of the *Dṛṣṭi-Sṛṣṭi-vāda*, which asserts the *Ajñāta Sattā* of the world. That is to say, it holds that the world exists even when it is not perceived. In opposition of this theory, the *Dṛṣṭi-Sṛiṭi-vāda* considerṣ the world as illusory as a dream, and negates its *Ajñāta Sattā*. It emphasizes that the world exists simultaneously with its perception (*Dṛṣṭi*), or *Dṛṣṭi* itself is *Sṛṣṭi*.

सृष्टियूर्द्धभाविनी दृष्टिः सृष्टिदृष्टिरितीर्य्यते ।
व्यावृत्तिर्व्यतिरेकः स्यादन्ययोऽनुगमस्तथा ॥

वेदान्तसिद्धान्तादर्शः, पृ. ६६।१९४३। काश्याम्

3. अत्र सङ्क्षेपशारीरकानुसारिणः केचिदाहुः शुद्धमेवोपादानम्, जन्मादिसूत्रतद्भाष्ययोरुपादानत्वस्य ज्ञेयब्रह्मलक्षणत्वोक्तेः ।

S.L.S. Ist Chapter, p.58.

Siddhāntaleśasaṁgraha — *Chawkhamba Sanskrit Series* Office Benaras, (1916).

साभासमेतदुपजीव्य चिदद्वितीया ।
संसारकारणमिति प्रवदन्ति धीरा : ।

Saṁkṣepaśārīraka, I.323.

संक्षेपशारीरकारानुयायिन ईश्वरस्य चैतन्यमेव विवर्तयोपादानकारणं माया तु केवलं द्वारकारणमेवेति वदन्ति ।

Si-Bi Introduction, p.11.

Abhyankar, Vasudeva Shastri, (ed.), *Siddhāntabindu*, 2nd edition (1962), Bhandarkar Oriental Research Institute.

4. विवरणानुसारिरणस्तु — 'यः सर्वज्ञः सर्ववित् यस्य ज्ञानमयं तपः । तस्मादेतद् ब्रह्म नामरूपमन्नं च जायते' इति श्रुतेः सर्वज्ञत्वादिविशिष्टं मायाशबलमीश्वररूपमेव ब्रह्म उपादानम् ।

S.L.S., Ist chapter, p.59.

5. यथा वियदादिप्रपञ्च ईश्वराश्रितमायापरिणाम इति तत्र ईश्वर उपादानम्, तथाऽन्तःकरणादि जीवाश्रिता विद्यामात्रपरिणाम इति तत्र जीव एव उपादानम् ।

S.L.S., Ist chapter, p.67.

6. Mahadevan, T.M.P., *The Philosophy of Advaita*, Ch.8, p.229, Fourth Edietion (1976), Arnold-Heinemann.

7. सत्त्वशुद्धविशुद्धिभ्यां मायाविद्ये च ते मते ।
मायाबिंबो वशीकृत्य तां स्यात्सर्वज्ञ ईश्वरः ॥
- अविद्यावशगसत्वन्यस्तद्वैचित्र्यादनेकधा ।

P.D. I.16, 17 (ab).

Pañcadaśī (Gujarati edition) 1st edition, Sastu Sahitya Vardhaka Karyalaya.

8. . . . मास्तु पृथगविद्या; मायां तु प्रकृतिमिति सर्वोपादानत्वश्रुतेः । अतो लाघवान्मायैवाविद्या ।

*Vivaraṇaprameyasaṁgraha, Sū.*1, *Varṇaka.*1, p.134.

संवत् । १९९६ । अच्युतग्रन्थमाला कार्यालय, काशी also मायाविद्ययोश्चैकत्वमवोचाम । p.174.

9. Mahadevan, T.M.P., *The Philosophy of Advaita*, Ch.7, p.192, Fourth Edition (1976), Arnold-Heinemann.

10. एतस्माज्जायते प्राणो मनः सर्वेन्द्रियाणि च। . . . इत्यादिश्रुतेः कृत्स्नव्यावहारिकप्रपञ्चस्य ब्रह्मैव उपादानम् । जीवस्तु प्रातिभासिकस्य स्वप्नप्रपञ्चस्य च ।

S.L.S. Ist chapter, p.69.

11. सङ्क्षेपशारीरककृतस्तु— ब्रह्मैवोपादानम् ।
कूटस्थस्य स्वतः कारणत्वानुपपत्तेः माया द्वारकारणम् ।

S.L.S., Ist chapter, pp.75-76.

12. वाचस्पतिमिश्रास्तु — जीवाश्रितमायाविषयीकृते ब्रह्म स्वत एव जाडयाश्रयप्रपञ्चाकारेण विवर्तमानतयोपादानमिति माया सहकारिमात्रम्, न कार्यानुगतं द्वारकारणमित्याहुः ।

    S.L.S., Ist chapter, p.77.

13. Bhāmati on the *Br. Sū. Śā. Bhā.* I.4.3, p.378, *The Brahmasūtra Śāṅkara Bhāṣya with the commentaries*, Bhāmati, Kalpataru and Parimala (1981), Parimala Publications; *Siddhāntabindu,* Introduction, p.11. Abhyankar Vasudeva Shastri (ed), 2nd edition (1962), Bhandarkar Oriental Research Institute.

14. तच्चाज्ञानं स्वात्ममात्रनिमित्तं न सम्भवतीति कस्यचित्कस्मिंश्चिद्विषये भवतीत्यभ्युपगन्तव्यम् । इह च पदार्थद्वयं निर्द्धारितमात्मानात्मा च । तत्रनात्मनस्तावन्नाज्ञानेनाभिसम्बन्धः । तस्य हि स्वरूपमेवाज्ञानं न हि स्वतोऽज्ञानस्याज्ञानं घटते । सम्भवदप्यज्ञानस्वभावेऽज्ञानं कमतिशयं जनयेत् । न च तत्र ज्ञानप्राप्तिरस्ति येन तत्प्रतिषेधात्मकज्ञानं स्यात् । अनात्मनश्चज्ञानप्रसूतत्वात् । न हि पूर्वसिद्धं स्ततो लब्धात्मलाभस्य सेत्स्यत आश्रयस्याश्रयि संभवति । तदनपेक्षस्य च तस्य निःस्वभावत्वात् । एतेभ्य एव हेतुभ्यो नानात्मविषयमज्ञानं सम्भवतीति ग्राह्यम् । एवं तावन्नानात्मनोज्ञानित्वं नापि तद्विषयमज्ञानम्। पारिशेष्यादात्मन एवास्त्वज्ञानं तस्याज्ञोऽस्मीत्यनुभवदर्शनात् । . . . . न चात्मनोऽज्ञानस्वरूपता तस्य चैतन्यमात्रस्वाभाव्यादतिशयश्च सम्भवति ज्ञानविपरिलोपो ज्ञानाप्राप्तेश्च सम्भवस्तस्य ज्ञानकारित्वात् । न चाज्ञानकार्यत्वं कूटस्थात्मस्वाभाव्यादज्ञानानपेक्षस्य चात्मनः स्वत एव स्वरूपसिद्धेर्युक्तमात्मन एवाज्ञत्वम् ।

    Jacob, G.A. (ed), *Naiṣkarmyasiddhi* III, pp.106-109, *Bombay Sanskrit and Prakrit Series* XXXVIII, 1925.

    Translation from Potter, Karl H., '*Encyclopedia of Indian Philosophies,* Vol. III, p.542 (1981), Motilal Banarsidass.

15. अत एवाऽर्थाज्जीवे ब्रह्मस्वरूपप्रकाशाच्छादिकाऽविद्या कल्प्यतेऽन्यथापरमार्थस्तत्स्वरूपत्वे तदवबोधोऽपि यदि नित्यसिद्धः स्यात्तदा तादात्म्योपदेशो व्यर्थः स्यात् ।

    P.D. p.14, Rāmaśāstrībhagavatācārya (ed). १९४२काश्साम् ।

16. आश्रयत्वविषयत्वभागिनी निर्विभागचितिरेव केवला ।
    पूर्वसिद्धतमसो हि पश्चिमो नाश्रयो भवति नापि गोचरः ॥

    Saṁkṣepaśārīraka, I.319.

17. अतश्चिन्मात्राश्रितमज्ञानं . . .

    V.P.S. Sūtra I, *Varṇaka* I, p.171.

18. अविद्यास्वरूपं तु साक्षिचैतन्यादेव सिध्यति ।

    V.P.S. Sūtra I, *Varṇaka* I,p.164.

19. विमतमज्ञानमाश्रयविषयभेदं नापेक्षते, अक्रियात्मकत्वाद् घटादिवत् ।

    V.P.S. Sūtra I, *Varṇaka* I, p.164.

20. तथा विमतमेकपदार्थमेवाऽऽश्रयत्यावृणोति च आवरकत्वादपवरकस्थतमोवदिति . . .

    V.P.S. Sūtra I, *Varṇaka* I, p.164.

21. नापि ब्रह्मणः सर्वज्ञत्वादिहानिरिति . . . यथा सत्यपि बिम्बप्रतिबिम्बयोरैक्ये मलिनदर्पणगत-प्रतिबिम्बेऽध्यस्तेन श्यामत्वादिना न बिम्बस्यावदातताहानिः तथा जीवस्याऽविद्याश्रयत्वेऽपि न ब्रह्मणः सर्वज्ञत्वादिहानिरिति वक्तुं शक्यत्वात् ।

    V.P.S. Sūtra I, *Varṇaka* I,p.166.

22. एको जीवः, तेन चैकमेव शरीरं सजीवम् । अन्यानि स्वप्नदृष्टशरीराणीव निर्जीवानि। तदज्ञानकल्पितं सर्वं जगत्, तस्य स्वप्नदर्शनवद्यावदविद्यं सर्वो व्यवहारः । बद्धमुक्तिव्यवस्थाऽपि नास्ति,

जीवस्यैकत्वात् । शुकमुक्त्यादिकमपि स्वप्नपुरुषान्तरमुक्त्यादिकमिव कल्पितम् । अत्र च सम्भावितसकलशङ्कापङ्कप्रक्षालनं स्वप्नदृष्टान्तसलिलधारयैव कर्तव्यमिति ।

S.L.S. Ist chapter, pp.124-25.

23. अन्ये त्वस्मिन्नेकशरीरैकजीववादे मनः प्रत्ययमलभमानाः 'अधिकं तु भेद-निर्देशात्'। उ. मी. अ. पा. १. सू. २२। 'लोकवत्तुलीला कैवल्यम्' । उ. मी. अ. २ पा. १ सू. ३३। इत्यादिसूत्रैर्जीवाधिक ईश्वर एव जगतः स्रष्टा, न जीवः । तस्याप्तकामत्वेन प्रयोजनाभावेऽपि केवलं लीलयैव जगतः सृष्टिरित्यादि प्रतिपादयद्भिर्विरोधं च मन्यमाना हिरण्यगर्भ एको ब्रह्मप्रतिबिम्बो मुख्यो जीवः। अन्ये तु तत्प्रतिबिम्बभूताश्चित्रपटलिखितमनुष्यदेहार्पितपटाभासकल्पाः जीवाभासाः संसारादिभाज् इति विशेषानेकशरीरैकजीववादमातिष्ठन्ते ।

S.L.S. Ist chapter, pp.125-26.

24. अपरे तु हिरण्यगर्भस्य प्रतिकल्प भेदेन कस्य हिरण्यगर्भस्य मुख्यं जीवत्वमित्यत्र नियामकं नास्तीति मन्यमाना एक एव जीवो विशेषेण सर्वं शरीरमधितिष्ठति। न चैवं शरीरावयवभेद इव शरीरभेदेऽपि परस्परसुखाद्यनुसन्धानप्रसङ्गः । जन्मान्तरीयसुखाद्यनुसन्धानादर्शनेन शरीरभेदस्य तदननुसन्धान-प्रयोजकत्वक्लृप्तेः ।

S.L.S. Ist chapter, p.127.

25. अज्ञानप्रतिबिम्बितं चैतन्यं जीव इति वा अज्ञानानुपहितं शुद्धं चैतन्यमीश्वरः अज्ञानोपहितं च जीव इति वा मुख्यो वेदान्तसिद्धान्त एकजीववादाख्यः । इयमेव च दृष्टिसृष्टिवादमाचक्षते ।

Abhyankar, Vasudev Shastri (ed.), *Siddhāntabindu*, pp.48-49 (1962), Bhandarkar Oriental Research Institute.

26. Divanji, P.C. (ed.), *Siddhāntabindu*, p.94 (1933), Baroda Oriental Institute.

27. तेषु केचिदेवमाहुः - यद्यपि शुद्धब्रह्माश्रयविषयमेकमेवाज्ञानम्, तन्नाश एव च मोक्षः, तथापि जीवनमुक्तो अज्ञानलेशानुवृत्यभ्युपगमेन अज्ञानस्य सांशत्वात् तदेव क्वचिदुपाधौ ब्रह्मावगमोत्पत्तौ अंशेन निवर्तते, उपाध्यन्तरेषु यथापूर्वमंशान्तरैरनुवर्तते इति ।

S.L.S. Ist chapter, pp. 129-30.

28. अपरे तु नाज्ञानं शुद्धचैतन्याश्रयम् किं तु जीवाश्रयं ब्रह्मविषयम् । अतश्चान्तःकरणप्रतिबिम्बरूपेषु सर्वेषु जीवेषु व्यक्तिषु जातिवत् प्रत्येकपर्यवसायितया वर्तमानमुत्पन्नविद्यं कंचित् त्यजति नष्टा व्यक्ति मिव जातिः । स एव मोक्षः । अन्यं यथापूर्वमाश्रयतीति व्यवस्थेत्याहुः ।

S.L.S. Ist chapter, pp.132-33.

29. इतरे तु प्रतिजीवमविद्याभेदमभ्युपगम्येव तदनुवृत्तिनिवृत्तिभ्यां बद्धमुक्तव्यवस्थां समर्थयन्ते ।

S.L.S. Ist chapter, pp.132-33.

30. न वयं प्रधानवदविद्यां सर्वजीवेष्वेकामाचक्ष्महे, चैनेवमुपालभ्येमहि, किंत्वियं प्रतिजीवं भिद्यते । तेन यस्यैव जीवस्य विद्योत्पन्ना तस्यैवाविद्याऽपनीयते न जीवान्तरस्य, . . .

Bhāmati on the *Br. Sū. Śā. Bhā.* I.4, pp.378-79.

The Brahmasūtraśāṅkarabhāṣya with commentaries (1981), Parimala Publications.

31. अस्मिन् पक्षे कस्याविद्यया प्रपञ्चः कृतोऽस्त्विति चेत्, विनिगमकाभावात् सर्वाविद्याकृतोऽनेकतन्त्वारब्धपटतुल्यः । एकस्य मुक्तौ तदविद्यानाशे एकतन्तुनाशे पटस्येव तत्साधारणप्रपञ्चस्य नाशः । तदैव विद्यमानतन्त्वन्सरैः पटान्तरस्येव इतराविद्यादिभिः सक्लेतरसाधारणप्रपञ्चान्तरस्योत्पादनमित्येके ।

S.L.S. Ist chapter, p.132.

32. यदि तत्र युगपद्भ्राम्यद्बहुपुरुषाविद्यकृतमेकमेव रजत कस्यचिद् भ्रमनिवृत्तौ पुनर्भ्रमानुवृत्तिस्तदा तदितरसकलपुरुषाविद्याकृतं अतान्तरमिति साधरण्यमुपपाद्यते तदा स एव न्याय: प्रपञ्चे योजनीय:। Kalpataru Parimala, on the *Br. Sū. Śā. Bhā.* I.4.3, p.379, *The Brahmasūtraśāṅkarabhāṣya with the commentaries* (1981), Parimala Publications.

33. अनेकैकत्वविषयिणी बुद्धि: अपेक्षाबुद्धि:।

SL.S. Ist Chapter, p. 133

34. तत्तदज्ञानकृत प्रातिभासिकरजतवत्, न्यायमते तत्तदपेक्षाबुद्धिजन्यद्वित्यवच्च तत्तदविद्यावृतो वियदादिप्रपञ्च: प्रतिपुरूषं भिन्न: । शुक्तिरजते त्वया यद् दृष्टं रजतं, तदेव मयाऽपीतिवदैक्यभ्रममात्रमित्यन्ये ।

S.L.S. Is chapter, p.134.

35. द्विविधेऽपि दृष्टिसृष्टिवादे मन:प्रत्ययमलभमाना: केचिदाचार्या: सृष्टिदृष्टिवादं रोचयन्ते ।

. *S.L.S.* 2nd chapter, p.356.

36. श्रुतिदर्शितेन क्रमेण परमेश्वरसृष्टमज्ञातसत्तायुक्तमेव विश्वं तत्तद्विषयप्रमाणावतरणे तस्य तस्य दृष्टिसिद्धिरिति ।

S.L.S. 3rd chapter, p.356.

37. . . . प्रपञ्चस्य कल्पितत्वाभावे श्रुत्यादिप्रतिपन्नस्य सृष्टिप्रलयादिमत: प्रत्यक्षादिप्रतिपन्नार्थक्रियाकारिणश्च तस्य सत्यत्वमेवाभ्युपगतं स्यादिति . . .

S.L.S. 2nd chapter, pp. 356-57.

38. . . . कल्पनासमसमयत्वाभावेऽपि ज्ञानेकनिवर्त्यत्वरूपस्य, सदसद्विलक्षणत्वरूपस्य, प्रतिपन्नोपाधिगतत्रैकालिकनिषेधप्रतियोगत्वरूपस्य वा मिथ्यात्वस्याभ्युपगमात् ।

S.L.S. 2nd chapter, p.357.

39. सत्यत्वपक्षे प्रपञ्चे उक्तरूपमिथ्यात्वाभावेन ततो भेदात् ।

S.L.S. 2nd chapter, p.358.

40. *Siddhāntabindu*, p.49.

10

Dṛṣṭi-Sṛṣṭi-Vāda in the *Vedānta Siddhānta Muktāvalī*

IN the previous chapter it has been discussed how *Sṛṣṭi-Dṛṣṭi-vāda* in the Absolutistic philosophy of *Kevalādvaita Vedānta* peresents an apparently Realistic trend in solving the riddle of the world existence in consonance with the belief in *Advaita*. It recognises the Objective Empirical (Phenomenal) Reality of the world in all its aspects, and thus would appeal to many from the common-sense point of view.

On the other hand *Dṛṣṭi-Sṛṣṭi-vāda*, the rival theory, puts forth an Idealistic explanation regarding the world of appearance; and denounces its empirical reality. Of course, *Sṛṣṭi-Dṛṣṭi-vāda* as well as *Dṛṣṭi-Sṛṣṭi-vāda* are both just *Vedāntic* theories meant to establish the unreality of the phenomenal world and thus uphold the *Advaita-Vāda* of *Vedānta*; yet the *Dṛṣṭi-Sṛṣṭi-vāda* can be said to have presented a more logical solution, if we keep in mind that the *Kevalādvaita* philosophy admits the reality of just one non-dual pure sentiency — the Absolute principle.

It may be noted that the actual development towards what is known as the *Dṛṣṭi-Sṛṣṭi-vāda* took place during the post-Śaṅkara period. In the works before Śaṅkara, we find scattered glimpses of Idealism, or not a very systematic exposition of it, which nevertheless could be said to lead steadily towards *Dṛṣṭi-Sṛṣṭi-vāda*. This has been already dealt with in the previous chapters. The present chapter deals with the post-Śaṅkara development and the establishment of the *Dṛṣṭi-Sṛṣṭi-vāda* as presented in the *Vedānta Siddhānta Muktāvalī*.

As has been already stated that after Śaṅkara, it was Maṇḍana Miśra who initiated a Subjectivistic trend in regarding the *Jīva* as the locus of *Avidyā*; and this was strengthened by Vācaspati Miśra. Since the *Sṛṣṭi-Dṛṣṭi-vāda* emphasizes *Brahman* as the locus of *Avidyā*, there is left no role for the *Jīva* to play, so far as the creation of the world is concerned. And as *Brahman* is the creator of the world, it is not possible to eradicate the empirical reality of the phenomenal world. On the other hand, Maṇḍana Miśra and Vācaspati Miśra both consider the *Jīva* as the locus of *Avidyā* and thus the *Jīva* tends to assume the role of the creator. Now, in regarding the *Jīva* as the creator, there arise many complications. In other words, it invites the problem of oneness and manyness of the *Jīva*, as well as of *Avidyā*. If the *Jīva* is one, and it is the creator of the world, then when the *Jīva* gets liberated, the world also should simultaneously vanish with its liberation. But this is something which we never experiences in the phenomenal world. On the contrary we see that when one *Jīva* is liberated, the world still remains there with many other *Jīvas*. This compels one to think in terms of the manyness of the *Jīvas*. Now, if there is one *Avidyā*, common amongst many *Jīvas*, a common world experience becomes possible. But at the same time the problem regarding liberation remains unsolved as mentioned above. On the other hand, if may *Jīvas* possessing many *Avidyās* are accepted, then the problem about one common world experience remains unsolved.

The Śaṅkarites have applied themselves to the explanation of such problems as already seen in the previous chapter. Even risking repetition, a bird's eye view of the *Jīvāśrita-Avidyā-vāda* is presented here as it helps us to march ahead towards *Dṛṣṭi-Sṛṣṭi-vāda*.

Jīvāśrita-Avidyā-Vāda

In order to give a rational explanation of the problem of bondage and liberation, the *Jīvāśrita-Avidyā-vāda* is put forth with variations, such as *Anekajīvāśrita-Eka-Avidyā-Vāda, Aneka-*

jīvāśrita-Aneka-Avidyā-vāda, Ekajīvāśrita-Eka-Avidyā-vāda. Besides, these variations are meant to solve the problem of a common world experience.

According to the *Anekajīvāśrita-Eka-Avidyā-vāda,* a common world experience becomes possible, as there is one common *Avidyā.* But this view has to face the difficulty that when one *Jīva* is emancipated, at that very moment all the *Jīvas* should be emancipated, as the *Avidyā* located in each and every *Jīva* has been eradicated.

In order to avoid this difficulty, another view was formulated, according to which *Aneka Avidyās* reside in *Aneka Jīvas.*

Vācaspati Miśra holds the view that *Avidyā* is not one but many, and each *Jīva* has its own *Avidyā* located in it.[1] In holding this view, there arises no problem of the destruction of the mundane world and the emancipation of all the *Jīvas.* But as Appaya Dikṣita has explained, the *Avidyās* jointly give rise to the phenomenal world and *Brahman* remains a witness. When the *Avidyā* of one *Jīva* is destroyed, the world is destroyed but simultaneously another world is brought about by the *Avidyās* of the remaining *Jīvas.* This is explained by the analogy of threads and cloth.[2]

After Maṇḍana Miśra and Vācaspati Miśra, it was Prakāśānanda, who was the pioneer in propounding-*Eka-Jīvāśrita-Eka-Avidyā-vāda,* which represents the last stage of development of *Jīvāśrita-Avidyā -vāda.* This shall be examined at some length later while dealing with the *Dṛṣṭi-Sṛṣṭi-vāda* in the *Vedānta Siddhānta Muktāvalī.*

The *Vedānta Siddhānta Muktāvalī,* written in the sixteenth century A.D. by Prakāśānanda presents the *Dṛṣṭi-Sṛṣṭi-vāda* in its full bloom. It would not be out of place to state that in the early *Vedāntic* works we find only scattered Idealistic thoughts, and the actual term *Dṛṣṭi-Sṛṣṭi* is also not used. It is true that in the *Yoga-Vāsiṣṭha,* we find the term, but we cannot arrive at its specific meaning or interpretation from the expressions used in that work. The actual establishment of *Dṛṣṭi-Sṛṣṭi-vāda* occurred in the latter half of the sixteenth century.[3]

At the outset, one may see how Prakāśānanda tries to reject the unapprehended existence (*Ajñāta Sattā*) of the world, in what way he logically refutes the validity of the means of knowledge and the theory of Causation, how he emphasizes the highest *Vedāntic* position of the non-duality or oneness of the *Jīva* (*Ekajīva-vāda*), which all together constitute the doctrine, viz. *Dṛṣṭi-Sṛṣṭi-vāda* in the *Vedānta Siddhānta Muktāvalī*.

Locus of *Avidyā*

Since Prakāśānanda holds that there is nothing existing other than the attributeless, immutable, eternal and Absolute Ultimate Reality viz. *Brahman*, everything apart from *Brahman* must be regarded as unreal, so he firmly refuses to accept any compromising stand meant to explain the position of the world, God, *Jīvas*, etc. Hence the problem of the locus of *Avidyā* is immaterial for him. Nevertheless, he has presented the views of the Śaṅkarites about the locus of *Avidyā*.

Some Śaṅkarites, keeping in mind the system of bondage and liberation try to propound *Anekajīvāśrita-Aneka-Avidyā-vāda*. They hold that the *Jīva* is the locus of *Avidyā*, while *Brahman* is its object. Moreover, the *Jīvas* are many, otherwise the system of bondage and liberation would not be possible.[4] The *Jīva*, which attains the knowledge of *Brahman* through hearing etc. gets liberation, while the rest of the *Jīvas* still remain in bondage. Hence, many *Avidyās* are hypostatised. Otherwise, if one *Avidyā* is recognised, the whole phenomenal world established by perception etc. should not be experienced when the *Avidyā* is destroyed by true knowledge. And it is also not possible to hold that yet no one has obtained true knowledge, for in that case, no one would try to get liberation through "hearing" etc., thinking that those were performed by ancient sages like Vyāsa, Vasiṣṭha etc. and still they did not attain liberation.[5]

In the context of worldly experience, a question is posed, "On the base of the means of knowledge, viz. perception why should not the duality of the world be regarded real?" Then it is stated, "If the trustworthiness of perception is proved by any other means then the fault of Infinite Regress (*Anavasthā*) would be itself unavoidable, and if it is proved by itself only, then also there would be a suspicion of fault."[6]

How is the trustworthiness of perception proved? Does perception make its object the things of practical dealings or the things which can never be proved unreal? In accepting the first alternative, it could be applied to the imaginary things also, as they also serve practical dealings. Now, the second alternative is also not possible, nor it is proved by another as this involves the fault of Infinite Regress.

Moreover, the scriptures themselves declare the untrustworthiness of the means of knowledge and show the unreality of the world.

Further, the plural (*Māyābhiḥ*) statement of the scripture, "Due to *Māyās*, Indra imagines various forms" establishes the plurality of *Avidyā*, and that these *Avidyās* reside in the *Jīvas* making *Brahman* their object.[7]

The above-mentioned view is held by some Śaṅkarites. Some other Śaṅkarites emphasize the view that *Avidyā* resides in the *Ātman* making it its object.

First it is asked whether both the *Jīva* and *Brahman* are meant by the term *Ātman*, or only the *Jīva* is known as *Ātman* and *Brahman* is signified by another term. Now, if the first alternative is accepted, then it is favourable, as *Ātman* becomes the object of *Avidyā*. It may be objected that being an object of *Avidyā*, the *Ātman* would not shine forth for it would be concealed by *Avidyā*, as the pot concealed by the darkness is not seen. The answer to this objection is that the *Ātman* becomes the object of *Avidyā* with respect of its non-duality and bliss only. Its virtue of consciousness (*caitanya*) never becomes the object of *Avidyā*, otherwise *Avidyā* itself could not be proved.[8] Moreover, the differentiation of the Absolute into its parts viz. bliss etc. is falsely imagined, as the ignorant people imagine that only consciousness shines forth and not bliss. Hence, the locus and object of *Avidyā* are identical. *Avidyā* is a kind of darkness, as darkness makes the locus its object, so is in the case of *Avidyā* also.[9]

Now, if *Brahman* and the *Jīva* (*Ātman*) are different, then their difference would be either natural or conditional. If the first alternative is accepted, *Brahman* would be non-sentient, for the self is sentient, and the scripture declaring "*Vijñānaṁ ānandaṁ Brahma*" would be contradicted. Furthermore, it (*Brahman*) would not be the object of *Avidyā* for whatever is unintelligent is *Avidyā* and to assume that *Avidyā* invests itself is idle. And it would follow that the self, as being different from *Brahman* would abandon its selfhood to become like earthen pots etc. (in other words, non-sentient). In accepting the second alternative, does this limitation consist in the difference being an effect produced by the limiting condition as its cause, or in the difference being made known through the limiting condition, or is it some other kind of dependence on the limiting condition? It must be premised that *Avidyā* is the only limiting condition possible with regard to the difference between *Jīva* and *Brahman* for the effects of *Avidyā* as being occasional (not permanent) cannot be the conditions determining the difference between the *Jīva* and *Brahman.*[10] Amongst the above-mentioned alternatives, the first one is not admitted, since *Avidyā* has been proved to have existed in the undifferenciated self even before the difference between the *Jīva* and *Brahman* was brought about, the differentiation is unnecessary, nor is *Avidyā* admitted as an independent entity.[11] The second alternative is also not admissible: for *Avidyā* being non-sentient can make known nothing.[12] Nor is the third alternative possible : for the kinds of dependence commonly recognised are three viz. the production of an effect from a cause, the attachment of an attribute to a substrate, the cognitional relation between something made known and that which makes it known. Here, none of these kinds of dependence is possible with regard to *Avidyā*, so dependence on a limiting condition cannot determine the difference between the *Jīva* and *Brahman.*[13]

Nor can it be urged that the difference between the *Jīva* and *Brahman* is dependent on *Avidyā*, like the relation which exists between *Avidyā* and the self, as with regard to relation the restrictive rule is that relation is dependence on the things related, and difference is not relation. Hence, *Avidyā* resides in the *Ātman* which is devoid of differentiation into the *Jīva* and

Brahman, and makes it its object. Thus, the self has been proved to be the object of *Avidyā*.[14]

The above-mentioned *Jīvāśrita-Avidyā-vāda* and *Brahmāśrita-Avidyā-vāda* are related to the rival theories, namely *Dṛṣṭi-Sṛṣṭi vāda* and *Sṛṣṭi-Dṛṣṭi-vāda* respectively.

Here, a curiosity may arise to know the view of Prakāśānanda about the locus of *Avidyā*. But for Prakāśānanda, only one sentiency exists which due to *Avidyā* assumes the state of *Jīva* and imagines itself variously in the form of the world, God, the *Jīva* etc. so, as soon as the sentiency is conditioned by *Avidyā*, it is called the *Jīva*.

As there is only one sentiency, naturally there is only one *Avidyā*, due to which this complex network of the phenomenal world is imagined.

Eka-jīva-Eka-Avidyā-vāda

We have already stated that in order to make the system of bondage and liberation tenable, some of the Śaṅkarites recognise manyness of the *Jīvas* as well as of *Avidyā*.

On the other hand, Prakāśānanda seems to be of the view that as there is only one *Jīva*, there is only one *Avidyā*. It is stated in the *Vedānta Siddhānta Muktāvalī*, "There is no evidence either worldly or *Vedic* for *Avidyā*. If it is imagined through its effects, then it is better to hold *Avidyā* as one according to the law of parsimony."[15]

Avidyā is neither established by the *Veda* nor by perception etc. The earlier portion of the *Veda* is concerned with action, while the later portion asserts the reality of Absolute-Existence-Consciousness-Bliss, i.e., *Brahman*. If *Avidyā* is proved by perception, there would remain no controversy. So, as there is unrelated, passive, ever blissful and satisfied being only, recognition of *Avidyā* is the only acceptable alternative for explaining the production of the inexplicable world, which is a complex network of joys and pains. Now, is this hypostatised *Avidyā* one or many? It is better to recognise one *Avidyā* possessing manifold powers as the fault of sleep though one is seen to produce manifold effects in a dream.[16]

This one *Avidyā* is the limiting condition (*upādhi*) of the one *jīva*. This is the view of the *Ekajīvavādins*, who quote a statement from the scripture in their support: *"Ajāṁ ekāṁ lohita-śukla-kṛṣṇām bahvīḥ prajāḥ sṛjamānām sarūpaḥ, ajo hy eko juṣamāno nuśete jahāty enām bhuktabhogām ajo'nyaḥ" Śve.Up*. IV.5.

Here the word *aja* which shows that *Avidyā*, from which the world is produced, is unborn. The term *Ekāṁ* negates the plurality. Further, the word *Aja* also negates the origination of the *Jīva*, which is conditioned by *Avidyā*. And the term *Eka* negates the plurality of the *Jīva*.

The doubt as to how the *Jīva* could be one when its plurality is experienced in the phenomenal world, is set aside by the term *hi* signifying that the unity of the *Jīva* is well-known in the *Upaniṣads*, and is proved by argument also.[17]

Now, in this context a doubt may arise that if there is only one *Jīva*, how would the system of bondage and liberation be possible, as the whole phenomenal world would come to an end along with the liberation of the one *Jīva*. Such a doubt is set aside by stating that inasmuch as many internal organs are admitted, the so-called fault would not arise. In short, it is not possible to talk in terms of 'all' in the presence of the *Ekajīvavādin*, who recognises only 'one' *Jīva*. Eventhough the plurality of *Jīvas* is experienced, this should be considered possible as in a dream.[18]

Here, a further doubt arises. As in a dream, the perceiver of the dream is considered to be real, and all else as imagined, so in the waking state also one is real and all the rest are imagined. But which *Jīva* should be considered real amongst all the *Jīvas*.

The answer to this is that this experience (of many *Jīvas*) is based on the illusion that the body is the self.[19] If it is argued that the plurality of the *Jīvas* is inferred from the different activities of various bodies, then the answer is that diverse activities are possible in spite of there being one *Jīva* as in the case of the *Kāyavyūha* (manifestation of different bodies) of the *yogin*.

In short, the plurality of the *Jīva* is experienced only due to the wrong conception of the body as the self. As a matter of fact, there is one self, in its own nature eternal, absolute, intelligent, free, made known in the *Upaniṣad* only. This self, associating itself with *Avidyā* becomes *Jīva* and falsely surmises the bodies of gods, men, etc., for whose enjoyment it creates, as means, the 'egg of *Brahman*' and the fourteen worlds. Of these bodies one is a god, another is a man. There is Hiraṇyagarbha the creator of all things. Viṣṇu the preserver, and Rudra who destroys the world at the *pralaya* or final resolution. These three have the *rajas, sattva* and *tamas* respectively as their limiting conditions, to which all their powers are due. Then again there is the individual man who thinks within himself "I am the son of *Brahman*; having served the Gods in *pūjā* and acquired 'hearing' and the other prescribed means. I shall gain emancipation. In all these forms the self, though really *Īśvara* is deceived in the waking state. Again, the self having put and end to the world of waking consciousness as described above, and aided by the defects of sleep, surmises in dreams a world precisely similar to that of waking, falsely imagining thus: "Vasiṣṭha and other sages won emancipation, when through their bodies and sense-organs they had experienced the results of their actions, other men are bound; I too am bound, miserable in the bonds of transmigration, I shall obtain emancipation." Then again the self puts an end to this dream and enters on the waking state, or that of dreamless sleep in which there is an end to all such false imaginings. Hence, there is only one Absolute, self-luminous and blissful self, which is known as the transmigrant *Jīva* due to its associate *Avidyā*. There is no other transmigrant *Jīva* other than this one, this has been clearly proved.[20]

Here, it can be clearly seen that the *Ekajīva-vāda* plainly puts the phenomenal world on the same footing as the dreaming state, and rejects outright the existence of the many *Jīvas*. It thus tries to remain faithful to the *Kevalādvaitavedānta*, which forcefully puts forth *Brahman* as the only Ultimate Reality. Since only one sentiency viz. *Brahman* is all-pervading, how could there be another thing?

Ekajīva-vāda has been discussed by Madhusūdana Sarasvatī, in the *Siddhāntabindu* and in the *Advaitasiddhi*. In the *Siddhāntabindu* he has stated, "According to the *Ekajīva-vāda* the *Jīva* itself, due to ignorance becomes the mterial (*upādāna*) as well as the efficient (*nimitta*) cause of the world.[21] And this one, the only *Jīva*, gets liberation on performing 'hearing' etc. based on the instruction of the teacher and the scripture etc. which are also imagined by itself only.[22] All the other *Jīvas* are unreal appearances imagined by this only *Jīva*. Since rightly speaking there is absence of many *Jīvas*, the liberation of Śuka and others is stated only as an eulogy.[23] If Śuka is considered that particular *Jīva*, then by virtue to its liberation, the whole world imagined by it should have been dissolved at that very moment of liberation, as elephant, horse, etc. imagined in the dreaming state are dissolved the very moment the person wakes up. So Śuka cannot be considered the main *Jīva*, and the liberation of Śuka is mentioned only as eulogy.[24]

In the *Advaita Siddhi* also we find *Ekajīva-vāda* discussed at some length. But in order to avoid repetition, we do not ponder longer over this here.[25]

Since the *Ekajīva-vāda* treats the phenomenal dealings just like a dream, that is to say, as illusory (*prātibhāsika*), it can be said to be identical with *Dṛṣṭi-Sṛṣṭi-vāda*. As already stated, Madhusūdana Sarasvatī does not recognise any difference between the *Ekajīva-vāda* and the *Dṛṣṭi-Sṛṣṭi-vāda* and consider them as identical.[26] But it seems that the *Ekajīva-vāda* is one of the aspects of the *Dṛṣṭi-Sṛṣṭi-vāda*. *Dṛṣṭi-Sṛṣṭi-vāda* is a theory, which emphasizes that nothing exists independently apart from its perception. While the *Ekajīva-vāda* is its metaphysical aspect upholding the highest *Vedāntic* position that nothing exists except the non-dual sentiency viz. *Brahman*. *Brahman* is the only Ultimate Principle, which by virtue of *Avidyā* becomes *Jīva* and imagines God, other *Jīvas* and the world. Hence, the seeming plurality of *Jīvas* and the world is nothing but an illusion. Of course, *Dṛṣṭi-Sṛṣṭi-vāda* may comprehend the *Ekajīva-vāda*, but that does not necessarily make them totally identical theories.

Nevertheless, it is noteworthy that according to the

Ekajīva-vāda the *Jīva* itself becomes the material (*upādāna*) cause of the world. In this context, in the commentary on the *Siddhāntaleśasaṁgraha* it is stated, "The Absolute self becoming *Jīva* due to *Avidyā*, even without limitation (*avaccheda*) and reflection (*pratibimba*) imagines itself to be God. And thus becoming God it imagines the creation of the world consisting of sky etc. from itself only. It gradually imagines man etc. Thus, *Brahman* which has become the *Jīva* is the material cause because it imagines the entire phenomena in itself only. This is the view of the *Dṛṣṭi-Sṛṣṭi-vādins*.[27]

It is to be mentioned here that Sadānanda in his *Advaita Brahma Siddhi* has stated that *Dṛṣṭi-Sṛṣṭi-vāda* is based on *Avacchedavāda* whereas *Sṛṣṭi-Dṛṣṭi-vāda* is associated with *Pratibimbavāda*.[28]

In short, we can consider the *Ekajīva-vāda* as one of the facets of the *Dṛṣṭi-Sṛṣṭi-vāda*. Nevertheless, among the *Vedāntins* those who recognise *Dṛṣṭi-Sṛṣṭi-vāda*, would necessarily resort to *Ekajīva-vāda* in order to maintain their doctrine of non-duality and also to explain the worldly phenomena.

Rejection of *Ajñāta Sattā*

Usually we feel that the things which we perceive, do not merge into nothingness after our perception. The garden, the buildings which we visit do not disappear after our visit. To a layman, it seems absurd to consider that things vanish after their perception.

Strikingly enough, the *Dṛṣṭi-Sṛṣṭi-vāda* strongly negates the unapprehended existence (*Ajñāta Sattā*) of this phenomenal world; and tries to emphasize that the things disappear when we do not perceive them. It may be mentioned that Śaṅkara and his followers generally accept the empirical existence (*Vyāvahārika Sattā*) of the world. Besides, the *Mādhyamika* Buddhists recognise the Ultimate existence (*Pārmārthika Sattā*) as well as the empirical existence (*Saṁvṛti Satya*). And the *Yogācārins* (*Vijñānavādins*) also, though from a different angle, recognise three types of natures (*trisvabhāva*) namely, the Ultimate (*pariniṣpanna*), the dependent (*paratantra*), and the illusory (*parikalpita*).

What is meant by this is only that generally the objective existence of the world is not denounced. Though it is negated from the ultimate point of view, it is accepted for practical dealings.

Now, amongst the Śaṅkarites, Prakāśānanda is the only exception who has boldly enough denied the objective existence of the world.[29]

In the *Vedānta Siddhānta Muktāvalī* it is stated, "Orthodox Śaṅkarites admit three types of existence[30] viz.:

(i) the ultimate existence (*pārmārthika*)

(ii) the empirical existence (*vyāvahārika*)

(iii) the illusory existence (*prātibhāsika*).

Amongst these, *Brahman* has ultimate existence; while the world of appearance has empirical existence. Orthodox Śaṅkarites believe that the world exists until the dawn of knowledge. When the Ultimate Reality is realised, then only it is negated as unreal (*mithyā*). On the other hand, dream, snake appearing in the rope, silver appearing in the mother of pearl have illusory existence, as they are sublated at once.

It is interesting to know that early *Vedāntic* works namely the *Gauḍapādakārikā*, the *Vivekacūḍāmaṇi* etc. do not specifically state that the world does not have unapprehended existence eventhough they compare the world with a dream. Nevertheless, in the *Yoga-Vāsiṣṭha* we get a hint from a verse which seems to indicate negation of the unapprehended existence that, "All things have *Avidyā* as their source : bubble, like they spring up for a moment and are refunded into the great ocean of knowledge."[31]

So, perhaps following the *Yoga-Vāsiṣṭha*, Prakāśānanda admits only two types of existence namely the ultimate and the illusory, and thus simply negates the empirical existence of the world. In other words, according to Prakāśānanda, things exist only when they are perceived. That is to say, the phenomenal world has only illusory existence just like a dream.

In this context, it might be argued that if *Ajñāta Sattā* of the world is rejected, then a man gone out of the house would become very miserable and would die weeping, knowing that his house, son, beasts, etc. do not exist when they are not perceived.[32] So before self-realisation, the world is not sublated.

Prakāśānanda very logically asserts that the world has got only illusory existence, and so it does not exist when not perceived. A question is posed before the holders of three types of existence. "Is duality real or unreal? If it is unreal, then how could it be three-fold?"[33]

Does an object exist even when not perceived by maintaining that duality is either real or is what is technically termed inexplicable?

The first alternative will not hold, for an absolutely real duality must be rejected on the rejection of the trustworthiness of perception, inference and other sources of evidence.

If the last alternative is adopted, it may be asked whether this merely apparent existence was observed in any instance prior or not? If not observed, how, in the absence of an instance confirmatory of the inference, is the merely apparent existence of the world beginning with the subtle element sky to be proved. If it is to be replied that the snake, which erroneously appears in place of the rope seen at night, is a well-known instance, among others, of a merely apparent object, then it being premised that the existence of the world beginning with sky is precisely similar to the existence of the snake; the question remains to be discussed whether the objective world exists even when not perceived, or only so long as perceived. If the unapprehended existence be surmised for the world, the example (the existence of the snake) and the case in point (the existence of the world) do not sufficiently correspond, because of the dissimilarity.[34]

That is to say, here the analogy of the snake, presented to show the inexplicable existence of the world consisting of sky etc. is not proper; but contradictory. On the contrary the snake appearing in the place of the rope indicates its illusory (*prātibhāsika*) existence.

Nor would the man who has gone out of the house die weeping because of being certain of their non-existence, for he is not convinced of their non-existence so long as no evidence subversive of his belief in their existence is forthcoming, and, further because it is shown that all experience is like that of the dream.[35]

There is no difference between the dreaming state and the waking state, for in neither case, while the error lasts, any sublation is admitted. Nor is there any inconsequence in holding that there is a sublation of error on the application of evidence, for none would say that, when the error has been removed, there can be any further dealings with the erroneously surmised objects.[36]

Besides, there is no contradiction with the view of the holders of three-fold existence, as they have recognised the empirical existence of things only for the satisfaction of the ignorant people without abandoning the illusory existence of duality. Though *Prapañca* is illusory, there is no contradiction in their speaking of its empirical existence due to intermediate differences as it is recognised by the ignorant people.[37]

Now, in our daily life the unapprehended existence of the world is experienced. Everyday we experience the very same world. If the unapprehended existence of the world is rejected, then what about the experience of the man who recognises the same world after waking up from the dreaming state?[38]

This doubt is set at nought by stating the analogy that in dim light, ten people simultaneously running away on account of the illusion of a snake, know from each other's statements that they all had experienced the same (illusory) snake. In this case, each had a different experience of the illusory snake, as no one is able to experience the illusion of another person. But due to non-discrimination all knew that each one had experienced the same snake.[39]

Similarly, the *Prapañca* which is experienced after waking up from the deep sleep is absolutely different from the previously experienced *Prapañca*. But due to non-discrimination one feels that it is the very same *Prapañca*.[40]

Moreover, there is no lack of testimony about the dissolution of *Prapañca* during deep sleep. The scripture asserts the absence of *Prapañca* in deep sleep.[41]

Here, one may be confused since the world consisting of earth, water etc. is obviously different from the illusory snake. How could a very big stone, hitting the head of a man be considered illusory, as it causes severe pain? Objects, fulfilling our practical usages could not be just compared with illusory things. The 'difference' between them is that the world is perceived by the sense-organs, while the illusory things are perceived due to *Avidyā*. Moreover, illusory things do not exist before their actual perception, on the other hand, the world seems to be existing even when not perceived. Hence, one has to admit the unapprehended existence of the phenomenal world.

In answer to this objection it is stated that as a matter of fact, the sense-organs are not the causes of the knowledge of the world. If the reason is asked, then a counter question could be asked whether the sense-organs are instruments of valid knowledge or of just knowledge which is common to both valid knowledge and false knowledge or of false knowledge only.[42]

Here, none of the alternatives is acceptable. The sense organs are not the causes of valid knowledge, as the truth of the knowledge effected through the sense-organs would have to be proved by ascertaining that the object of this knowledge was something different from what is known by false knowledge. And its being a different object from the object of false knowledge would have to be determined by its being an object of valid knowledge. So the fault of mutual dependence would arise. And the fact that it is the object of valid knowledge does not prove that the object known by it really exists for the knowledge. "This silver is unreal" has an unreal thing for its object.[43]

Moreover, since it must be held that the sense-organs as

sources of knowledge must have for their objects things which are not known, it follows that sense-organs can have as their only object the substratum of all things viz. *Brahman*, for the world being non-sentient could not be something that is 'not known'.[44] The whole word of objects being non-intelligent (*jada*, i.e., *Avidyā* when considered apart from self, intelligence, the substrate), it cannot be what is termed *ajñāta* (unknown, i.e., invested by *Avidyā*), for the objects are *Avidyā* itself, and *Avidyā* could only invest or make unknown intelligence and not itself).

Accordingly, since the fact of being the locus of the world can apply satisfactorily to the self only, it would have to declare that the sense-organs as sources of knowledge have the self within as their object, and such a declaration is not possible, for attributeless self cannot be an object for the sense-organs.[45] The scripture also anounces this.[46] Nor can it be said that this *Śruti* passage declares that the sense-organs have the world as their object. For while the passage re-states the instrumentality is commonly regarded as proved by a method of conjoint presence and absence which is really false, as (the presence and absence of) sense-organs in dream (is purely imaginary). The real meaning of the passage lies in showing that the self is not an object for the sense-organs. Thus, the second alternative is refuted by showing that the sense-organs cannot be instruments of true knowledge.[47]

The third alternative also will not hold for *Avidyā* alone is the cause of false knowledge. And in the case of the dreaming state it happens that though no sense-organs act, the presence and absence of the sense-organs is seen. Thus, to meet the expectation of a cause for all effects such as earthen pots etc., *Avidyā* alone is to be accepted as their cause. But the acceptance of special causes for each of these effects by those who desire these effects can be proved to be precisely similar to the acceptance during the dreaming state.[48]

Hence, everything else other than *Brahman* in the form of *jñāna-jñeya* are the effects of *Avidyā*, and their existence has been proved to be apprehensional only.[49]

Thus, in the exposition of *Dṛṣṭi-Sṛṣṭi-vāda* it is repeatedly stated that this manifold phenomena exists only when perceived, it is imagined by *Avidyā* like the snake and the silver appearing in the rope and in the mother of pearl respectively, and like *gandharvanagara* and a dream.[50]

In short, the sole intent of the *Dṛṣṭi-Sṛṣṭi-vāda* is to reject the unapprehended existence of the phenomenal world, and to assert that it exists only when it is perceived.

Dṛṣṭi itself is *Sṛṣṭi*

By denying the unapprehended existence of the worldly phenomena, Prakāśānanda simply shows that the world exists simultaneously with its perception.

Now, we shall examine how he emphasizes that there is no creation (*Sṛṣṭi*) apart from its percipi (*Dṛṣṭi*). In other words, *Dṛṣṭi* itself is *Sṛṣṭi*. This resembles the theory of *Sahopalambhaniyama* of the *Yogācāra* Buddhism, which asserts that both *jñāna* and *jñeya* are cognised simultaneously. The *jñeya* has no existence apart from the *jñāna*, and so is of the nature of consciousness.

Perception, inference and the scripture are not able to establish the 'difference' between the object and the knowledge of the object (*jñāna-jñeya*).

Perception

Perception is considered the most direct means of valid knowledge. Through perception we all become aware of the things around us. Usually, we believe that we perceive things that are different from its knowledge or awareness. Realists hold that the phenomenal world exists independently of its awareness, for which they consider perception as an appropriate means.

But this view is refuted by Prakāśānanda.

Is the perception, "this is a pot" able to distinguish the pot as different from itself or is it so distinguished by some other perception? If that very perception declares the 'difference' then is this perception self-known or known or known through some other perception?[51] If self-known, and if the view be adopted that a determinate knowledge (*Viśiṣṭhajñāna*) is effected through a knowledge of the attribute portion — then, although in this case the difference is known as the attribute of the object made known by the perception itself, it follows that the perception is self-originated in that which it makes known an attribute, viz. the 'difference' and this is the fault of self-dependence.[52]

Now, if it is held that the difference of pot and knowledge is known as the subject portion (*ghaṭa jñānayor bhedaḥ*), then the intercourse of the sense-organs with both the subject and attribute portions would be the only cause of this determinate perception. So in this situation the difference must be stated to be existing before the origination of its knowledge. And when the difference itself is non-existent before the origination of knowledge, how would it become the object of the knowledge?[53]

And since a second perception cannot be known a self-known perception, it cannot be known as a difference which has as its counter-entity a self-known perception.[54] If it is argued that perception in other than present time is known by another cognition, then the self-luminous virtue is made to depend on present time which would be its limiting condition. If it is held that in the present time, the very nature of knowledge is self-luminous, then this would hold good of the knowledge of past and future also, as there is no difference in their being knowledge.[55] Nor is a change in the nature of knowledge possible according to the change in time, for a pot perceived as a pot never becomes a non-pot. It may be argued that merely by the fact of its own and existence (i.e., without being perceived), the difference (between the pot and the perception of the pot), with which difference the sense-organs were in contact, produced the perception in which the difference was declared. But such a view is a bare statement, for in the absence of evidence, the mere fact of existence of the difference is not proved.[56]

The view that knowledge is made known through another

knowledge also cannot establish the difference of knowledge and its object (e.g. pot). In this case, it should be decided whether or not the knowledge of the difference was preceded by the knowledge of the reciprocally different counter entity and locus. If not, then how could it make known the difference? For nobody is conscious of a difference which is devoid of locus and counter entity. Everyone experiences that 'this' is different from 'that'. On the other hand, if it is admitted that the knowledge of difference was preceded by a knowledge of the reciprocally different counter entity and locus, then the fault of Infinite Regress would be unavoidable. And if it is held that the knowledge of the reciprocal difference was brought about by this same second knowledge, then the fault of self-dependence would be there. Hence, it is proved that perception grasps just the thing and knows nothing of the difference (of thing perceived and the perception).[57]

Inference

Inference also does not establish the difference between the knowledge and the object of knowledge. If it is argued that Inference proves the difference as follows:

(i) *Pratijñā*: The thing under discussion differs from the perception which makes it known.
(ii) *Hetu*: Because this thing is the substrate of attributes which are opposed to the attributes of the perception which makes this thing known.
(iii) *Udāharaṇa*: Whatever is the substrate of attributes which are opposed to the attributes of some other thing is different from that other thing : viz. a piece of cloth is different from a pot.
(iv) *Upanaya*: The thing under discussion is similar to the piece of cloth.
(v) *Nigamana*: Therefore, the perceived object is different from the perception of the object.[58]

The above-mentioned syllogism is rejected. Since the opposition is to be known through the difference, it follows that while the difference is unproved, the opposition is also unproved; hence this thing is the substrate of attributes which is opposed to the attributes of the perception which makes this thing known as invalid. And because as long as the *Sādhya* is unsupported, so long the universal concomitance is unproved. Nor can the difference between a pot and a piece of cloth be proved by any evidence so as to support the *Sādhya*. And if in the absence of perception, recourse is had to a second inference to prove it, the fault of Infinite Regress will continue to haunt the argument.[59]

Thus, inference also cannot prove the difference between *jñāna-jñeya*.

Verbal Testimony

The scriptures repeatedly emphasize non-duality, so the question of their establishing the difference does not arise at all.[60]

It may be argued that, in teaching the emanation of the world from *Brahman*, the scriptures also teach that all products are different from *Brahman*; for if not different, their emanation from *Brahman* could not be mentioned.[61]

This argument is set aside by stating that since every *Vedic* passage bearing on creation is devoted to the refutation of those other causes of the world viz. *Pradhāna* etc. assumed by other thinkers, by showing that just as in such cases as that of earth and the earthen pot, it is impossible to explain what the difference is between earth, the cause, and the pot, the effect, so too it is not possible to explain what the difference is between *Brahman*, the cause, and the whole world which is an effect from *Brahman*, it follows that every such passage finds its real meaning only in giving the knowledge of *Brahman* the one without a second. Otherwise, if the *Vedas* were devoted to teaching difference, the prohibition with regard to duality would be purposeless.[62]

Further, passages dealing with creation do not directly teach 'difference'; for no word bearing the sense of difference occurs in such passages. These cannot declare a meaning which the words composing them do not bear, because it is only what is meant by the words that a sentence can directly be known, either by showing syntactical relation between the words or by conveying the simple notion of identity (of subject and predicate in the sentence). And an inference (from *Vedic*) passages bearing on creation of the world to the difference between *Brahman* and the world is inadmissible as contradictory of (such) prohibitive passages.[63]

Thus, Prakāśānanda emphasizes that neither perception, nor any of the other means of valid knowledge is able to establish the 'difference'.

It may be argued that as the knowledge is not possible without an object different from itself, it follows that knowledge (*jñāna*) makes a thing different from itself its object. Moreover, objectless knowledge is not possible, nor is it experienced. It is knowledge accompanied by its object and that is experienced, otherwise objectless knowledge would be experienced, for apart from an object cognised, there is nothing to determine the cognition. This view is rejected by stating that there is absence of impossibility of the knowledge without its object.[64]

Scrutinising this argument, Prakāśānanda says: Is it meant that the production of knowledge is impossible or the persistence of knowledge is impossible or that secondary knowledge (awareness of knowledge) is impossible without the object being different? The first altenative is not acceptable as knowledge in its essential nature is not a product at all. And if it is believed to be a product, then as its production it is possible through the means of knowledge or through their counterfeits; an object would not be necessary to produce it. And it is not the rule that knowledge is produced by an object.[65]

Nor is the second alternative tenable, as the object to be known is not the locus of the knowledge. If the object is believed to be the locus of the knowledge, then it would not remain an object, (but would become the knower). It might be argued that there is impossibility of the awareness of knowledge, in the absence of an object to be known, since aquaintance of knowledge is dependent on the knowledge of an object. But this is not proper, since knowledge is self-luminous, it does not require the aid of anything for its *Vyavahāra*. If this is not recognised, then the fault of Infinite Regress could not be avoided, and as a result, knowledge would not be established and the world would be merely blank darkness. If it is believed that an 'unknown' knowledge testifies to the reality of the object that is known, then in the absence of evidence knowledge would become an absolutely non-existing entity like the horns of a man.[66]

It may be granted that knowledge needs a second knowledge to make it known, yet it may be asked as to why an object is needed, for only knowledge of the object is necessary. Against this, it might be asked by the opponent: since the necessity of cognition in general (apart from some object cognised) is not here postulated. It follows that there is a necessity for a cognition as determined by some cognised object, and hence the demand for an object is inevitable. But this argument is not tenable, for cognition is self-differenced, as are the categories of generality (*sāmānya*) etc. recognised by the other Schools of Philosophy.[67]

Again it might be argued that the very fact of cognition leads us to infer the existence of some object, because of the universally established concomitance of cognition and cognised object. Such an argument is put aside as follows: Such universal concomitance cannot be proved because cognition and cognised object cannot exist together in the same locus; since their spatial positions are distinct. Moreover, their temporal co-existence cannot be proved, since cognition of a past and future object is a matter of common experience.[68]

In short, the difference between the knowledge and the object to be known cannot be proved.[69] The whole world is stationed in the self only, it exists only when perceived and arises, persists and perishes again and again.[70]

It is stated that there is no duality over and above the existence of the self. This whole world of appearance is seen and heard when the self is seen and heard. Here, the analogy of *rajju* is presented, that when *rajju* is known, all its appearances like garland, stick etc. are known. Similarly, when the self is known, everything is known.[71]

To a layman, a question certainly occurs, "If everything is the self, then who is the seer of the duality?" But in the realm of non-duality, such a question has no scope. When everything is the self, the question of its seer does not arise at all. It can only be stated that through induction (*Prāptāprāptaviveka*) *Dṛṣṭi* alone could be the material modification (*Pariṇāma*), for no perceptible thing other than it is existent.[72]

Further, it is impossible that this vision or product, as included within the self, should be a *pariṇāma* of self, since a thing is not a *pariṇāma* of itself, and because the *pariṇāma* view is vitiated by the alternative assumptions of whole or a part of self undergoing *pariṇāma*. It cannot be argued that the same fault attaches to the *vivarta* view, for the meaning of *vivarta* is not understood. A *vivarta*, is no reality existing, apart from its substrate, in regard to which the above-mentioned alternatives may find place, but what is termed as *vivarta* is nothing but the substrate itself, which through some defect appears under a different form.[73]

Prakāśānanda rejects even *Vivartavāda* the ultimate standpoint. While demolishing the theory of Causation, he propounds the acme of *Vedāntic* thought viz. *Ajātivāda* which has been discussed below.

Rejection of the theory of Causation

Since nothing exists except the non-dual sentiency viz. *Brahman*, there is no use of talking about the theory of Causation. In the chapter, namely — "Idealistic thought in the *Gauḍapādakārikā*", Gauḍapāda has forcefully rejected the theory of Causation and has established Acosmism (*Ajātivāda*). On the other hand, Śaṅkara and most of his followers have admitted the theory of Causation, though only from the empirical standpoint.

In our daily life we see that a particular effect is produced from a particular cause. For example, a pot is produced from clay. Here, the pot is the effect and clay is the cause. It is seen that a pot is always produced from clay and not from milk. Hence, a specific order is maintained in the theory of Causation. Thus, from our empirical experience we assume that there must be some cause of the world. It is noteworthy that each system of thought recognises a cause of the world in its own way. The *Vaiśeṣika* system considers atoms as the cause of the world. While the *Vedāntic* thought regards *Brahman* as the material as well as the efficient cause of the world. *Brahman* is the very cause, from which everything has emerged. This concept may lead towards the theory of Transformation (*Pariṇāmavāda*), but it is noteworthy that the *Kevalādvaita* philosophy accepts the theory of Appearance (*Vivartavāda*). But from the ultimate standpoint, even *Vivartavāda* is not recognised. The *Smṛti* declares that the theory of Appearance is taught only to people with a lower intellect.[74]

As already seen that most of the Śaṅkarites regard *Brahman* as the cause of the world, while Prakāśānanda asserts *Avidyā* (*Māyā*) as the material cause of the world, and that is only to avoid an awkward silence, for Idealism does not allow the theory of Causation to enter into its realm.

In the *Vedānta Siddhānta Muktāvalī* this problem is put forth in an interesting manner. Since it is maintained that all the things have *Avidā* for their cause, it is asked, whether the causal relation is recognised as real or not. If not, then the causality of *Avidyā* could not be affirmed. If it is recognised then the method of conjoint presence and absence would alone be the means of knowledge, for no other method could be applied to the causal relation. In this case, it would not be proper to maintain the causality of *Avidyā*, having rejected the causality of clay, threads etc., which has been proved by inductive methods.[75]

Another doubt is put forth as to whether *Avidyā* is the sole cause, independent of all others, or *Avidyā* accompanied by others viz. God etc. is the cause. The first alternative is not possible, for variety in the effects is impossible in the absence of variety in the cause. Moreover, *Avidyā* which is non-sentient, cannot produce the effect without being monitored by someone who is sentient.[76] Nor is the second alternative acceptable for those who hold the view that *Avidyā* is the cause will have to regard God etc. as the cause also to account for the variety in the world, so there is no use of considering *Avidyā* as the cause, for according to the law of Parsimony, the effects could be established by *Adṛṣta* etc.[77] Moreover, the trustworthiness of perception and the other means of human knowledge, and the earlier portion of the *Veda* as the means of obtaining sons, cattle, paradise would have to be aceepted. If it is denied then which view could be adopted in opposition of the *Veda* and human experience? Hence, "*Avidyā* is the sole cause" is a hasty statement.[78]

The above-mentioned arguments are refuted as follows: "As an existent thing is not produced, similarly, a non-existent thing also is not produced. The bare fact of production proves that the product is the work of *Māyā*.[79]

Now, is an effect something real or unreal? It is not something real, for this is opposed to the purely monistic teaching of the *Śruti* in such passages as 'one only without a second'. Nor can an effect be proved to be something real. To explain: previous to its production is an effect existent, or non-existent? If non-existent, then the horn of a hare ought to be produced through the agency of the cause, for it is alike non-existent. If the effect was something previously existent, then causal agency is not necessary, for the effect existed previous to the exercise of this function, and the nature of the effect is thus overthrown.[80]

If it is argued that it is merely the manifestation of the thing that is brought about through the causal agency, then it is replied that even on this assumption there is no getting rid of the evil fate, whichever of the alternatives be assumed. Grant then (it may be said) that an effect is something inexplicable either as existent or non-existent. Then as an answer it is stated that it is fitting to maintain, as the only cause *Avidyā* inexplicable, beginningless, and of the same nature as its effects, for it is impossible that entity should be the cause of non-entity, and common experience vouches for this impossibility.[81]

It cannot be said that a variety of effects is impossible, for there is presumptive evidence for *Avidyā* as a unity possessing manifold powers.[82]

Nor is the authoritativeness of the earlier portion of the *Veda* impossible, for the real aim of this portion is to teach *Brahman* indirectly by teaching that certain means bring about certain results through the performance of which the intellect is purified, or through which one becomes possessed with the desire to practice the means, of attaining the knowledge of *Brahman*. And because the authoritativeness of the *Veda* is in respect of its purport viz. *Brahman* alone.[83]

Hence, it is rightly said that the *Avidyā* is the cause of things.[84]

Now, a doubt may arise regarding the cause of the world, as the scriptural passages declare both *Brahman* as well as *Avidyā* as the cause of the world.[85]

But the *Śruti* passages describing *Brahman* and *Avidyā* as the cause would not be contradicted, for "*Brahman* is not the cause of the world, but the world is produced through *Avidyā* regarding *Brahman*. *Brahman* is regarded as the cause inasmuch as it is substratum."[86]

As *Brahman* is immutable (*kūṭastha*), and virtually different from cause effect, it cannot be considered as the cause of the world. So beginningless and inexplicable *Avidyā* is the cause (of the world) and not *Brahman*.[87]

It is very clearly stated that the scripture has secondarily or figuratively declared *Brahman* as the cause in the sense that it is the substratum of all. Even *Avidyā* is not meant to be the cause of the world. It is mentioned only as the factor responsible for illusion. So rightly speaking the theory of the Causation lies outside the scope of *Vedānta*, and the theory of Appearance is the only teaching of the *Upaniṣads*.[88]

Hence, if it is asked as to what is the cause of the world, then only to avoid an awkard silence, *Ajñāna* is stated to be the cause of the world.[89]

Thus, the theory of Causation remains totally expelled from the realm of *Dṛṣṭi-Sṛṣṭi-vāda*. It may be said that so far as it negates the theory of Causation, *Dṛṣṭi-Sṛṣṭi-vāda* supports Acosmism (*Ajātivāda*) established by Gauḍapāda, and this reveals the highest *Vedāntic* position.[90] Potter says, "His (Prakāśānanda's) position represents the logical resting place of *Advaita Vivartavāda* in *Ajātivāda* and Solipsism. . ."[91]

In the context of solipsim we would like to quote the statement of Umesh Chandra Das. "The theory of *Dṛṣṭi-Sṛṣṭi* propounds that one *Jīva* is absolute in essence. His egotism is illusory, thanks indeed to the suicidal yet self-centered concept of the theory. The charge of solipsism does not here hold good. That charge would be warmly welcomed by *Ekajīva-vādins* or *Dṛṣṭi-Sṛṣṭi-vādins*."[92]

But as the author of the *Siddhāntaleśasaṁgraha* has said, all the theories of the Śaṅkarites have the sole purpose of maintaining and establishing the Sole Reality of pure consciousness, the *Sṛṣṭi-Dṛṣṭi-vāda* or the *Dṛṣṭi-Sṛṣṭi-vāda* are but attempts to give an explanation of the world-phenomena and our empirical experiences even when nothing else exists other than *Brhaman*. Even if *Dṛṣṭi-Sṛṣṭi-vāda* may appear to be allied to solipsism, it is not final doctrine of the *Advaita-vedāntin*, which is beyond all empirical proof and vertbal usage; and has therefore to be differently communicated.

While Summing up, it may be said that in the *Vedānta Siddhānta Muktāvalī*, Prakāśānanda has propounded the *Dṛṣṭi-Sṛṣṭi-vāda* which has opened a new vista in the history of *Vedāntic* thought. It tries to solve the riddle of world-existence in its own way. This theory can give rise to many questions which may seem difficult to solve. Yet it would not be wrong to repeat that it puts forth the highest *Vedāntic* position very logically.

References

1. Bhāmati on the *Br. Sū. Śā. Bhā.* I.4.3.
2. *S.L.S.* Chapter I, p. 133.

3. "Prakāśānanda's doctrine of *Dṛṣṭi-Sṛṣṭi* is apparently unknown to the earlier *Vedāntic* works and even the *Vedānta-Paribhāṣā,* a work of early sixteenth century, does not seem to be aware of him, and it appears that the earliest mention of his name can be traced only to Appaya, who lived in the sixteenth and the seventeenth centuries. Prakāśānanda may thus be believed to have lived in the latter half of the sixteenth century."
— Dasgupta, S.N., *History of Indian Philosophy,* Vol.II, Ch. XI, p. 17, Footnote, (1975), Motilal Banarsidass.

4. आत्मशब्देन जीवः कथ्यते स चाज्ञानस्याश्रयो न तु विषयः,
विषयत्वं तु ब्राह्मण एव । स च जीवोऽनेकोऽन्यथा व्यवस्थानुपपत्तिः ।
V.S.M., p. 5.
Venis Arthur (tr.). *The Vedānta Siddhānta Muktāvalī* (1975), Chawkhamba Orientalia, Varanasi.

5. यस्य तु श्रवणाद्यभ्यासपाटवेन ब्रह्मात्मावबोधस्तस्य मोक्षस्तदितरस्य बन्ध इति । अत एवाज्ञानान्यनेकानि कल्प्यन्ते । अन्यथा ज्ञानस्यैकत्व एकज्ञानेनाज्ञानतत्कार्यस्य कृत्स्नस्य निवृतौ प्रत्यक्षादिसिद्धस्य जगतोऽननुभवप्रसङ्गः । न चैतावता कालेन कस्यापिज्ञानं न जातमिति साम्प्रतम् प्राचीनानां सम्यक् साङ्गोपाङ्गसाधनानुष्ठातृणां व्यासवसिष्ठादीनामपि ज्ञानानुत्पत्ताविदानीन्तनानां ज्ञानोत्पत्तेः सम्भावयितुमप्यशक्यत्वेन श्रवणाद्यप्रवृत्तावनिर्मोक्षप्रसङ्गात् ।
V.S.M., pp. 5-6.

6. प्रत्यक्षादिप्रमाणानां प्रमात्वं परतो यदि ।
अनवस्था स्फुटा तत्र स्वतस्त्वे दोषसंशयः ॥४॥
V.S.M., p. 7.

7. . . . इन्द्रो मायाभिः पुरुरूप ईयते 'इति मायाभिरिति बहुवचननुरोधेन च जीवाश्रयाणि ब्रह्मविषयाण्यनेकान्यज्ञानानीति . . .
V.S.M., p. 8.

8. ननु आत्मनोऽज्ञानविषयत्वे कथं तस्य भानं तमसाऽऽवृत्तत्वात्, नह्यन्धकारावृतो घटो दृश्यते इति चेत्? न, अद्वयानन्दरूपेणैव तस्याज्ञानविषयत्वात् चैतन्यमात्रस्यैव भासमानत्वात् तस्य चाज्ञानविषयत्वात् अन्यथा ज्ञानस्याप्यसिद्ध्यापत्तेः ।
V.S.M., p. 9.

9. अविद्या स्वाश्रया भिन्नविषया स्यात्तमोः यतः ।
यथा बाह्यं तमो दृष्टं तथा चेयं ततस्तथा ॥
V.S.M., p. 10.

10. जीवब्रह्मभेदस्य उपाधिरप्यज्ञानमेव वक्तव्यम्, : अज्ञान कार्यस्य कदाचित्कत्वेन जीवब्रह्मविभागानुपाधिकत्वात् ।
V.S.M., p. 12.

11. तत्र नाद्यः, भेदोत्पत्तेः पूर्वमेव केवल आत्मन्यज्ञानसिद्धेर्भेदानपेक्षणात् स्वतन्त्रज्ञानानङ्गीकारात् ।
V.S.M., p. 12.

12. न द्वितीयः, अज्ञानस्य जडत्वेन मासकत्वानुपपत्तेः ।
V.S.M., p. 12.

13. नापि तृतीयः, तन्त्रत्वं हि त्रिधा दृष्टं लोके जन्यत्वेन आश्रितत्वेन भास्यत्वेन च । तत्र अन्यतमस्यापि प्रकारस्याज्ञाननिरूपितस्य प्रकृत्तेऽसम्भवात् तन्त्रत्वानुपत्तिः ।
V.S.M., p. 13.

14. न चाज्ञानात्मसम्बन्धवत् अज्ञानतन्त्रत्वं ब्रह्मात्मभेदस्येति वाच्यम्; सम्बन्धस्य सम्बन्धितन्त्रत्वनियमात् भेदस्य च तथात्वाभावात् । तस्माज्जीवब्रह्मविभागशून्यमात्मानमाश्रित्य तमेव विषयीकरोतीत्यज्ञानविषयत्वमात्मनः सिद्धम् ।

V.S.M., p. 13.

15. लौकिकी वैदिकी चापि नाज्ञाने दृश्यते प्रमा ।
कार्यदृष्ट्याऽथ कल्पयं चेल्लाघवादेकमेव तत् ॥८॥

V.S.M., p. 14.

16. तस्मात्स्वतोऽसङ्गोदासीनस्य सदा स्वानन्दतृप्तस्यासत्यानेकविधसुख- दुःखाद्यात्मकप्रपञ्चरचनानुपपत्त्याऽज्ञानं कल्प्यत इत्येव वाच्यं गत्यन्तराभावात् । तथा च कल्प्यमानमज्ञानमेकमनेकं वेति विवादे एकस्यापि निद्रादोषस्यानेकविधकार्यजनकत्वस्य स्वप्ने द्रष्टत्वाल्लाघवसहकृतान्यथानुपपत्ति विचित्रशक्तिकमेकमज्ञानमादाय विश्राम्यतीति युक्तम् ।

V.S.M., p. 15.

17. ननु जीवगतमनेकत्वं लोकेऽनुभूयते तत्कथमेकत्वमित्याशङ्कयाऽभेदस्योपनिषत्प्रसिद्धत्वं युक्तिसिद्धत्वं च प्रसिद्धार्थेन हि शब्देनाह — इति

V.S.M., p. 17.

18. एकत्ववादिनं प्रति सर्वत्वस्य निरूपयितुमशक्यत्वात् । तथापि बहवो जीवा अनुभवसिद्ध । इति चेत् १ भवतु तर्हि स्वप्नवद् व्यवस्था ।

V.S.M., p. 20.

19. तथा च देहात्मभ्रममाश्रित्यैव जीवभेदानुभव इति स्थितम् ।

V.S.M., p. 23.

20. एक एव नित्यशुद्धबुद्धमुक्तस्वभाव उपनिषन्मात्र गम्यो वस्तुतोऽस्ति । स एवाज्ञानमाश्रित्य जीवभावं लब्ध्वा देवतिर्यङ्मनुष्यादिदेहान् परिकल्प्य तदुपकरणत्वेन ब्रह्मण्डादिचतुर्दशभुवनं सृष्टवा तेषु तेषु देहेषु कश्चिद्देवः कश्चिन्मनुष्यः कश्चिद्धिरण्यगर्भः सर्वेषां स्रष्टा कश्चिद्विष्णुः पालकः कश्चिदन्यः सर्वसंहारकर्ता रूद्रः प्रलये । तेषामुपाधयः सत्त्वादिगुणाः तद्वशात्तेषां सर्वे सामर्थ्यम् । अहं पुनः कश्चिद् ब्राह्मणकुमारस्तेषां भक्तिं पूजानमस्कारादिनाऽनुष्ठाय श्रवणादिसाधनं सम्पाद्य मोक्षं साधयिष्यामीतीश्वरोऽपि सन् भ्रान्तो भवति जागरे । पुनर्यथोक्तजागरप्रपञ्चमुपसंहृत्य स्वप्ने निद्रादोषसहकृतः तादृशमेवप्रपञ्चं परिकल्प्य तत्तदेहेन्द्रियसाध्यभोगं भुक्त्वा वसिष्ठादयो मुक्ता अन्ये बद्धा अहमपि कश्चिद् बद्धः दुःखी संसारी मुक्तो भविष्यामीति च कल्पयित्वा पुनस्तामवस्थामुपसंहृत्य जागरं सुषुप्तिं वा सर्वभ्रमनिवृत्तिरूपां प्राप्नोतीति । एवं सति एक एवात्मा परिपूर्णः स्वयंप्रकाशानन्देकस्वभावः स्वाज्ञानवशाज्जीवः संसारीत्यादिशब्दाभिधेयो भवति । न तदन्यः कश्चित् संसारी सम्भावयितुमपि शक्य इति स्थितम् ।

V.S.M., pp. 23-24.

21. अस्मिंश्च पक्षे जीव एव स्वाज्ञानवशाज्जगदुपादानं निमित्तं च ।

Si.Bi., p. 9.

Abhyankar Vasudev, Shastri (ed), *Siddhantabindu*, 2nd edition (1962). Bhandarkar Oriental Research Institute.

22. एकस्येव च स्वकल्पितगुरुशास्त्राद्युपबृंहितश्रवणमननादिदाढर्यादात्मसाक्षात्कारे सति मोक्षः ।

Si.Bi, p. 50.

23. . . . अन्यस्य जीवस्येवाभावात् । तथा च शुकवामदेवादयोनेके मुक्ता इति यदुच्यते तत्प्ररोचनमेव केवलं न तु वस्तुस्थितिः ।

Abhayankar's Commentary on *Si.Bi.*, p. 50.

24. किं च योसावेको मुख्यो जीवः स यदि शुकः स्यात्तर्हि तस्य मोक्षे तत्कल्पितस्य सर्वस्येवास्य प्रपञ्चस्य विलयः स्यात् । यथा स्वप्ने कल्पितानां गजाश्वादीनां सर्वेषामेव स्वप्नद्रष्टुर्जागृतो विलयो भवति तद्वत् । ततश्च नेदानीं जगद् दृश्येत । अतः स मुख्य एको जीवः शुको नेत्यवश्यं कल्पनीयमिति शुको मुक्त इति व्यवहारः केवलमर्थवाद एव ।

Abhyankar's commentary on *Si.Bi.*, p. 50.

25. Sastri, N.S., Ananta Krishna (ed.), *Advaitasiddhi* pp. 539-42, (1982), Parimal Publications.

26. अज्ञानप्रतिबिम्बितं चैतन्यं जीव इति वा अज्ञानानुपहितं शुद्धं चैतन्यमीश्वरः अज्ञानोपहितं च जीव इति वा मुख्यो वेदान्त सिद्धान्त एकजीववादाख्यः । इममेव च दृष्टिसृष्टिवादमाचक्षते ।

Si.Bi., p. 49.

27. परिपूर्णश्चिदात्मा अविद्यया अवच्छेदप्रतिबिम्बभावो विनाऽपि प्राप्तजीवभावः सन् आत्मानमेव सर्वेश्वरं कल्पयति । प्राप्तेश्वरभावात् स्वस्मादेव गगनादिसृष्टिं कल्पयति । . . . तथा क्रमेण मनुष्यादिभावं कल्पयति । . . . तथा च स्वस्मिन्नेव सर्वप्रपञ्चकल्पकत्वात् जीवभावापन्नं ब्रह्म सर्वोपादानमिति दृष्टिसृष्टिवादिन आहुरित्यर्थः ।

Kṛṣṇānandatīrtha's Commentary on *S.L.S.*, p. 71 (1916), *The Chawkhamba Sanskrit Series.*

28. भवतु अवच्छेदवादपूर्वक दृष्टिसृष्टिवादः ।
सृष्टिदृष्टि संमत प्रतिबिम्बवादे तु कथं निर्वाहः ।

Advaita Brahma Siddhi, p. 216 (1981), Parimal Publication.

29. "Prakāśānanda was probably the first who tried to explain *Vedānta* from a purely Sensationalistic viewpoint of idealism and denied the objective existence of any stuff. The existence of objects is nothing more than their perception."
Dasgupta, S.N., *History of Indian Philosophy*, Vol. II, Ch. XI, p. 221 (1975), Motilal Banarsidass.

30. अत एव विविध (त्रिविध) सत्वमङ्गीकुर्वन्ति वृद्धाः ।

V.S.M., p. 25.

31. अविद्यायोनयो भेदाः सर्वेऽमी बुद्बुदा इव ।
क्षणमुद्भूय गच्छन्ति ज्ञानेकजलधौ लयम् ॥

Yv. VI (A), 127.20

32. अन्यथा गृहान्निर्गतस्य पुत्रपश्वादिसकलसाधनजातमपश्यतस्तदभावनिश्चयेन शोकाग्निना दह्यमानस्य रुदतो मरणप्रसङ्गः ।

V.S.M., pp. 25-26.

33. सत्त्वत्रयं वदन् वादो प्रष्टव्योऽत्राधुना मया ।
सत्यं द्वैतमसत्यं वा नाऽसत्ये विविधंकुतः ॥

V.S.M., p. 26.

34. किं द्वैतं पारमार्थिकेमाश्रित्य अज्ञातसत्त्वं साध्यते, उतानिर्वचनीयम् ? नाद्यः, प्रत्यक्षादिप्रामाण्यनिरासेन निरस्तत्वात् । अन्त्ये अनिर्वचनीयं प्रथमतः क्वचित्सिद्धं न वा ? न चेत् तर्हि दृष्टान्ताभावात् कथमाकाशादेरनिर्वचनीयत्वं साधनीयम् ? सिद्धं रज्जुसर्पादिकमिति चेत् तर्हि तत्र यादृशं सत्त्वं तादृशमेवाकाशादेः प्रपञ्चस्येति स्थिते विवेचनीयं किमज्ञातसत्त्वं किं वा प्रातीतिकमेव ? यद्यज्ञातमपि सत्त्वमाकाशादेः कल्प्येत तदा कथमयं दृष्टान्तो दार्ष्टान्तिके सामञ्जस्येनोपसंह्रियेत विरोधात् ।

V.S.M., pp. 26-27

35. न च गृहान्निर्गतस्यासत्त्वनिश्चयेन रोदनादिप्रसङ्गो दोषः, बाधकप्रमाणस्याप्रवृत्तत्वेन, अभाव-निश्चयानङ्गीकारात् स्वप्नवत्सर्वव्यवहारस्योपपादितत्वाच्च ।

V.S.M., p. 28.

36. न च तत्र बाधोऽस्तीति वैषम्यम्; प्रभावस्थायां कुत्रापि बाधस्यानङ्गीकारात् । प्रमाणप्रवृतो बाधेऽपि न कश्चिच्दोषः; तदानीं भ्रमसिद्धेन व्यवहारनभ्युपगमात् ।

V.S.M., p. 28.

37. न च त्रिविधसत्त्वाभ्युपगमविरोधः; सर्वस्य द्वैतस्य प्रातीतिकसत्त्वमपरित्यज्य ते भ्रन्तिसन्तोषमात्रस्य कृतत्वात् प्रातीतिकत्वेऽपि प्रपञ्चस्य भ्रान्तबुद्धिसिद्धावान्तरवैषम्यमाश्रित्य व्यावहारिकसत्त्वाभिधान-विरोधात् ।

V.S.M., p. 28.

38. तथाऽपि अज्ञातसत्त्वानभ्युपगमे सुप्तप्रबुद्धस्य स एवायं प्रपञ्च इति प्रत्यभिज्ञाने का गतिरिति चेत् ?

V.S.M,. p. 29.

39. एकस्यामेव रज्ज्वां मन्दान्धकारवर्तिन्यां दशानां युगपत्सर्पभ्रमेण पलायमानानां परस्परं संवादेन एक एव सर्पः सर्वैरनुभूत इति प्रत्यभिज्ञायां या सेवेति सन्तोष्टव्यम् । तत्र हि स्वस्वभ्रमसिद्धः सर्वैः पृथक् पृथगेवानुभूयते विषयः; अन्यभ्रमसिद्धस्यान्येन ज्ञातुमशक्यत्वात् अन्यभ्रमस्याज्ञानवत् । अविवेकादेव तु तत्र प्रत्यभिज्ञानमेक एव सर्पः सर्वैरनुभूयत इति ।

V.S.M., pp. 29-30.

40. एवं जाग्रदवस्थायां प्रपञ्चमनुभूय सुषुप्तिं गत्वा पुनरुत्थाय योऽयं प्रपञ्चानुभवः स प्रपञ्चान्तरमेव विषयीकरोति प्रत्यभिज्ञानं त्वविवेकादेव ।

V.S.M., p. 30.

41. न च सुषुप्तौ प्रपञ्चप्रलये प्रमाणाभावः,न हि द्रष्टुर्दृष्टेर्विपरिलोपोविद्यते अविनाशित्वात्, न तु तद्द्वितीयमस्ति ततोऽन्यद्विभक्तं यत् पश्येदिति श्रुत्या सुषुप्तौ द्वितीयाभावं वदन्त्या तत्र सर्वप्रपञ्चाभावस्य दर्शितत्वात् ।

V.S.M., p. 30.

42. इन्द्रियादेर्वस्तुतः प्रपञ्चज्ञानं प्रत्यकारणत्वात् । कुत इति चेत् तत्र वक्तव्यं किमिन्द्रियादेः प्रमितिमात्रे कारणता किं वा भ्रमप्रमासाधारणज्ञानमात्रे भ्रममात्रे वा ?

V.S.M., p. 32.

43. नाद्यः; इन्द्रियादिजन्यज्ञानप्रामाण्यं भ्रमविषयव्यावृत्तार्थविषयत्वेन साधनीयं भ्रमविषयव्यावृत्तार्थत्वं च प्रमितिविषयत्वेनेत्यन्योन्याश्रयात् । न च प्रमितिविषयत्वेमर्थसत्यत्वेहेतुरपि; मिथ्येदं रजतमिति प्रमित्याऽस्त्यस्यापि विषयीकरणात् . . .

V.S.M., p. 33.

44. किञ्च इन्द्रियाणाम् प्रमाणत्वेन अज्ञातार्थविषयत्वे वक्तव्येऽधिष्ठानमात्रविषयत्वं प्राप्तम्; प्रपञ्चस्य सर्वस्य जडत्वेन अज्ञातत्वाभावात् ।

V.S.M., p. 33.

45. तथा चाधिष्ठानत्वस्यात्मन्येव विश्रान्तत्वेन प्रत्यगात्मविषयाणीन्द्रियाणि प्रमाणानीति वक्तव्यम्, तच्च नोपपद्यते; प्रत्ययात्मन इन्द्रियाविषयत्वात्, तस्य निर्धर्मकत्वात् ।

V.S.M., p. 34.

46. तथा च श्रुतिः 'न सन्दृशे तिष्ठति रूपमस्य च चक्षुषा पश्यति कश्चिदेनम् , (*Kaṭh .U.p.* II.6.9.) पराञ्चि खानि व्यतृणत् स्वयंभूस्तस्मात्पराङ पश्यति नान्तरम्'(*Kaṭh Up.* II.4.1)

V.S.M., p. 34.

47. न चानयैव श्रुत्येन्द्रियाणां प्रपञ्चविषयत्वं दर्शितमिति वाच्यम्; स्वप्नेन्द्रियवदन्वयव्यतिरेकभ्रमसिद्धप्रपञ्चज्ञानकारणत्वानुवादेनात्मन इन्द्रियाविषयत्वप्रदर्शने तात्पर्यात् । एतेन भ्रमप्रमासाधारणज्ञानकारणत्वमप्यपास्तम् ; प्रमाकरणत्वस्य निरूपयितुमशक्यत्वात् ।

V.S.M., p. 34.

48. ततो ब्रह्मातिरिक्तं कृत्स्नकार्यजातं ज्ञानं ज्ञेयरुपं तत्सर्वमाविद्यकमेव इति प्रातीतिकमेय सत्वं सर्वस्येति सिद्धम् ।

V.S.M., p. 35.

49. न; भ्रमज्ञानस्याऽविद्यामात्रयोनित्वस्य त्वयैवोक्तत्वात्, ज्ञानं प्रतीन्द्रियान्वयव्यतिरेकयोश्च स्वप्नेन्द्रियान्वयव्यतिरेकवदुपपत्ते: । एवं घटादिकार्य्यमात्रे कारणाकाङ्क्षायां कारणत्वेनाविद्यैवोपसंहर्तव्या । तत्तदर्थिनां तत्कारणविशेषोपादानं तु तथैव स्वप्नवदुपपदनीयम् ।

V.S.M., p. 35.

50. अतोऽविद्याकल्पितस्य जगत: प्रतीतिसमकालीनमेव सत्वमुचितम्; रज्जुसर्पशुक्तिरजतगन्धर्वनगरस्वप्नप्रपञ्चेषु तथा दर्शनात् ।

V.S.M., p. 40.

51. प्रत्यक्षमिति चेत् तत्र घटोऽयमिति यत्प्रत्यक्षमिदमेव स्वस्याद् घटस्य भेदं विषयीकरोति प्रत्यक्षान्तरं वा ? स्वयमेव स्वविषयोदं गृहणाति प्रत्यक्षमिति चेत् तत्किं स्वप्रकाशं परप्रकाशं वा ?

V.S.M., p. 61.

52. तत्राद्ये स्वविषयविशेषणत्वेन भेदस्य मानेऽपि विशिष्टज्ञानस्य विशेषणज्ञानजन्यत्वपक्षे स्वेनैव भेदलक्षणविशेषणविषयेण स्वयं जन्यत इति प्राप्तं तथा चात्माश्रय: ।

V.S.M., pp. 41-42.

53. विशेष्यत्वेन भेदस्य भानै विशेषणविशेष्येन्द्रियसन्निकर्षमात्रं विशिष्टज्ञानकारणमिति पक्षे ज्ञानोत्पत्ते: पूर्वं भेदोऽस्तीति वाच्यं तथा च तस्यैव ज्ञानस्य कथं स भेदो विषय: स्यात्; स्वोत्पत्ते: पूर्वं एवस्येवाभावात्, . . .

V.S.M., p.43.

54. . . . ज्ञानान्तरस्य च स्वयंप्रकाशज्ञानाविषयत्वेन तत्प्रतियोगिकभेदाविषयत्वात् ।

V.S.M., p.43.

55. अवर्तमानस्य ज्ञानस्य परप्रकाश्यत्वे वर्त्तमानकालोपाधिकं स्वप्रकाशत्वमिति स्यात् । वर्तमानकाले ज्ञानस्वरूपमेव स्वप्रकाशमिति चेत् ? न ; अतीतानागतयोरपि तथात्वापत्ते: ।

V.S.M., p. 43.

56. नहि घट: कदाचिदघट इति स्यात् ।
इन्द्रियसन्निकर्षाश्रियस्य भेदस्य स्वसत्तामात्रेण
प्रमाणसत्तामात्रेण स्वविषयकज्ञानजनकत्वमित्यपि
प्रक्रियामात्रं प्रमाणाभावेन सत्तामात्रस्याप्यसिद्धे: ।

V.S.M., p. 44.

57. अस्तु तर्हि परप्रकाशज्ञानपक्षे प्रत्यक्षान्तरेण ज्ञानाज्ज्ञेयस्य भेदग्रह: । सोऽपि व्यावृत्तप्रतियोग्यादिग्रहपूर्वको न वेति विवेचनीयम् । न चेत् कथं भेदं विषयीकुर्यात् ? नहि निर्धर्मिकं निष्प्रतियोगिकं वा भेदं कश्चित्प्रत्येति; अयमसमाद्भिन्न इत्यनुभवात् । व्यावृत्तप्रतियोग्यादिग्रहपूर्वकत्वे तु व्यावृत्तिग्राहकप्रत्यक्षान्तरान्वेषणेऽनवस्था । तेनेव व्यावृतिग्रहे आत्माश्रय: । तस्माद्वस्तुमात्रावगाहि प्रत्यक्षं न भेदवार्ता जानातीति सिद्धम् ।

V.S.M., pp. 44-45.

58. अस्तु तर्ह्यनुमानाज्ज्ञानज्ञेययोर्भेदग्रहः । तथाहि विमतो विषयः स्वविषयज्ञानाद्भिद्यते, तद्विरुद्धधर्माश्रियत्वात्, यो यद्विरुद्धधर्माश्रयः स ततो भिद्यते, यथा घटात्पटस्तथाचायं तस्मात्तथा ।

V.S.M., pp. 45-46.

59. मैवम्; विरोधस्य भेदनिरूप्यत्वेन भेदासिद्ध्या विरोधासिद्धौ तद्विरुद्धधर्माश्रयत्वस्याप्यसिद्धेः, साध्याप्रसिद्ध्या व्याप्त्यसिद्धेश्च । नहि घटपटयोर्भेदः केनचिन्मानेन सिद्धो येन साध्यं प्रसिद्ध्येत् । प्रत्यक्षाभावेऽनुमानान्तरानुसरणेऽप्यनवस्थादिदोषस्य तादवस्थ्यात् ।

V.S.M., p. 46.

60. आगमस्याभेदमात्रे तात्पर्य्येण पर्यवसनस्य भेदबोधकत्वं शङ्कितुमप्यशक्यम् ।

V.S.M., p. 47.

61. ननु ब्रह्मणः सकाशात् सृष्टिं प्रतिपादयन्नागमः कार्यजातस्य ततो भेदमपि प्रतिपादयति । अभेदे ततो जन्मैव न स्यादिति चेत् ?

V.S.M., p. 47.

62. न; सृष्टिवाक्यस्य सर्वस्य प्रधानादिपरपरिकल्पितकारणान्तरनिराकरणपरस्य मृद्घटादौ कारणात् कार्य्यस्य भेदेनानिरुपणवद् ब्रह्मणः कारणात् कार्य्यजातस्य सर्वस्य भेदेनानिरुपणेनाद्वितीयब्रह्मसम्भावनामात्रे तात्पर्य्यात् । अन्यथा भेदपरत्वे तन्निषेधोऽनर्थकः स्यात् ।

V.S.M., p. 47.

63. किञ्च सृष्टिवाक्यं न तावत्साक्षाद्भेदं प्रतिपादयति; भेदवाचकपदाभावेनापदार्थस्य वाक्यार्थत्वाभावात् पदार्थस्येव संसृष्टत्वेन वा धर्मिमात्रपरत्वेन वा वाक्यप्रतिपाद्यत्वात् कल्पनायाश्च निषेधवाक्यविरोधेनानुत्थानात् ।

V.S.M., pp. 47-48.

64. न च ज्ञानमेव स्वातिरिक्तज्ञेयव्यतिरेकेणानुपपन्न स्वभिन्नं ज्ञेयं विषयीकरोति, न हि निर्विषयं ज्ञानं सम्भवति दृष्टं वा; सविषयस्येव भासमानत्वात्, अन्यथा निष्प्रकारकमेव भासेत । ज्ञाने विषयातिरिक्तस्यप्रकाशस्याभाववादिति वाच्यं, ज्ञेयव्यतिरेकेण ज्ञानस्यानुपपत्यभावात् ।

V.S.M., p. 48.

65. तथाहि तत्किं ज्ञानस्य ज्ञेयव्यतिरेकेणोत्वत्यनुपपत्तिः स्थित्यनुपपत्तिर्ज्ञप्तयनुपपत्तिर्वा ? नाद्यः, ज्ञानस्य स्वरूपत उत्पत्यभावात् , भावे वा प्रमाणतवाभासाभ्यामेव तदुत्पादनसम्भवे विषयानपेक्षणात्, ज्ञानस्य सर्वत्र विषयजन्यत्वे नियमाभावात् ।

V.S.M., p. 49.

66. ज्ञानविषयकज्ञानस्य विषयज्ञानाधीनत्वेन ज्ञेयं विना ज्ञप्त्यनुपपत्तिरस्त्विति चेत् ? न, ज्ञानस्य स्वयंप्रकाशमानत्वेन स्वव्यवहारार्थं स्वातिरिक्तानपेक्षणात्, परप्रकाशत्वेन ज्ञानान्तरापेक्षायां तस्याप्यन्यतस्तस्याप्यन्यतइत्यनवस्थित्या ज्ञानासिद्धौ जगदान्ध्यप्रसङ्गत्, अज्ञायमानस्यैव ज्ञानस्य स्वविषयसाधकत्वे प्रमाणाभावेन नरशृङ्गतुल्यस्य स्वरूपसत्वासिद्धेः ।

V.S.M., pp. 49-50.

67. अस्तु वा ज्ञानस्य स्वज्ञानार्थं ज्ञानान्तरापेक्षा तथापि विषयापेक्षणं कुतः विषयज्ञानस्येवापेक्षणात् ? ज्ञानसामान्यस्यानपेक्षणे स्वविषयव्यावृत्तज्ञानापेक्षायां विषयापेक्षाऽप्यवश्यसम्भाविनीति तत्तुच्छम्; ज्ञानस्य स्वत एव व्यावृत्तत्वात् परसिद्धजात्यादिवत् ।

V.S.M., p. 50.

68. तथापि ज्ञानस्य ज्ञेयव्याप्तत्वाज्ज्ञेयं बोधयतीति चेत् ? न; व्याप्त्यसिद्धेः ज्ञानज्ञेययोर्विभिन्नदेशत्वेन सामानाधिकरण्याभावात्, अतीतानागतार्थज्ञानदर्शनैनैककालत्वस्याप्यसिद्धेः ।

V.S.M., p. 51.

69. Prakāśānanda has given some stanzas which clearly emphasize the — non-difference between *jñāna* and *jñeya* :

प्रत्येतव्यप्रतीत्योश्च भेदः प्रामाणिकः कुतः ।
प्रतीतिमात्रमेवेतद्भाति विश्वं चराचरम् ॥१८॥
ज्ञानज्ञेयप्रभेदेन यथा स्वप्नं प्रतीयते ।
विज्ञानमात्रमेवेतत् तथा जाग्रच्चराचरम् ॥१८॥

V.S.M., p. 51.

70. आत्मन्येव जगत्सर्वं दृष्टिमात्रं सतत्वकम् ।
उद्भूय स्थितिमास्थाय विनश्यति मुहुर्मुहुः ॥२२॥

V.S.M., p. 52.

71. आत्मसत्तातिरिक्ताया द्वैतसत्ताया अभावात् आत्मनि दृष्टे सर्वं द्वैतं दृष्टं भवति, यथा रज्जुस्वरूपे दृष्टे तत्राध्यस्तानां स्रग्दण्डादीनां स्वरूपं दृष्टं भवति तद्वत् आत्मनि दृष्टे सर्वं दृष्टं भवतीति नानुपपन्नम् ।

V.S.M., p. 164.

72. प्राप्ताप्राप्तविवेकेन दृष्टिरेव परिणामोऽस्तु तदरिक्तदृश्याभावात् ।

V.S.M., p. 167.

73. . . . दृष्टेः फलरूपाया आत्मरूपान्तर्भावेन तत्परिणामत्वनुपपत्तेः । न हि स्वयं स्वस्य परिणामः, कात्स्न्र्येकदेशविकल्पेन परिणामपक्षानुपपत्तेश्च । ननु वितर्तेपक्षेऽयं दोषः समान इति चेत् .१ न, विवर्तस्वरूपापरिज्ञानात् । न ह्यधिष्ठानस्वरूपातिरिक्तं विवर्तो नाम किञ्चिद्वस्त्वस्ति यदाश्रित्य कात्स्न्र्यैकदेशविकल्पावतारः स्यात् । किन्त्वधिष्ठानमेव दोषवशाद्विलक्षणाकारेण भासमानं विवर्त इत्युच्यते ।

V.S.M., p.168.

74. बालान् प्रति विवर्तोऽयं ब्रह्मणः सकलं जगत् ।

V.S.M., p. 172.

75. नन्वविद्यायोनित्वं भावानां कार्य्यकारणभावमङ्गीकृत्य न वा ? न चेदविद्यायोनित्वमपि कथम् ? अस्ति चेत् कार्य्यकारणभावस्तदा यथायथमन्वयव्यतिरेकादिरेव प्रमाणम्; तत्र प्रकारान्तरासम्भवात् । तथा चान्वयव्यतिरेकादिसिद्धं मृदा विकारणत्वमपहाय अविद्याकारणंत्वामिद्यानमनुचितमेव ।

V.S.M., p.36.

76. . . . कारणवैचित्र्याभावेन कार्य्यविचित्र्यानुपपत्तेः, चेतनाछिष्ठानमन्तरेण जडशकतेः कार्य्यकारित्वानुपपत्तेश्च ।

V.S.M., p. 37.

77. अविद्याकारणवादिनाऽप्यदृष्टेश्वरादेः कारणत्वस्यावश्यं वक्तव्यत्वाल्लाघवातत एव विचित्रकार्योपपत्तौ किमज्ञानेन कारणत्वाभिमतेन कल्पितेन ।

V.S.M., p. 37.

78. तथा च प्रत्यक्षादेलौकिककस्य प्रमाणस्य पूर्वकाण्डस्य च पुत्रपशुस्वर्गादिकं प्रति यागादेः साधनताबोधकस्य प्रामाण्यं समर्थितं भवति । अन्यथा लोकवेदविरुद्धः कथं पक्षमवलम्बेत । तस्मादविद्यामात्रकारणकं जगदिति साहसमात्रम् ।

V.S.M., pp. 37-38.

79. यथा सतो जनिर्नैवमसतोऽपि जनिर्न च ।
जन्यत्वमेव जन्यस्य मायिकत्वसमर्पकम् ॥ १६॥

V.S.M., p. 38.

80. किमिदं कार्यं सत्यमसत्यं वा ? नाद्यः, एकमेवाद्वितीयमित्यद्वैतमात्रपर्यवसितागमविरोधात्, अनुपपत्तेश्च । तथाहि कियुत्पत्तेः पूर्वं कार्यं सदसद्वा ? असच्चेत् तर्हि शशविषाणमपि कारणव्यापाराज्जायेत; असत्वाविशेषात् । सच्चेत् किं कारणव्यापारेण पूर्वमपि तस्य सत्त्वात् कार्य्यत्वप्याघातच्च ।

V.S.M., pp. 38-39.

81. अभिव्यक्तिमात्रं कारणव्यापाराज्जायत इति चेत् ? न; तथापि सत्वासत्वविकल्पग्रासत्रासानपायात् । अस्तु तर्हि सदद्विलक्षणमनिर्वचनीयमेव कार्यम् । एवं चेत्तर्हि कार्यानुरूपानाद्यानिर्वचनीयाज्ञानमेव कारणमुचितम्; सत्यस्यासत्यहेतुत्वानुपपत्तेः लोके तथा दर्शनात् ।

V.S.M., p. 39.

82. न च कार्यवैचित्र्यानुपपत्तिः, विचित्रशक्तिकस्यैवाज्ञानस्य कल्पनादित्युक्तम् ।

V.S.M., p. 39.

83. न च पूर्वकाण्डस्य प्रामाण्यानुपपत्तिः । तस्यापि साध्यसाधनभावमुखेन सत्त्वशुद्धिद्वारेण प्रवृतिद्वारेण वा ब्रह्मण्येव तात्पर्य्यात् तात्पर्य्यार्थे श्ब्दस्य प्रामाण्यात् ।

V.S.M., pp. 39-40.

84. तस्मादविद्यायोनित्वं भावानां सुष्ठूक्तम् . . .

V.S.M., p. 40.

85. *Śruti* statements describing *Brahman* as the cause of the world.

सदेव सोम्येदमग्र आसीत्

Chā. Up. VI-2-1.

यतो वा इमानि भूतानि जायन्ते

Tai. Up. III.1.

तत्माद्वा एतस्मादात्मन आकाशः संभूतः

Tai Up. II.1.

— *Śruti* statements describing *Avidyā* as the cause of the worlds:

इन्द्रो मायाभिः पुरुरूप इयते

Ṛg. Veda. IV. 47-48.

मायां तु प्रकृतिं विद्यात्

Śve. Up. IV.10.

86. ब्रह्मज्ञानाज्जगज्जन्म ब्रह्मणो कारणत्वतः ।
अधिष्ठानत्वमात्रेण कारणं ब्रह्म त्रीयते ॥३८॥

V.S.M., p. 116.

87. . . . जगतोऽनाद्यनिर्वचनीया अविद्यैव कारणं न ब्रह्म, तस्य कूटस्थस्य कार्यकारणविलक्षणत्वात् . . .

V.S.M., p. 116.

88. न चाज्ञानमपि जगत्कारणं श्रुत्या विवक्षितम् ।
तस्य भ्रमनिमित्तमात्रत्वेनैवोक्तत्वात् कार्यकारणवादस्य
वेदान्त बहिर्भूतत्वात् विवर्तस्येव वेदान्तवादत्वात् ।

V.S.M., p. 117.

89. किं जगतः कारणमिति पृष्टे प्राप्ताप्रतिभानिवृत्तिमात्रप्रयोजनतया अज्ञानं कारणमित्यभिहितत्वाच्च ।

V.S.M., p. 118.

90. न निरोधो न चोत्पत्तिर्न बद्धो न च साधकः ।
न मुमुक्षुर्न वै मुक्तः इत्येषा परमार्थता ॥
V.S.M., p. 179.

91. Potter, Karl. H., *Presuppositions of India's Philosophy*, Ch. XI, p. 246, (1965), Prentice Hall of India (Private Ltd.) New Delhi.

92. Das, Umeshchandra, "Problems and justifications of the theory of *Dṛṣṭi-Sṛṣṭi*", In *Journal of Indian Philosophy*, Vol, V, p. 159, Sep.-Dec. (1977), D. Reidel Publishing Company, Holland, U.S.A.

11

Defence of *Dṛṣṭi-Sṛṣṭi Vāda*

THE meaning of the term *Dṛṣṭi-Sṛṣṭi-Vāda* and how it can be said to be the culmination of the *Vedāntic* thought is the matter of discussion here. Besides, the arguments put forth by the Realists in opposition to the *Dṛṣṭi-Sṛṣṭi-Vāda* and how ingeniously *Dṛṣṭi-Sṛṣṭi-Vāda* answers them will also be examined. But before entering into details the main aspects of the *Dṛṣṭi-Sṛṣṭi-Vāda* as emphasized in the *Vedānta Siddhānta Muktāvalī* by Prakāśānanda will be reviewed so that it becomes easier to understand the theory.

(i) *Dṛṣṭi-Sṛṣṭi-vāda* forcefully negates the unapprehended existence (*Ajñāta sattā*) of the world. It asserts that the creation (*Sṛṣṭi*) takes place only when it is seen. In other words, *Dṛṣṭi* itself plays the role of *Sṛṣṭi*. There is no creation apart from *Dṛṣṭi*.

(ii) Considering the world as illusory (*prātibhāsika*), *Dṛṣṭi-Sṛṣṭi-vāda* puts it on the same footing as a dream.

(iii) According to the *Dṛṣṭi-Sṛṣṭi-vāda* in deep sleep (*Suṣupti*), the world (*Prapañca*) is merged or disappears and on waking up from deep sleep, a completely new *prapañca* arises. But due to non-discrimination one is not able to distinguish between the two.

(iv) *Dṛṣṭi-Sṛṣṭi-vāda* holds that there is only one sentiency, which due to *Avidyā* (Nescience) becomes the *Jīva* and imagines itself variously in the form of God, the world, the *Jīvas* etc. Thus, it shows its preference for *Ekajīva-vāda*.

(v) The theory of Causation is absolutely rejected by the *Dṛṣṭi-Sṛṣṭi-vāda*. Only in order to avoid an awkward silence, it considers *Avidyā* or *Māyā* as the material (*Upādāna*) cause of the world. As a matter of fact, nothing is ever born, but due to *Avidyā* things seem to be existing, but this is merely an illusion. Thus, *Dṛṣṭi-Sṛṣṭi-vāda* ultimately ends in Acosmism (*Ajātivāda*), and presents the culmination of the *Vedāntic* thought.

This gives a bird's eye view regarding *Dṛṣṭi-Sṛṣṭi-vāda* as propounded in the *Vedānta Siddhānta Muktāvalī*.

As already stated that before the sixteenth century A.D., nowhere does one get a systematic exposition of *Dṛṣṭi-Sṛṣṭi-vāda*. It was Prakāśānanda who discussed the *Dṛṣṭi-Sṛṣṭi-vāda* in all its aspects for the first time in the *Vedānta Siddhānta Muktāvalī*. After that, one finds this theory mentioned as an established theory by Madhusūdana Sarasvatī, Appaya Dikṣita and others.

In the *Advaita-Siddhi* of Madhusūdana Sarasvatī, the pros and cons of the *Dṛṣṭi-Sṛṣṭi-vāda* is found. But, before one peeps into these details, it is necessary to make it clear as to what is meant by the term *Dṛṣṭi-Sṛṣṭi*.[1]

The Term *Dṛṣṭi-Sṛṣṭi*

Usually, the term *Dṛṣṭi* stands for visual knowledge while creation is meant by the term *Sṛṣṭi*.

The above-mentioned is the etymological meaning of the term *Dṛṣṭi-Sṛṣṭi*. But, here we are not much concerned with its etymological meaning. So the question arises as to what the philosophical term *Dṛṣṭi-Sṛṣṭi* stands for. We find the term defined in the *Advaita Siddhi*, in the *Siddhāntaleśasaṁgraha*, in the *Vedānta Siddhāntādarśa* etc. As mentioned in the *Advaita Siddhi*, the term *Dṛṣṭi* stands for consciousness conditioned by, or reflected on the mode (*vṛtti*) of *Avidyā*.[2] Hence, it is the mode of *Avidyā* that projects the illusory creation (*Sṛṣṭi*). *Avidyā* by its very nature is misleading. It conceals the real nature of a thing and projects it wrongly. *Brahman*, the Ultimate Spiritual Reality is all-pervading. But due to *Avidyā* it imagines itself as the *Jīva* and being the *Jīva,* it imagines various forms. So, *Avidyā* is the very root of the creation. It may be said that consciousness reflected on the mode of *Avidyā* takes the form of the things. That is to say, in the illusion of the snake, the mode of *Avidyā* is transformed into the snake, snakeness and its misconception. Thus, consciousness reflected on the mode of *Avidyā* itself acts as *Sṛṣṭi.* So *Dṛsti* itself is *Sṛṣṭi.* There is no *Sṛṣṭi* existing independently of its *Dṛṣṭi.*

In the *Siddhāntaleśasaṁgraha,* the term *Dṛṣṭi-Sṛṣṭi* is explained in two ways:

(i) *Sṛṣṭi* is created simultaneously with *Dṛṣṭi.*[3] That is to say, creation takes place at the very moment of perception.

(ii) *Dṛṣṭi* itself is *Sṛṣṭi.*[4] Here, *Dṛṣṭi* and *Sṛṣṭi* are considered identical.

In the *Vedānta Siddhāntādarśa* also these two types of *Dṛṣṭi-Sṛṣṭi-vāda* are mentioned.[5] so far as the *Dṛṣṭi-Sṛṣṭi-vāda* regards *Sṛṣṭi* as identical with *Dṛṣṭi,* it can be said that it comes very close to the *Sahopalambhaniyama* of the *Yogācāra Buddhism* (*Vijñānavāda*)[6] except that the *Vijñānavāda* does not recognise one universal consciousness as the Ultimate Principle or one *Jīva.*

In short, *Dṛṣṭi-Sṛṣṭi-vāda* is an Idealistic theory, which shows the relation of perception and creation. That is to say, it asserts that there is no creation (*Sṛṣṭi*) apart from its *Dṛṣṭi.* Existence is perception itself. (We can compare this concept with Berkeley's *"Esse est percipi"*).

It would not be wrong to state that the *Vedāntic* thought has acquired subtlety in the form of the *Dṛṣṭi-Sṛṣṭi-vāda.* But that does not mean that before the actual establishment of the theory this subtlety was utterly lacking in *Vedāntic* thought. In earlier *Vedāntic* works we positively get scattered glimmerings of the Idealistic thought, which ultimately resulted in *Dṛṣṭi-Sṛṣṭi-vāda* in the sixteenth century A.D.

It may now be examined how *Dṛṣṭi-Sṛṣṭi-vāda* is defended in the *Advaita Siddhi* against the attacks of the Realists.

Defence of *Dṛṣṭi-Sṛṣṭi-vāda*

In he *Advaita-Siddhi,* Madhusūdana Sarasvatī has prapared a safe ground for the *Dṛṣṭi-Sṛṣṭi-vāda* while rejecting the arguments of the Realists with full force.

The very first attack of the opponent is on the term *Dṛṣṭi-Sṛṣṭi.* Since the *Sṛṣṭi-Dṛṣṭi-vāda* holds that there is *Sṛṣṭi,* and so it is seen; it comes in direct opposition to the *Dṛṣṭi-Sṛṣṭi-vāda,* which emphasizes that there is no *Sṛṣṭi* other than *Dṛṣṭi. Sṛṣṭi* exists only when it is seen.

So, the first question is asked, "what is meant by the term *Dṛṣṭi-Sṛṣṭi?*

(i) *Is Dṛṣṭi itself Sṛṣṭi?*

Here, is *Dṛṣṭi* meant to be of the form of *vṛtti,* physics or is it of the form of *caitanya*? Neither of these alternatives is acceptable, as in the former case, even *Brahman,* which is the object of the final *vṛtti* would be *Dṛṣṭi-Sṛṣṭi* while in the second case, there would be the contingency of *Sṛṣṭi* existing at all times.[7]

(ii) *Or does it signify negation of Sṛṣṭi apart from Dṛṣṭi?*

In this second alternative, there would be the untenability of the usage as distinct viz. 'created by *caitra,* seen by me'.[8]

(iii) *Or does it signify the negation of the thing to be created apart from Dṛṣṭi?*

This also could not be accepted, for there would be contradiction of our experience viz. 'The jar is known but not the knowledge.'[9]

(iv) *Or does it mean that Sṛṣṭi is created by the causal assemblage of Dṛṣṭi?*

This alternative is also not admissible, for in this case jar is non-different from its perception on account of its being produced by the same causal complex and there would be the fault just mentioned.[10]

(v) *Or does it mean that Sṛṣṭi is simultaneous with Dṛṣṭi?*

This also is not tenable, for in the case of jar, etc. produced simultaneously with verbal knowledge, it would be a case of providing what is already produced and there would be the contingency elsewhere of the two being different things as in the case of jar and *śabda-jñāna.*[11]

(vi) *Or does it mean that Sṛṣṭi has the same existence as Dṛṣṭi?*

No, for this would be tenable even if both were real and so would be a case of *Siddha Sādhana.*[12]

(vii) *Or does it signify that it is different from sat and asast* ?

This alternative is also not acceptable, for this is itself of the form of *mithyātva,* and it is not proper to put it forth in order just to prove that very thing only.[13]

(viii) *Or does it signify that it is different from sat and asat being something outside the three-fold existence, viz. Pāramārthika, vyāvahārika and prātibhāsika* ?

No, since illusory existence (*prātibhāsika sattā*) is included in the three-fold existence, it is not possible for the world of this type to be beyond the scope of three-fold existence in the *Dṛṣṭi-Sṛṣṭi* view.[14]

(ix) *Or does it signify the absence of unapprehended existence* (*Ajñāta Sattā*)?

This alternative is not possible for this would hold good of utterly non-existent (*tuccha*) things also.[15]

(x) *Or does it signify existence, which can be known only?*

No, for in the case of happiness it would be equivalent to proving what is already proved and in other cases there would be the contingency of *Dṛṣṭi* and *Sṛṣṭi* being two different things like happiness and its knowledge.[16]

The above-mentioned arguments are refuted by the Idealist: What is meant is Existence which is a thing that is known only, it being based on its being occasioned by a fault; or absence of existence that is not known, or existence which is a thing that is known only, being produced by *Dṛṣṭi* of the substrate of what is known (*pratipannopādhi*), or existence that can be only known while not being capable of being known by any other seer. Thus the fault of *Siddhasādhana* in respect of the aspect of happiness etc., or the contingency of its being a different object will not arise.[17] (According to *Dṛṣṭi-Sṛṣṭi-vāda,* happiness etc. belonging to another person is not known, but is imagined in oneself only as belonging to another.[18]

Another objection put forth by the Realist is that, *Dṛṣṭi-Sṛṣṭi-vāda* would come into conflict with the statement of the ancient, viz. "*Jīva Īśo Viśuddhā cit tathā jīveśayorbhidā | Avidyā tacchitor yogaḥ ṣaḍasmākama anādayaḥ* || (Jīva, God, pure consciousness, the difference of *Jīva* and God, *Avidyā,* and its relation with consciousness these six are beginningless) as also with the texts of the *Brahmasūtra, Śāṅkarabhāṣya* and *Vivaraṇa* and the like, which recognise the enduring nature of the world on the strength of the fact of recognition, etc. as against the Buddhist.

In answer to this it is stated that *Dṛṣṭi-Ṣṛṣṭi* is accepted only in respect of *Sṛṣṭi* other than what is beginningless; and permanence is accepted in its nature as the cause. By this much only, refutation of the Buddhist theory of momentariness is possible and there is no contradiction of the basic texts, on the contrary one finds *Dṛṣṭi-Sṛṣṭi* justified at a number of places in the basic texts.[19]

As *Dṛṣṭi-Sṛṣṭi-vāda* asserts that *Dṛṣṭi* itself is *Sṛṣṭi,* and strongly negates the theory of Causation, another objection of the Realist is that if things are constituted of just knowledge, and are not produced by their respective causes, the injunction of *jyotiṣṭoma* for heaven in the *Veda* and the injunction of 'hearing' for the realisation of *Brahman,* and also the statements regarding the sky etc. being the causes of air etc. would all not be proper.

In answer to this it is stated, that such statements could be justified like the statement instructing about causality pertaining to a dream. And even then *Upaniṣadic* sentences and their critique would not come to be fully on par with a dream-statement and its explanation, for their difference is tenable by virtue of the sublation and non-sublation of their objects.

It may be argued that if *Dṛṣi-Sṛṣṭi* is accepted, it would no longer be necessary to indulge in the activity of eating for one's satisfaction, or in the activity of using articulate sounds for communication, and this activity would then be contradicted.

The answer to this is that this charge is set aside by looking upon this behaviour as possible like dream-behaviour.[20]

As the *Dṛṣṭi-Sṛṣṭi-vāda* negates the unapprehended existence (*Ajñāta sattā*) of things, the Realist in this context argues that since jar etc. would be non-existent before their knowledge, systematic ordering that each knowledge has its object would not be possible. Moreover, like silver etc. the substratum also viz. the 'this' element (of the mother of pearl) would also be non-existent before the knowledge 'this is silver', and so the *Taṭastha lakṣaṇa* of superimposition, viz. being produced by the causes. viz. contact of the sense-organs and the like or its *Svarūpa lakṣaṇa* viz. the appearance of a true thing (consciousness limited by 'this') as mixed up with a false thing would not be possible.

For this objection, the *Dṛṣṭi-Sṛṣṭi-vādin*'s answer is that this *Pratikarmavyavasthā* and the *Taṭastha lakṣaṇa* of superimposition are meant for people with lower intellect. And the *Svarūpa lakṣaṇa* has nothing in it that is contradictory to the *Dṛṣṭi-Sṛṣṭi* view. It is not that consciousness limited by the 'this' aspect, is not a thing; and it is not that a false form which does not appear as mixed up with it.[21]

In this very context the Realist again raises a doubt that at the time of the knowledge 'this is silver', nacreness etc. would be absent, so this contradicts the theory put forth that superimposition is the effect of its ignorance and so on.

This doubt is set at nought by saying that though nacreness may be absent at the time of the knowledge 'this is silver', yet there is nothing to contradict the existence of its ignorance.

Further, it may be argued that 'This is silver', 'This is not silver' — these knowledges have different objects and so they cannot possibly be related as sublated-sublator.

This argument can be refuted by saying that though the two knowledges may have different objects, since the objects are similar in form, the relation of sublated-sublator is possible, as in the case of the sublated-sublator of the dreaming state.[22]

It may be argued that if even the sublation of silver etc. is *Dṛṣṭi-Sṛṣṭi*, the unreality of the silver etc. cannot be proved by it.

This is refuted by saying that having 'not a lower' degree of existence is what accounts for its being the sublator and not having a higher grade of reality. So as the empirical is sublated by the empirical, there is no contradiction if the illusory is sublated by the illusory.[23]

Now, according to the *Dṛṣṭi-Sṛṣṭi-vāda*, the *Prapañca* is merged during deep sleep, and a completely new *Prapañca* is created while waking up from it. In this context, the opponent argues that since in deep sleep and dissolution etc. the division of the *Jīva* and *Brahman* is not known, it would be absent, so at the time of every deep sleep and dissolution the soul would come to be released and it would have to be accepted that it returns again to the mundane existence.

The answer to this objection is that since the division of the *Jīva* and *Brahman* is beginningless, it is not accepted as *Dṛṣṭi-Sṛṣṭi*. It is not true to say that since in the case of a sleeping person even the impressions are absent, it is not proper for him to awake again. This cannot be true for the impressions are present in their causal forms. (And this form is not *Dṛṣṭi-Sṛṣṭi*, for the *Jīva* cannot know the subtle state in the form of impression in deep sleep and dissolution).[24] Since liberation is of the nature of *Brahman*, it is not something other than consciousness and so unlike the liberation in a dream it would not come within the range of *Dṛṣṭi-Sṛṣṭi*.[25]

Another objection of the opponent is against the definition of the term *Dṛṣṭi-Sṛṣṭi*. It is argued that *Dṛṣṭi* of the form of just consciousness is not *Sṛṣṭi*, but *Dṛṣṭi* of the form of consciousness qualified by psychosis, or *Dṛṣṭi* of the form of psychosis should be regarded as *Sṛṣṭi* and in its case also another *Dṛṣṭi* would be its *Sṛṣṭi* and so there would be the fault of Infinite Regress.[26]

In reply to this it is stated that this argument is not proper. It is true that if consciousness alone be regarded as *Dṛṣṭi*, jar etc. having the same grade of reality should be regarded as everlasting. But what the term *Dṛṣṭi* signifies is consciousness having psychosis as its adjunct. Even in respect of *vṛtti* (mode), the psychosis or mode itself having its own nature would be the adjunct of consciousness; and so there would not be the fault of Infinite Regress. This also refutes the argument that if there is the non-existence of defect, ignorance, *adṛṣṭa*, body, sense-organs etc. there would be no illusion and therefore if they also are accepted as *Dṛṣṭi-Sṛṣṭi*, there would be the fault of Infinite Regress. Like dream-illusion the empirical illusion would be possible independently of body, sense-organs etc. that is to say, even in their absence. The argument noticed in presence and absence is as in a dream.[27]

It may be further argued that if *Dṛṣṭi-Sṛṣṭi* itself is *Dṛṣṭi-Sṛṣṭi*, jar etc. would cease to be *Dṛṣṭi-Sṛṣṭi*.

Such an argument is set aside by stating that even if the knowledge is the object to be known, the object of the knowledge does not cease to be something known, similarly even if *Dṛṣṭi-Sṛṣṭi* is *Dṛṣṭi-Sṛṣṭi*, jar etc. can be *Dṛṣṭi-Sṛṣṭi*.[28]

It could be further argued that there would be contradiction of the recognition of oneness if what was apprehended earlier is not now present; but this is not an illusion, for there is no sublating knowledge as there is in the case of lamp etc. regarding its different modifications, the flame being produced every moment. And if even then it is regarded as an illusion, then jar etc. also should be regarded as different in each moment, as also the self (*Ātman*) in every moment.

This argument is set aside by saying that the unreality of the world is determined by the *Śruti* passage, "Here, there is nothing like many . . . " so that the *Prapañca* is of the nature of just an illusion like *rajju-sarpa*, which is sublated as being existent at a time other than when it appears. So the recognition of things other than the self of different times is an illusion. The apprehension of 'one' in respect of *Ātman* and recognition of 'oneness' in jar etc. as conditioned by one time is not an illusion, for there is no sublation of the non-difference of the self, and of the jar etc. conditioned by one time. But the recognition of non-difference of jar as perceived by one man and another man at the same time is an illusion, for the appearance is different. Ten persons in slight darkness may have the illusion of the snake in respect of the same rope at the same time and start running. Because of the mutual agreement in regard to this experience, if they have the feeling or recognition that the same snake has been experienced by all, it is an illusion, for what is established by the illusion of one cannot be known by another. Similarly the jar perceived by one and the same person at two different periods of time could not be one and the same.[29]

In this context, again it may be asked as to how there could be the illusion of non-difference, when its cause similarity or the like is not at all there in anyone.

The answer to this is that like the illusion of non-difference in a dream, there is the possibility of similarity etc. as established by *Dṛṣṭi-Sṛṣṭi*.[30]

It should not be said that in that case non-difference alone should be produced, as this is something that is welcomed, for the restriction is in respect of a produced things only that they must be grasped ones. Moreover, there is no absence of the deciding factor as to where a known thing is produced and where it is not produced, for *Māyā* is admitted as having diverse powers.[31]

Now, it may be objected that on the basis of the illustration "This is that Devadatta", it is not proper to take the sentence *tat-tvam-asi* as meant to state oneness by *jahadajahallakṣaṇā*.

The answer to this objection is that as the time and place on the two occasions are different, so Devadatta also is different, so *jahadajahadlakṣaṇā* cannot, as a matter of fact, operate here. Still where *Dharmyabheda* is not grasped because of sublation or contradiction, but only *Dharmyabheda* is grasped, there

Jahadajahallakṣaṇā is possible; and so the illustration. "This is that Devadatta" is justified. It is not proper to say that even non-difference is *Dṛṣṭi-Sṛṣṭi,* so its knowledge cannot serve as a sublating factor. This is so because non-difference of *Ātman* is the very nature of *Ātman* and so is not *Dṛṣṭi-Sṛṣṭi,* and a thing can serve as a sublator by virtue of having a grade of reality that is not less.[32]

It may be further argued that even direct realisation is *Dṛṣṭi-Sṛṣṭi* and so is not produced by the means of knowledge and hence in the absence of knowledge, liberation should not be possible.

This argument is refuted by stating that even because its object is not sublated, the said knowledge is possible; and this remains intact even if it be *Dṛṣṭi-Sṛṣṭi.* Moreover, this does not contradict the *śruti* — The sky is firm, earth is firm, these mountains are permanent (firm), this entire world is firm.[33] Even those who regard things as non-eternal, have to explain the term *Dhruva* differently (not as eternal, but as lasting, possessing long life); it is better to explain it as conveying non-discontinuity of continuum till the end of the *kalpa.* Otherwise it would be difficult to expalin the expression *Dhruvo rājā*: The *Śruti*—"Thus only from this self — emerge all vital airs, all worlds, all *Vedas,* all elements, all these selves" — which says that the creation of vital airs etc. is from the *Jīva,* which wakes up after sleeping, in an authoritative statement supporting *Dṛṣṭi-Sṛṣṭi.*[34]

Here, it is noteworthy that the *Dṛṣṭi-Sṛṣṭi-vādins* quote the *Śruti* passage (*Bṛ. Up.* II. 1.20) in support of their theory that after waking up from deep sleep, new *prapañca* is created from the *Jīva.* From its previous context (*Atha yadā syuṣupto bhavati*) it seems that after deep sleep, the *Jīva* creates the whole *prapañca.* Moreover it shows that after the absolute absence of everything mundane, a completely new *prapañca* is created. Here, it would not be out of place to state that according to Śaṅkara, no role is performed by the *Jīva* in the act of creation. In the commentary upon the *Bṛ. Up.* II. 1.20. Śaṅkara has clearly stated that creation is strictly from the supreme self, for there is no capacity in the *Jīva* regarding the knowledge of creation, sustenance and destruction."[35] So we can see that Śaṅkara's way of presentation indicates his inclination towards *Sṛṣṭi-Dṛṣṭi-vāda,* as no role is assigned to the *Jīva* with regard to creation etc. but rather the supreme self is believed to be the creator of the world. On the other hand, the *Dṛṣṭi-Sṛṣṭi-vādins* quote this passage in support of the theory. Of course! one cannot state with certitude that this passage is the very root of the *Dṛṣṭi-Sṛṣṭi-vāda;* nevertheless, one can consider it as an expression, which must have finally resulted in the *Dṛṣṭi-Sṛṣṭi-vāda.*

The *Dṛṣṭi-Sṛṣṭi-vāda* asserts that all vital airs, worlds etc. emerge from the *Jīva* after deep sleep. In this connection, an objection may be raised by the opponent that the vital airs etc. are existent in the state of deep sleep, so it is not necessary to create them again.

In answer to this it is stated that the *Śruti* clearly says that everything of the nature of effect is dissolved in sleep. This does not contradict the *Śruti* affirming the existence of *Nāḍīs* in sleep.[36] Here, as a matter of fact, the gradual process of sleep is described. The arteries called *hitā* go from the heart to the *puritat;* moving through them the soul sleeps in *puritat.* This *Śruti* speaks of the existence of arteries in order to show the gradual stages in the period immediately preceding sleep and not also at the time of sleep for this would contradict another *Śruti* statement that there is nothing else.

It is further argued that the *Śruti* sentence "*Yatra eṣa etat supto'bhud ya eṣa vijñānamayaḥ purusaḥ kva eṣa tadābhut kuta etadāgata*" refers to *Brahman* which is the abode of the sleeping one and so *Ātman* should signify *Brahman* and hence the creation of the vital airs etc. should be the function of *Brahman* and not of the *Jīva* who rises from sleep; otherwise the statement of production of threads from the spider, sparks from the fire, etc. and the statement about the creation of the world would be false in meaning, for in the theory of *Dṛṣṭi-Sṛṣṭi* there is neither the production of threads etc. from the spider etc. nor the creation of the world.

This argument is refuted by saying that here the word *yatra* signifies time and so there is no reference to *Brahman.* In the next sentence, there is the use of two words. *'kva eṣa tadābhut'*. If *'yatra'* were to signify *Brahman* or place, the question *'kva'* regarding place would be unnecessary; and if time were not mentioned earlier, the late reference *'tadā'* would be out of place. The *Bhāṣyakāra* and others have explained it in this way, keeping in view the dull student. The statement regarding the production of threads from the spider etc. is made keeping in view the well-known theory of Causation established by worldly illusion.[37]

The creation of the world is in view of the manifestation of the different perceptions or knowledge. What is meant is that whatever he sees, he at the same time creates. It should not be argued that if the *Jīva* along with *Avidyā* is the cause, the diversity of the world would not be possible. This is not proper, for *Avidyā* which is the constituent cause of the world has diverse powers. Besides, other arguments in support have been given in the *Siddhāntabindu* and *Vedānta Kalpalatikā* etc.[38]

In the *Siddhāntabindu* as well as in the *Vedānta Kalpalatikā;* Madhusūdana Sarasvatī has put forth *Avidyā* as the constituent cause of the world.[39]

So, the entire assemblage of duality of the nature of *jñāna-jñeya,* apart from *Brahman,* is just a production of *Avidyā.* It has illusory existence. It is proved that like rope-snake, the world is not existent when it is not cognised; since it is the *Dṛṣṭi-Sṛṣṭi* of the one who is awake, and the *Śruti* speaks of its dissolution in sleep.[40]

It may be stated here regarding the *Dṛṣṭi-Sṛṣṭi-vāda,* as mentioned in the *Advaitasiddhi* that though the theory strictly adheres to the *Kevalādvaita Vedāntic* thought, it seems to be failing in satisfying the mundane mind; as it puts each and every practical dealing on a par with the dream. Every now and then, when contradictions with the worldly phenomena are put forth as objections, the *Dṛṣṭi-Sṛṣṭi-vādin* seems to give an evasive answer comparing everything with a dream. Of course, the *Dṛṣṭi-Sṛṣṭi-vādin* speaks only from the pedestal of the ultimate standpoint while regarding everything simply as an illusion. Outright rejection of the empirical existence has invited much criticism, and has not allowed the doctrine to be acceptable without reluctance, though it could be said to be the most logical outcome of the *Kevalādvaita* view.

Besides Madhusūdana Sarasvatī, Appaya Dikṣita has also given a brief presentation of the *Dṛṣṭi-Sṛṣṭi-vāda* in the *Siddhāntaleśasaṁgraha*,[41] which shall be stated here avoiding repetition as far as possible.

In Kṛṣṇānandatīrtha's commentary on the passage regarding the *Dṛṣṭi-Sṛṣṭi-vāda* it is stated that the early teachers have propounded the *Dṛṣṭi-Sṛṭi-vāda* following the *Śruti* which speaks of the origination and dissolution of the entire world in the waking state and state of deep sleep respectively. This *Śruti* is meant for those, who are desirous of Brahma-knowledge, such persons being those who see no difference even in the waking condition from the dream, as they have minds thoroughly purified by virtue of the fullest grace of God attained by diverse pursuits of knowledge and action.[42]

Explaining the absence of the unapprehended existence (*Ajñāta Sattā*) it is stated that a thing does not exist before it is actually apprehended. Moreover, it mentions that the experience of the elephant etc. even in the waking state is not one produced by the organ of vision.[43] On the contrary like the dream experience, it is of the nature of just 'witness'.[44]

Now, as the whole waking world is held to be an imagined one by the *Dṛṣṭi-Sṛṣṭi-vādin,* it may be doubted as to who imagines it — whether the unconditioned self or the self-conditioned by ignorance. But neither of the two alternatives is acceptable. For in the first case the unconditioned self-requiring no means would be present even in the state of liberation on the imaginary; and so the world would continue and there would be no difference from the mundane state. In the second case; ignorance also being something that is to be imagined; its imaginer should be said to be present even before its imagination.[45]

As a solution to such on objection, it is stated by some that every preceding soul conditioned by ingnorance is the imaginer of each succeeding ignorance; and as there is no beginning of this chain of imaginers and imagined objects, they would not creep in the fault of Infinite Regress. An objection may be raised that since *Avidyā* is accepted as beginningless it cannot be something imagined like nacre-silver, for otherwise the division of things into these having a beginning and these are beginningless would not be tenable. But this argument is not proper.[46]

In a dream, temples etc. are imagined as previously established, and some things are imagined as originating; so also in the waking state something are imagined as having a beginning and others differently, and this justifies the division of things into these having a beginning and these that are beginningless. This also explains the division of cause-effect. It may be noted that other thinkers of this school regard eternal things like *Jīva,* God, *Avidyā* as beyond the scope of *Dṛṣṭi-Sṛṣṭi-vāda.* The unreality of these, excluding *cit* (consciousness) can be proved on other grounds.

It may be further asked as to who is the imaginer of the creation of the elements viz. sky etc.; and their order, whichcan be known only from the scripture. If it is said that no one is the imaginer, then what is the basis of the *Śruti* stating the creation of the element from the self. The answer to this is that through the method of superimposition and negation the attributeless *Brahman* can be known.[48]

Thus, the statements regarding creation etc. are not meant to instruct us in regard to creation etc. but are meant only to give us knowledge of the Absolute *Brahman* devoid of any diversity.

The above exposition of the *Dṛṣṭi-Sṛṣṭi-vāda* reveals the facets of the theory already established in the *Vedānta Siddhānta Muktāvalī* by Prakāśānanda. Of course, it openly states that the *Dṛṣṭi-Sṛṣṭi-vāda* is grasped by those with absolutely purified intellect. Such a statement plainly puts the *Dṛṣṭi-Sṛṣṭi-vāda* on the zenith of the *Vadāntic* thought.

No doubt, the *Dṛṣṭi-Sṛṣṭi-vāda* is a unique solution to the riddle of the world, though it seems to be contradicted by our practical life and behaviour. This is especially so in the case of people engrossed in the reality of the mundane world, who cannot think of regarding the world as being like a dream.

It may be objected that the dreaming state is a result of the memories of the weking state. So it is possible to consider dream objects as unreal, but things perceived in the waking state cannot be unreal.

But this charge could be put aside by stating that the dreaming state is not based on the memories resulting from the waking state. In a dream, we experience the things never experienced before.[49] Besides, dream objects never come in contact with empirical sense-organs, which remain inoperative in sleep; and yet we imagine that we perceive through our sense-organs. This could be true of the waking state also.

In short, what is intended by this is to show that like the dreaming experience, the waking experience is also *Sākṣīrūpa.* Moreover, the motive behind this comparison is to show the illusory character of the phenomenal world, taking the extreme view, and that is why this theory remains far away from the scope of the common-intellect. As a matter of fact, it is the only theory which can be said to be the very culmination of *Vedāntic* thought.

The one pervading sentiency conditioned by *Avidyā-Vṛtti* is the agent of numerous creations. As Umesh Chandra Das puts it: "Sometimes it assumes the form of a fragrant flower and sometimes the smaller of that flower. Sometimes it turns into a melodious tune and sometimes the musician himself . . . At times it plays the part of a thief and at times the part of a judge punishing the theif. The Sun, the Moon and various other planets and stars all are part and parcel of it. How wonderful is its operation: Thus the theory of *Dṛṣṭi-Sṛṣṭi* presents us a view which is undoubtedly novel.[50]

Dṛṣṭi-Sṛṣṭi-vāda prefers only one sentiency conditioned by *Avidyā* known as the *Jīva.* Which is the creator of the world. This may seem to resemble monotheistic Idealism which recognises only one God as the creator of the world. But there is this difference that in *Dṛṣṭi-Sṛṣṭi-vāda*, the only *Jīva* is not regarded as God, who on the contrary is an imaginary construct along with other *Jīvas* and things.

Hence, *Dṛṣti-Sṛṣṭi-vāda* can be said to be an unparallel theory which has been described as the culmination of *Vedāntic* Idealism.

References

1. दृष्टिः— बुद्धिः । (दृश + भावे + क्तिन्।) दर्शनम्.

   शब्दकल्पद्रुम - द्वितीयः काण्डः, पृ. ७८०

   सृष्टिः निर्म्मितिः । (सृज् + क्तिन्।)

   शब्दकल्पद्रुम - पञ्चमः काण्डः, पृ. ८०७

2. वृत्त्युपहितचैतन्यमेव दृष्टिशब्दार्थः ।

   Ad. Si, p. 535.

   Sastri, N.S. and Ananda Krishna (ed.), *Advaita Siddhi* (1982), Parimal Publications.

3. अयमेको दृष्टि समसमया विश्वसृष्टिरिति — दृष्टिसृष्टिवादः ।

   *S.L.S.*Ch. II, p. 355.

4. अन्यस्तु दृष्टिरेव विश्वसृष्टिः।

   S.L.S., Ch. II, p. 355.

5. दृष्टिरेव भवेत्सृष्टिर्दृष्टिसृष्टिमते, तथा ।

   दृष्टिकालीनसृष्टिस्तु दृष्टिसृष्टिमतान्तरे ।।१।।

   — वेदान्तसिद्धान्तादर्शः, पृ. ६५ सं. १९४३

   - काश्याम्

6. Since *Sahopalambhaniyama* of the *Yogācāra* Buddhism emphasises that the knowledge of the object (*jñāna*) and the object to be known (*jñeya*) are identical, it comes very near to the *Dṛṣṭi-Sṛṣṭi-vāda*.

   See: Raval, C.V., *Philosophy of Śri Śankarācārya* (in Gujarati), Ch. III, p. 219, First Edition (1974), University Granth Nirmana Board.

7. दृष्टिरेव सृष्टिरिति — आद्ये वृत्तिरूपा, चैतन्यरूपा वा, दृष्टिरभिमता । प्रथमे चरमवृत्तिविषयब्रह्मणोऽपि दृष्टिसृष्ट्यापत्तिः । द्वितीये सर्वदापि सृष्ट्यापत्तिः ।

   Ad. Si., p. 533.

8. दृष्टिव्यतिरिक्तसृष्ट्यभावो वा — न द्वितीयः, चैत्रेण सृष्टो मया दृष्ट इति बैलक्षण्येन व्यवहारानुपपत्तेः।

   Ad. Si., p. 533.

9. दृष्टिव्यतिरेकेण सृज्याभावो वा— न तृतीयः

   ज्ञातो घटो न ज्ञानमिति अनुभवविरोधात् ।

   Ad. Si., p. 533.

10. दृष्टिसामग्रीजन्यत्वं वा — न चतुर्थः, एकसामग्रीप्रसूतत्वेन घटादेर्दृष्टयभिन्नत्वेनान्तरोक्तदोषात् ।

Ad. Si., p. 533.

11. दृष्टिसमानकालीनसृष्टिर्वा — न पञ्चमः, शाब्दाविज्ञानसमकालोत्पन्नघटादौ सिद्धसाधनात्, तद्वदन्यत्रार्थान्तरतापतेश्च ।

Ad. Si. p. 533

12. दृष्टिसमानसत्ताकसृष्टिर्वा — न षष्ठः, उभयसत्त्वेऽप्युपपत्तेः सिद्धसाधनात् ।

Ad. Si., p. 533.

13. सदसद्विलक्षणत्वं वा— न सप्तमः, अस्यैव मिथ्यात्वरूपत्वेन तत्साधनायैव तदुपन्यासानुपपत्तेः ।

Ad. Si., p. 533.

14. त्रिविधसत्त्वबहिर्भूतत्वे सत्यसद्विलक्षणत्वं वा नाष्टमः, त्रिविधसत्त्वमध्ये प्रातिभासिकसत्त्वस्याप्यन्तभावेन दृष्टिसृष्टिपक्षे तद्वति जगति तद्बहिर्भावानुपपत्तेः।

Ad. Si. p. 533.

15. अज्ञातसत्त्वाभावो वा — न नवमः, तुच्छसाधारण्यात् ।

Ad. Si., p. 533.

16. ज्ञातेकसत्त्वं वा न दशमः, सुखादो सिद्धसाधनात् तद्वन्यत्रार्थान्तराच्चेति ।

Ad. Si., p. 533.

17. दोषप्रयुक्तत्वनिबन्धनस्य ज्ञातेकसत्त्वस्याज्ञातसत्त्वाभावस्य वा, प्रतिपन्नोपाधिदृष्टिजन्यज्ञातेकसत्त्वस्य वा, द्रष्ट्रन्तरावेद्यत्वे सति ज्ञातेकसत्त्वस्य वा विविक्षितत्वात् । तथाच न सुखाद्यंशे सिद्धसाधनम् तद्वन्यत्रार्थान्तरं वा ।

Ad. Si., p. 533-34.

18. दृष्टिसृष्टिपक्षे पुरुषान्तरीयसुखादिकं न ज्ञायते, किंतु पुरुषान्तरीयत्वेन स्वस्मिन्नेव कल्प्यत इति भावः । Gauḍbrahmānandi commentary, p. 534, *Ad.Si.*, (1982), Parimal Publications.

19. अनाद्यतिरिक्तसृष्टिविषय एव दृष्टिसृष्टिस्वीकारात्, कारणात्मना स्थायित्वस्वीकाराच्च । तावतेव बौद्धाभिमतक्षणिकत्वनिराकरणोपपत्तेर्नाकरविरोधः, प्रत्युताकरेषु बहुशो दृष्टिसृष्टिरुपपादितेव ।

Ad. Si., p. 534.

20. . . . स्वप्नकार्यकारणभावबोधकवाक्यवदुपपत्तेः । न चैवं वेदांतवाक्यस्य सतन्मीमांसायाश्च स्वप्नवाक्यतन्मीमांसातुल्यतापत्तिः, विषयबाधाबाधाध्यां विशेषोपपत्तेः । अत एव — तृप्त्यर्थं भोजने परप्रत्यायनार्थं शब्दादौ च प्रवृत्तेरयोगेन स्वक्रियाव्याघात इति—निरस्तम्; स्वाप्नव्यवहारवदुपपत्तेः ।

Ad. Si., p. 534.

21. प्रतिकर्मव्यवस्थायाः संप्रयोगादिहेतुत्रयजन्यत्वरुपाध्यासतटस्थलक्षणस्य च मन्दाधिकारिविषयत्वात् । सत्यस्य वस्तुनो मिथ्यावस्तु संभेदावभास इति स्वरूपलक्षणं तु दृष्टिसृष्टिपक्षेऽप्यधिरुद्धम्, न हीदमंशावच्छिन्नं चैतन्यं न वस्तु; न वा मिथ्यारूपस्य तेन सह न संभेदावभासः ।

Ad. Si., p. 534.

22. भिन्नविषयत्वेऽपि विषययोः सारुप्यात् स्वप्नबाध्यबाधकयोरिव बाध्यबाधकभावोपपत्तेः ।

Ad. Si., p. 534.

23 बाध्यान्यूनसत्ताकत्वमेव बाधकत्वे प्रयोजकम्, न त्वधिकसत्ताकत्वमित्यस्योपपादितत्वेन व्यावहारिकेण व्यावहारिकबाधवत् प्रातिभासिकेन प्रातिभासिकबाधाविरोधात् ।

Ad. Si., p. 534.

24. तस्य च रूपस्य न दृष्टिसृष्टिः, असंभवात् न हि प्रलये सुषुप्तो वा संस्काररुपसूक्ष्मावस्था जीवेन ज्ञातुं शक्यते ।

Gauḍabrahmānandi Commentary, p. 534.

25. जीवब्रह्मविभागादेरनादित्वेन दृष्टिसृष्टित्वानभ्युपगमस्योक्तत्वात् । न च सुषुप्तं प्रति संस्कारादेप्यभावेन तस्य पुनः प्रबोधायोगः, कारणात्मना संस्कारादेः सत्त्वात् । न च मोक्षस्य दृगन्यत्वेन स्वाप्नमोक्षवत् दृष्टिसृष्टयापत्तिः, मोक्षस्य ब्रह्मस्वरुपत्वेन दृग्भिन्नत्वासिद्धेः ।

Ad. Si., p. 534-35.

26. चैतन्यमात्ररूपा दृष्टिर्न सृष्टिः, किंतु वृत्तिविशिष्टचैतन्यरूपा वा, वृत्तिरूपा वा, दृष्टिः सृष्टिः इति वाच्यम्; तथा च तस्या अपि दृष्टयन्तरं सृष्टिरित्यनवस्था इति . . .

Ad. Si., p. 535.

27. चैतन्यमात्रस्य दृष्टित्वे यद्यपि तत्समानसत्ताकतया घटादेः सदातनत्वापत्तिः, तथापि वृत्त्युपहितचैतन्यमेव दृष्टिशब्दार्थः । वृत्तावपि वृतिरेव स्वस्वरूपा चैतन्योपाधिरिति नानवस्था । अत एव दोषा ज्ञानदृष्टदेहेन्द्रियादीनामभावे न भ्रम इति तेषामपि दृष्टिसृष्टित्वे अनवस्थेति — निरस्तम्; स्वप्नभ्रमवद्देहेन्द्रियादिनैरपेक्ष्येणाप्युपपत्तेः। अन्वयव्यतिरेकानुविधानं न च तद्वदेव ।

Ad. Si., p. 535.

28. ज्ञानस्य ज्ञेयत्वेऽपि विषयस्याज्ञेयत्वा भाववत् दृष्टिसृष्टेर्दृष्टिसृष्टित्वेऽपि घटादेर्दृष्टिसृष्टित्वोपपत्तेः ।

Ad. Si., p. 535.

29. 'नेह नाने' त्यादिश्रुतिभिः प्रपञ्चस्य मिथ्यात्वेऽवधृते रज्जुसर्पादिवत् प्रतिभासमात्रशरीरत्वमेव प्रतिभासकालातिरिक्तकालसत्त्वे बाधकम्, अतो भिन्नकालानामात्मभिन्नानां प्रत्यभिज्ञा भ्रान्तिः । आत्मन्यैकप्रतीतिरेककालावच्छेदेन घटादौचैक्यप्रत्यभिज्ञा न भ्रान्तिः। एककालावच्छिन्नघटादावात्मनि चाभेदे बाधकाभावात् । पुरुषान्तर प्रतीतेन सहेककालावच्छदेनापि घटादौ प्रत्यभिज्ञानं भ्रम एव, प्रतिभासस्य भेदात् । यथा एकस्यामेव रज्जवां मन्दान्धकारवर्तिन्यां दशानां युगपत् सर्पभ्रमेण पलायमानानां परस्परसंवादेनेक एव सर्पः सर्वैरनुभूत इति प्रत्यभिज्ञा भ्रमः, अन्यभ्रमसिद्धस्यान्येन ज्ञातुमशक्यत्वात् ।

Ad. Si., p. 535.

30. स्वप्नभेदभ्रमवत् दृष्टिसृष्टिसिद्धसादृश्यादि संभवात् ।

Ad. Si. p. 535.

31. न चैवं—अभेद एवोत्पद्यतामिति— वाच्यम्; इष्टापत्तेः, रज्जुसर्पाधिवदुत्पन्नस्येव ग्रहण नियमान् । नच क्वचिदुत्पद्यते क्वचिन्नेत्यत्र नियामकाभावः मायाया विचित्रशक्तिकत्वाभ्युपगमात् ।

Ad. Si., p. 535.

32. यद्यपि धर्मवद्धर्म्यभेदोऽपि बाधित एवेति जहदजहल्लक्षणापि न युज्यते; तथापि यदा धर्मभेदो बाधान्न गृहीतः, किंतु धर्म्यभेद एव, तदा 'सोऽयमित्यादौ जहदजहल्लक्षणासंभवेन दृष्टान्तत्वोपपत्तिः । न चाभेदस्यापि दृष्टिसृष्टित्वेन तज्ज्ञानस्य बाधकत्वायोगः, आत्माभेदस्यात्मरूपत्वेन दृष्टिसृष्टित्वाभावात् अन्यूनसत्ताकत्वमात्रेण बाधकत्वोपपत्तेश्च ।

Ad. Si., p. 535-36.

33. न च 'ध्रुवाद्यौध्रुवा पृथिवी ध्रुवासः पर्वता इमे ध्रुवं विश्वमिदं जग' दित्यादिश्रुतिविरोधः, . . .

Ad. Si., p. 536.

34. दृष्टिसृष्टौ च 'एवमेवास्मादात्मनः सर्वे प्राणाः सर्वे लोकाः सर्वे वेदाः सर्वाणि भूतानि सर्व एत आत्मानो व्युच्चरन्तीति श्रुतिः सुप्तोत्थितजीवात् प्राणादिसृष्टिं प्रतिपादयन्ती प्रमाणाम् ।

Adl Si., p. 536.

35. तस्माद्युक्तं 'एवमेवास्मादात्मनः इति परमात्मन एव सृष्टिरिति ।
संसारिणः सृष्टिस्थितिसंहारज्ञानसामर्थ्याभावं चावोचाम ।
Śaṅkara's commentary on the *Br. Up.* II, 1.20.
Ten Principal Upaniṣads with Śāṅkarabhāṣya, p. 735, Reprint (1978), Motilal Banarsidass.

36. 'न तु तद्द्वितीयमस्ति ततोऽन्यद्विभक्तं यत्पश्ये'दित्यादिना सुषुप्तौ सकलकार्यप्रपञ्चलायश्रवणात् । न च सुषुप्तौ 'हिता नाम नाडय' इति नाडीसत्त्वप्रतिपादकवाक्यविरोधः . . .
Ad. Si., p. 536.

37. यत्रेत्यस्य कालपरत्वेन यच्छब्देन ब्रह्मणो निर्देशाभावात् । न च यत्रेत्यस्य ब्रह्मरूपाधिकरणपरत्वं कालपरत्वं वैत्यत्र विनिगमनाविरहः, अनन्तरवाक्ये क्वैष तदाभूदित्यत्र क्व तदेति पदद्वयोपादानस्यैव विनिगमकत्वात्, यत्रेत्यनेन देशनिर्देशे क्वेति देशप्रश्नानुपपत्तेः, कालनिर्देशे च तदेति प्रतिनिर्देशानुपपत्तेः, भाष्यकारादिभिश्च स्थूलाधिकारिणं प्रति तथा व्याख्यानात्, ऊर्णनाभ्यादेस्तन्त्वाधिजन्मोत्पतिस्तु लौकिकभ्रमसिधिद्धकार्यकारणभावप्रसिद्धिमनुरुध्य ।
Ad. Si., p. 536-37.

38. सर्वलोकादिसृष्टिश्च तत्तदृष्टिव्यक्तिममिप्रेत्यः यदा यत् यश्यति, तत्समकालं तत् सृजतीत्यत्र तात्पर्यात् । न चाविद्यासहकृतजीवकारणकत्वे जगद्वैचित्र्यानुपपत्तिः, जगदुपादानस्याज्ञानस्य विचित्रशक्तिकत्वात् । उपपत्त्यन्तरेचात्र सिद्धान्तबिन्दुकल्पलतिकादावस्माभिरभिहितम् ।
Ad. Si., p. 537.

39. अविद्यातद्द्वयाप्यतत्कार्यात्मकः प्रपञ्चो दृश्यपदार्थः ।
Si.Bi., p. 93.
अज्ञानस्य च विश्वभ्रमोपादानत्वेन, अद्वितीयचैतन्ये कल्पितत्व वक्ष्यामः ।
Vedānta Kalpalatikā, pp. 35-36.
Krmarkar, R.D. (ed.), *Vedānta Kalpalatikā*, (1962), Bhandarkar Oriental Research Institute.

40. तस्मात् ब्रह्मातिरिक्तं कृत्स्नं द्वैतजातं ज्ञानज्ञेयरूपमाविद्यकमेवेति प्रातीतिकसत्त्वं सर्वस्येति सिद्धम् । रज्जुसर्पादिवद्विश्वं नाज्ञातं सदिति स्थितम् । प्रबुद्धदृष्टिसृष्टित्वात्सुषुप्तौ च लयश्रुतेः ।
Ad. Si., p. 537.

41. The *Siddhāntaleśasaṁgraha*, ch. II, pp.350-56 (1916), The Chowkhamba Sanskrit Series Office.

42. ये त्वधिकारिणो बहुविधज्ञानकर्मानुष्ठानसाधितनिरतिशय परमेश्वरप्रसादमहिम्ना नितान्तनिर्मलीकृतान्तःकरणस्सन्तो जागरेऽपि स्वप्नाद्विशेषं न पश्यन्ति, तान् ब्रह्मविद्याकामानधिकृत्य प्रवृत्तां कृत्स्नस्य जगतः प्रबोधस्वापावस्थायोः प्रभवप्रलयप्रतिपादिकां श्रुतिमनुसृत्य दृष्टिसृष्टिवादः पूर्वाचार्यैर्निरुपितः ।
Kṛṣṇānandatīrtha's commentary on the *S.L.S.*, Ch. II, p. 350.

43. . . . जाग्रद्गजाद्यनुभवोऽपि न चाक्षुष इति . . .
S.L.S., Ch. II, p. 350.

44. किंतु स्वप्नानुभववदेव केवलसाक्षिरूप इत्यर्थः ।
Kṛṣṇānandatīrtha's commentary on the *S.L.S.*, Ch. II, p. 350.

45. ननु, दृष्टिसृष्टिमवलम्ब्य कृत्स्नस्य जाग्रत्प्रपञ्चस्य कल्पितत्वोपगमे कस्तस्य कल्पकः — निरुपाधिरात्मा वा, अविद्योपहितो वा ? नाद्यः । मोक्षेऽपि साधनान्तर निरपेक्षस्य कल्पकस्य सत्वेन प्रपञ्चानुवृत्त्या संसाराविशेषप्रसंङ्गात् । न द्वितीयः । अविद्याया अपि कल्पनीयत्वेन तत्कल्पनात्प्रागेव कल्पकसिद्धेर्वक्तव्यत्वात् ।
S.L.S., Ch. II, p. 351.

46. अत्र केचिदाहुः — पूर्वपूर्वकल्पिताविद्योपहित उत्तरोत्तराविद्याकल्पकः । अनिदंप्रथमत्वाच्च कल्पककल्पनाप्रवाहस्य नानवस्थादोषः । न चाविद्याया अनादित्वोपगमाच्छुक्तिरजतवत् कल्पितत्वं न युज्यते, अन्यथा साधनादिविभागानुपपत्तेरिति वाच्यम् ।

    S.L.S., Ch. II, p. 351-52.

    Mehta M.D. *Siddhāntabheda,* p. 64;
    Sujña Gokulji Zala Vedānta Prize Essay (1894).

47. यथा स्वप्ने कल्प्यमानं गोपुरादि किञ्चित् पूर्वसिद्धत्वेन कल्प्यते, किञ्चित्तदानीमुत्पाद्यमानत्वेन, एवं जागरेऽपि किञ्चित् कल्प्यमानंसादित्वेन कल्प्यते, किञ्चिदन्यथेति तावता साधनादिविभागोपपत्तेः। एतेन कार्यकारणविभागोऽपि व्याख्यात इति ।

    S.L.S., Ch. II, p. 352.

48. नन्वेवमपि श्रुतिमात्रप्रतीतस्य वियदादिसर्ग तत्क्रमादेः कः कल्पकः ? । न कोऽपि । किमालम्बना तर्हि, आत्मनः आकाशः सम्भूतः 'इत्यादिश्रुतिः ? । . . . अध्यारोपपवादाभ्यां निष्प्रपञ्चब्रह्मप्रतिपत्तिर्भवतीति . . .

    S.L.S., Ch. II, p. 353.

49. In the *Gauḍapādakārikā,* Gauḍapāda has emphasized this fact, and has emphasized the similar characteristics of the waking state as well as of dreaming state.

50. Das, Umesh Chandra, 'Problems and Justifications of the theory of *Dṛṣṭi-Sṛṣṭi*'. In *Journal of Indian Philosophy,* Vol. V, p. 152, Sept-Dec. 1977.

12

Résumé

DURING the span of eleven chapters the main aim has been to visualise a total picture of the origin, development and establishment of the *Dṛṣṭi-Sṛṣṭi-vāda*. *Dṛṣṭi-Sṛṣṭi-vāda,* the culmination of the *Vedāntic* thought, is not a sudden outcome, but is a gradual development starting from the *Vedic* period and ending with the post-Śaṅkara period. In this concluding chapter, the stages of the development of Idealistic thought and how the *Dṛṣṭi-Sṛṣṭi -vāda* tries to solve the riddle of the world appearance has been recapitulated.

It has been found that in the early *Vedic* period not a single hint can be detected which could suggest the unreality of the worldly phenomena. On the contrary, Nature in all its aspects is considered as having some super power. Of course, henotheistic views are found gradually transformed into monotheistic views. A very feeble hint appears in one philosophical hymn (X.129), in which some queries are put forth about the origin of the world. How has the world emerged? What was there in the beginning — *sat* or *asat*? But nobody knows. Who could know? Such doubts show that the human intellect is incapable of fathoming the mystery of the world of appearance. The human intellect can only imagine the various ways of solving the riddle of the world. Either there was something, from which the world emerged or there was nothing. But even this does not stand the test of reason. This world could be an unreal projection which appears as real due to some misguiding force.

This hymn can be said to have paved the ways for mysticism, scepticism and Idealism. In short though the unreality of the worldly phenomena is not indicated clearly, one can consider it as possessing an expression which can lead towards the type of Idealism which negates the reality of the world.

Then in the *Upaṇisads* one finds the final emphasis on the non-dual sentiency as the Ultimate Reality. Everything also apart from the non-dual sentiency; viz. *Brahman* is considered unreal. There are stray expressions related to the unreality of the phenomenal world. The *Chāndogya Upaniṣad* very clearly emphasizes that everything having name and form comes forth by speech. This could mean that only the non-dual sentiency is the basic Ultimate Reality, while everything else is just its transformation. This could lay the firm foundation of the theory of Transforamtion (*priṇāmavāda*). But the expression used is such that it was easily interpreted as asserting the Reality of the one Absolute principle and the unreality of everything else which is but a fabrication of speech. And thus interpreted, the *Upaniṣadic* expression became the very root-source of Idealistic *Advaitic* thought.

Strikingly enough, a statement of the *Bṛhadāraṇyaka Upaniṣad* (*Ātmanastu kāmāya sarvaṁ priyaṁ bhavati*) can be said to contain a germ of subjectivism. It states that everything is dear for the sake of the self. What does it indicate? That nothing is good or bad by itself. All the things are relative by nature. The way one looks at a thing makes it either good or bad. Hence it can be said that the world is a projection of the self. It appears as we imagine it. So here is the root of subjectivism, which might have led towards the type of Idealism that declares the world as a projection of the mind. Here it has been stressed that perhaps this was not what was meant by the *Upaniṣadic* sage as this world was too early in the development of the concept in Indian philosophical thought. Perhaps what he meant was that everything has value inasmuch as it is related to the underlying Absolute Reality, the Self. But the expression could also be easily interpreted on subjectivistic lines everything is dear not for its sake, but for one's own sake or pleasure.

Other Idealistic expression are found in the *Bṛhadāraṇyaka* as well as in the *Aitareya Upaniṣads,* which announce that the world emerged from the consciousness.[1] So everything is of the nature of consciousness. It can be said that nothing exists but the consciousness. Then it could be said that it must be the power of ones own nescience which projects unreal things.

In short, though the *Upaniṣads* do not emphasize the unreality of the phennomenal world clearly, it can be said that as showing the way towards Idealism. On the whole the *Upaniṣads* declare non-dual sentiency as the Ultimate Reality and emphasize the creation as emerging from the Supreme Self viz. *Brahman.* At the same time they negate everything else apart from *Brahman.* Hence it can be said that rejection of everything apart from *Brahman* might have led towards the type of Idealism which negates the reality of the world.

After the *Upaniṣadic* era, Idealistic thought is found developed in the Buddhist schools namely — the *Mādhyamika* and the *Vijñānavāda* (*Yogācāra*). Both the schools emphasize the unreality of the phenomenal world on the basis of theory of dependent origination. Moreover as the things are relative, it is not possible to state anything either positively or negatively about them. Nothing can be explained or understood by reason, and so the reality of anything cannot be accepted. Though the *Mādhyamika* school reveals Idealistic views, the *Vijñānavāda* school is more helpful in the direction of that type of Idealism which is putforth by the *Dṛṣṭi-Sṛṣṭi-vāda.* The *Vijñānavāda* school regards the world as something projected by the mind. Besides it compares the eternal world with a dream. Moreover, the law of simultaneous Apprehension (*Sahopalaṁbhaniyama)* emphasizes a view very similar to *Dṛṣṭi-Sṛṣṭi-vāda.* It asserts that a thing to be known (*jñeya*) and its knowledge (*jñāna*) are not known apart from each other and so must be identical. In other words, there is no difference between *jñāna* and *jñeya.* According to *Dṛṣṭi-Sṛṣṭi-vāda* also *Sṛṣṭi* and its percipi (*Dṛṣṭi*) are both identical. So it can be said that the *Vijñānavāda* and the *Dṛṣṭi-Sṛṣṭi-vāda* are parallel streams of the extreme Idealistic thought.

The influence of these Buddhistic schools on the *Vedāntic*

thought is conspicuous. The *Yoga-Vāsiṣṭha* as well as the *Gauḍapādakārikā* assert the world as unreal as it is projected by the mind. Both these works compare the waking world with the dreaming world and thus suggest its illusory character. Like the *Mādhyamika* school, Gauḍapāda has refuted the theory of Causation which shows that in no way is production justifiable or possible. The *Yoga-Vāsiṣṭha* contains Idealistic thought having some new dimensions. It tries to solve the problem of the common world experience. It declares the world as something created by the *Avidyā* of the cosmic soul (*Hiraṇyagarbha*). Due to cosmic *Avidyā* everyone experiences one common world. For the first time in Brahmanical philosophy one finds Idealistic thought attempted to be systematically presented in the *Yoga-Vāsiṣṭha* and the *Gauḍapadakārikā* though there is some vagueness in the expression. In the *Yoga-Vāsiṣṭha, Avidyā* is considered to be the material cause of the world of appearance.[2] It has been seen that according to *Dṛṣṭi-Sṛṣṭi-vāda, Avidyā* is the material cause of the world. Moreover, the term *Dṛṣṭi-Sṛṣṭi* is used for the first time in the *Yoga-Vāsiṣṭha*. Of course, its precise meaning cannot be determined. Still it can be said that the *Yoga-Vāsiṣṭha* contributes much to the onward march towards *Dṛṣṭi-Sṛṣṭi-vāda*.

It can be concluded from this that one current of pre-Śaṅkara *Vedāntic* thought was in favour of the unreality of the phenomenal world. The world is repeatedly compared with a dream, *gandharvanagara*, mirage and a barren woman's son. Of course, one does not find any hint which positively condemns the Objective Reality of the empirical world.

Śaṅkara, on the other hand clearly admits the Objective Reality of the empirical world. Before the dawn of knowledge, everything is considered real and meaningful. Refuting the *Vijñānavāda* school of Buddhism, he even differentiates the waking state from the dreaming state. So it can be stated that eventhough Śaṅkara negates everything apart from *Brahman*, he certainly affirms the empirical world as real from the phenomenal point of view. Moreover, he considers *Brahman* as the material cause of the world. These points do not agree with the *Dṛṣṭi-Sṛṣṭi-vāda*. In short, Śaṅkara's views would favour

Sṛṣṭi-Dṛṣṭi-vāda and not the *Dṛṣṭi-Sṛṣṭi-vāda.*

But after Śaṅkara the yet unsolved question about the locus of *Avidyā* was put forth by his followers, which gave scope to the two streams favouring *Sṛṣṭi-Dṛṣṭi-vāda* and *Dṛṣṭi-Sṛṣṭi-vāda.* Mostly all of the Śaṅkarites except Maṇḍana Miśra and Vācaspati Miśra consider *Brahman* as the locus of *Avidyā.* Thus *Brahman* becomes the meterial cause of the world. Then naturally the Objective Reality of the phenomenal world would be recognised. On the other hand Maṇḍana Miśra as well as Vācaspati Miśra regard the *Jīva* as the locus of *Avidyā.* Thus the *Jīva* can be said to be the one who projects the world of appearance. It may be said that this point is not found specifically discussed in the *Brahmasiddhi,* and unfortunately Vācaspati's commentary *Tattva Samikṣā* on it is irretrievably lost. This subjectivistic trend of thinking paved the way for *Dṛṣṭi-Sṛṣṭi-vāda* in the true sense. Of course, one does not find related problems discussed in detail — how the *Jīva* creates the world — how the world is common for all — whether it is created by many *Jīvas* or a single *Jīva.* Later Śaṅkarites attempted to give their own solutions is conformity with the fundamental principle of *Kevala-Advaita.* Appaya Dikṣita has compiled in his *Siddhāntaleśasaṁgraha* various views relating to creation, locus of *Avidyā,* manyness and oneness of the *Jīva* etc.

Before Appaya Dikṣita one finds these moot problems discussed and attempted to be solved in the *Vedānta Siddhānta Muktavalī* by Prakāśānanda, who has firmly established the *Dṛṣṭi-Sṛṣṭi-vāda.*

Who is the creator of the world? How is the world considered one and common for all? Is the plurality of the *Jīvas* real or unreal? Does the world exist or not when not perceived? *Dṛṣṭi-Sṛṣṭi-vāda* in its own way presents a unique solution for all these questions. It simply puts the world on a par with a dream. And thus considering all the things as illusory as the dream-world, it solves all the difficulties.

Dṛṣṭi-Sṛṣṭi-vāda adheres to the *Kevalādvaita Vedānta* in the true sense of the term. That is to say it condemns even the empirical existence of the world and emphasizes the reality of only the Ultimate Sentiency viz. *Brahman;* and thus has been said to present the culmination of the *Vedāntic* thought.

It has been seen that putting forth logical arguments, *Dṛṣṭi-Sṛṣṭi-vādin* shows that no means of knowledge is capable of proving the difference of thing to be known and its knowledge. As everything is consciousness, how can there be any other thing existing? Then this world of appearance must be fictitious or illusory. It is right to say that when *Dṛṣṭi* (mode of *Avidyā*) works, this *Sṛṣṭi* is projected. In other words, *Dṛṣṭi* itself is *Sṛṣṭi.* Thus the unapprehended existence of things is thoroughly rejected in the *Dṛṣṭi-Sṛṣṭi-vāda.*

It is noteworthy that according to *Dṛṣṭi-Sṛṣṭi-vāda,* the non-dual ultimate sentiency is the only reality, which due to *Avidyā* imagines itself as the *Jīva* and then it imagines various bodies of god, animals, human beings etc. so even *Īśvara* is an imagination of the *Jīva.* Even the alleged emancipation of individual *Jīvas* is considered imaginary; and so the liberation of *Śuka* etc. is said to be nothing else but eulogy.

Moreover, as *Dṛṣṭi-Sṛṣṭi-vāda* puts every practical dealing on a par with a dream, it faces many controversies. But for that it cannot be brushed aside. It should not be forgotten that it is a theory which solves the riddle of the world-appearances in its own way, and that is what each and every theory does to solve the problem in its own way.

To the lay man, the concept of the illusoriness of the world seems to be utterly absurd. The masses hold that the world which is so much with them, is a part and parcel of God's will, and God is the only creator of the world; they cannot consider the world to be illusory like a dream. But as claimed by Appaya Dikṣita, though *Dṛṣṭi-Sṛṣṭi-vāda* is difficult to understand for a lay man, since it reveals the highest *Vedāntic* thought, only one with a highly purified mind can follow it. Nevertheless, it is wonderful to live in this complex world regarding it a huge dream.

References

1. अस्मादात्मनः सर्वे प्राणाः सर्वे लोकाः सर्वे देवाः सर्वाणि भूतानि व्युच्चरन्ति . . .

   Br. Up. I.20.

   . . . यच्च स्थावरं सर्वन्तत्प्रज्ञानेत्रं प्रज्ञानं प्रतिष्ठितं . . .

   Ai. Up. II.6.3.

2. *Yv.* VI (A), 127.20.

Glossary

Ābhāsa: Illusion.

Ābhāsavāda: The theory of illusion.

Ācārya : Preceptor.

Adhiṣṭhāna : Substratum/Locus.

Ādi Prajāpati : Mythological God Brahmā.

Adṛṣṭa : Unapprehensible.

Adhyāropa-apavāda : Imposition and Negation.

Adhyāsa : Superimposition.

Advaita : Non-duality.

Advaita Prakaraṇa : The third chapter of the *Gauḍapādakārikā.*

Adhyāya : Chapter.

Agrahaṇa : Non-apprehension.

Ahaṁkāra : The third of the eight elements of creation according to the *Sāṁkhya* Philosophy.

Aja : Unborn.

Ajāti : Non-origination.

Ajātivāda : Acosmism/The theory of non-orgination.

Ajñāna : Ignorance.

Ajñāta Sattā : Unapprehended existence.

Ākāśa : One of the five gross elements of creation.

Ālaṁbanaparikṣā : A treatise of the *Vijñānavāda* Buddhism.

Alāta cakra : Fiery circle.

Ālaya-vijñāna : Store consciousness.

Aṁśa : Part.

Anādi : Beginningless.

Anātman : Non-sentient matter.

Anavasthā : The fault of Infinite Regress.

Anekajīva-vāda : The theory that holds that there are numerous souls.

Anekajīvāśrita-eka-Avidyā-vāda : The theory that holds that there are many *Avidyās* as there are many *Jīvas*.

Aṅgulas : A kind of measurement of a thumb.

Anirvacanīya : Inexplicable.

Anirvacanīya khyāti : Inexplicable illusory perception. It is a view of *Advaita Vedāntin*.

Anvaya-vyatireka : Positive and Negative limbs of the *Nigamana*. These are two limbs of the syllogism according to *Nyāya* system of thought.

Anyathāgrahaṇa : Misapprehension.

Āp : Water/one of the five gross elements of creation.

Apekṣābuddhi : The notion which refers to many unities.

Artha : object/purpose.

Arūpadhātu : The immaterial world or the realm of formlessness.

Asat kalpa : As good as non-existent.

Asat Kāryavāda : *Nyāya-Vaiśeṣika* theory of causation, according to which effect does not exist in the cause.

Āśrama : Stages of life according to the Brahmanical tradition.

Āśraya : Locus/substratum.

Asyavāmīya Sūkta : One of the philosophical hymns of the *Ṛgveda*.

Ātivāhika : Intermediary body which carries the soul to the other world.

Ātman : Spirit/soul.

Avacchedavāda : The theory of limiting-adjunct.

Āvaraṇaśakti : One of the powers attributed to *Māyā*.

Avayavin : The whole.

Avidyā : Nescience.

Avidyāpratyupasthāpita : Brought about by Nescience.

Avidyā Vṛtti : Residual impression of Nescience.

Aviśeṣa-aneka- śarīra-eka-jīva-vāda : The theory that holds that only one *Jīva* resides in numerous bodies.

Avyakta : The unmanifest.

Bhāṣya : Annotation.

Bhāva : Existing.

Bhedābheda : The *Vedāntic* concept of Bhāskarācārya according to whom an individual soul (*Jīva*) is different as well as non-different from *Brahman* — the Ultimate Reality

Bījāṅkūra-nyāya : The maxim of seed and sprout. It takes its origin from the relation of mutual causation which subsists between seed and sprout.

Brahmā : Mythological God.

Brahman : The *Vedāntic* term for the Ultimate Reality.

Brahma Kāṇḍa : The first chapter of *Brahmasiddhi*.

Brahmaloka : Mystical region which is the fruit of worshipping *Saguṃa Brahman.*

Brahmāśrita-eka-Avidyā-vāda : The theory that holds that one *Avidyā* resides in *Brahman.*

Brahmavidyā : That *Vidyā* (knowledge), according to which *Brahman* is the sole Reality and this phenomenal world is unreal.

Buddhi : Intellect.

Caitanya : Sentiency.

Candraloka : Mystical region which is the fruit of meritorious deeds.

Cārvāka : Materialistic system of philosophy.

Cāṇḍāla : The person belonging to the lowest caste.

Cidākāśa : Space reflected in consciousness.

Cit : Consciousness.

Citta : Mind.

Cittaspanditaṁ : The phenomenon taking place through vibrations of the mind.

Devayāna : One of the paths on which the soul moves after death according to its deeds.

Dharmyabheda : The difference an account of time and place in an individual.

Dṛṣṭi : Vision/perception. In the term of *Vedānta*- consciousness conditioned by *Avidyā.*

Dṛṣṭi-Sṛṣṭi-Vāda : The *Vedāntic* theory which empasizes that the creation takes place simultaneously with its perception/ perception itself is creation.

Drṣṭṛ : Perceiver/seer.

Dṛśya : Appearance.

Dṛśyadhi : The sequence of appearance.

Dṛśya prapañca : The appearance of the phenomenal world.

Dvāra karaṇa : The intermediate cause.

Dvaya : two.

Dvaya-kālika : Existing for two moments only.

Eka jīva : One soul.

Eka-Jīva-vāda: The *Vedāntic* theory of one soul.

Ekatva : Non-duality.

Gandharvanagara : An illusory city.

Ghatākāśa : Space confined within the pot.

Ghatajñānayorbhedaḥ : The difference between pot and knowledge.

Grāhya : Graspable.

Guṇa : Attribute.

Guṇamayī : With attributes.

Hetu : Reasoning/one of the five limbs of *Nyāya Vaiśeṣika* System.

Hetvābhāsa : Wrong perception according to *Nyāya-Vaiśeṣika* System.

Hiraṇyagarbha: The microcosmic spiritual principle of the cosmos.

Hiraṇyagarbha Sūkta : One of the philosophical hymns of the *Ṛgveda*.

Hitā : One of the veins.

Idealism : The theory which emphasizes that the Ultimate Reality is spiritual.

Ihāmutraphalabhogavirāga: Detachment of fruits regarding this world and hereafter/one of the four means of getting *Brahman*'s knowledge (*Brahmajñāna*).

Īśvara : The Supreme Soul or the reflection of *Brahman* in *Māyā*

Īva : As if.

Jaḍa : Non-Sentient.

Jagat : The world.

Jahadajahallakṣaṇā : Secondary sense of a word by which it looses some of the portion of the primary meaning, and at the same time it retains it.

Jaina : One of the heterodox systems of Indian Philosophy.

Janmādyasya yataḥ : The second aphorism of the *Brahmasūtra,* i.e., from which the origination of the world etc. takes place.

Jāti : A generic term of *Nyāya* Philosophy.

Jāti-jarā-maraṇa : Birth-oldage-death.

Jatu-kāṣṭha : Lac-wood.

Jīna putra : In Jainism and Buddhism, this addressing is done to Mahāvīra and Buddha respectively by their disciples, i.e., those, who have conquered their sense-organs.

Jīva : A living being soul.

Jīvanmukti : Liberation while living.

Jīvāśrita-Avidyā-Vāda : The *Vedāntic* theory which holds that *Avidyā* (Nescience) resides in the *Jīva.*

Jñāna : Knowledge.

Jñeya : The thing to be known.

Jyotiṣṭoma : Vedic sacrifice.

Kākatālīya : The maxim of the crow and the palm fruit. It is used to denote a very unexpected and accidental occurrence.

Kalpa : Epoch/era.

Kalpanā : Imagination.

Kalpita Saṁvṛtyā : From the empirical point of view.

Kāma : Desire.

Karma : Action.

Kārikā : Verse.

Kevalādvaita : The concept emphasized by Śaṅkara that *Brahman* is the absolute Non-dual Reality.

Kleśa : Defilements.

Kūṭastha : Immutable/Immovable.

Loksaṁvṛti Satya : Empirical truth.

Mādhyamika : One of the Schools of Buddhism.

Madhyāntavibhāgasūtra : The treatise of Subjective Idealism.

Mahābhūtas : Gross elements.

Mahākāśa : Space : without any limiting adjuncts.

Mahāpralaya : Great dissolution.

Mahat : The second of the twenty-five elements recognized by *Sāṁkhya* philosophy.

Maṇḍalas : Divisions of the *Ṛgveda*.

Mantra : verse.

Manovijñāna : Thought consciousness.

Manojijṛṁbhita : Projected by the Mind.

Māyā : Divine creative power of God.

Māyābhiḥ : With the help of *Māyā*.

Māyāhastin : An illusory elephant.

Mithyā : Unreal.

Mithyātva : Unreality.

Mithyājñānavijṛṁbhitaṁ : Projected by false or unreal knowledge.

Moha : Delusion.

Mūlamādhyamakakārikā : The verses composed by Nāgārjuna.

Mumukṣu : The person desirous of liberation.

Mumukṣutva : Desire of getting liberation.

Naiyāyika : Logician believing in the *Nyāya* system of thought.

Nāmadhātu : The world of mental elements.

Nāmarūpa-avagamo : The knowledge of diverse forms.

Nānātva : Manyness.

Nāsadīya Sūkta : One of the philosophical hymns of the *Ṛgveda*.

Nigamana : Conclusion/one of the five limbs of *Nyāya*-syllogism.

Niḥsvabhāvatā : Essencelessness.

Nimitta : Efficient.

Nimitta cause : Efficient cause.

Nirguṇa : Attributeless.

Nirguṇa Brahman : Attributeless *Brahman*.

Nirvāṇa : Extinction.

Nirvāṇa Prakaraṇa : One of the chapters of the *Yoga-Vāsiṣṭha*.

Nirvikalpa : Indefinite sensation.

Nirviṣaya : Objectless.

Nitya : Everlasting/permanent.

Nityānityavastuviveka : Discrimination between the eternal and the non-eternal/one of the four means of knowledge.

Nyāya-Vaiśeṣika : The systems of Indian Philosophy.

Pāda : Quarter.

Padārthatattvanirṇayakāra : The author of the *Padārthatattvanirṇaya*.

Pañcadaśī : The treatise composed by *Vidyāraṇya.*

Paramātman : The Supreme Soul.

Paratantra : The dependent/the name for the mundane truth in the *Vijñānavāda.*

Parikalpita : Imagined.

Parikalpita Svabhāva : Imagined nature.

Pariṇāmavāda : The theory of evolution.

Pariṇāmī-upādāna-kāraṇa : The modified material cause.

Pārmārthiki : Ultimate.

Pārmārthika Sattā : The Ultimate existence/transcendental reality.

Pārmārthika Satya : The Ultimate Reality.

Pitṛyāna : One of the paths on which the soul moves after death which leads to *Pitṛloka.*

Pradhāna : The first source of the material world. Out of which all material appearances are evolved, according to the *Sāṁkhya* philosophy. It is also called *prakṛti.*

Prajāpati : Mythological God *Brahmā.*

Prajñā : Knowledge.

Prakaraṇas : Chapters.

Prakāśātman : One of the disciples of Śaṅkara/the propounder of *Vivaraṇa* School of *Vedānta.*

Prakṛti : The original source of the material world consisting of the three essential qualities, i.e., *Sattva, Rajas, Tamas.* It is also called *Pradhāna.*

Pralaya : Dissolution.

Prātibhāsika Sattā : Illusory existence.

Prapañca : The world of appearance.

Prārabdha : One of the divisions of *Karma* (action) which has already started giving results.

Prasaṁkhyāna : Meditation.

Pratibiṁba : Reflection.

Pratibiṁbavāda : The *Vedāntic* theory of reflection.

Pratijñā : Statement of the thesis — one of the five limbs of *Nyāya* syllogism.

Pratikarmavyavasthā : Arrangement of action as to be performed by each and every soul.

Pratipannopādhi : Substrate of what is known.

Pratītyasamutpāda : Dependent origination.

Pravṛtti Vijñāna : Active consciousness.

Pṛthivī : The earth—one of the five gross elements.

Purāṇa : Mythological scripture.

Purītat : One of the veins.

Puruṣa : The soul acording to *Sāṁkhya* philosophy. It is neither a production nor productive. It is passive and a witness.

Pūruṣa Sūkta : One of the philosophical hymns of the *Ṛgveda*.

Pūrva Pakṣa : The opponent who presents the doubt.

Rajas : One of the attributes of *Prakṛti*.

Rūpadhātu : The physical world.

Śabda jñāna : One of the means of knowledge.

Sādhya : The thing to be proved.

Saguṇa : With attributes.

Saguṇa Brahman : *Brahman* with attributes.

Sahakārī Kāraṇa : Subordinate cause.

Sahopalambha : Simultaneous apprehension of knowledge and the thing to be known.

Sahopalambhaniyama : The law of simultaneous apprehension.

Sākṣirūpa : Witnessing.

Samaṣṭi : Cosmic.

Samaṣṭi-Avidyā : Cosmic nesceince.

Samaṣṭi-Jīva : Cosmic Soul.

Sāmānya : A generic term of *Nyāya* system.

Saṁbhūti : Becoming.

Saṁkalpanagara : The city of imagination.

Sāṁkhya : One of the Six Systems of Indian Philosophy.

Saṁkṣepaśārīraka : The treatise of *Vedānta* composed by Sarvajñātamuni.

Saṁsāra : The course of mundane existence.

Saṁskāra : Formative force in the life of an individual.

Saṁsthāna : Configuration.

Saṁvṛti Satya : Empirical Reality.

Śāṅkara Vedānta : *Vedānta* as propounded by Śaṅkara.

Sārūpya : Similarity.

Śāśvatavāda : Eternalism of Buddhism.

Satkāryavāda : *Sāṁkhya* theory of causation, according to which effect exists subtly in the cause.

Sattva : One of the three attributes of *Prakṛti*.

Sautrāntika : One of the Schools of Buddhism.

Savikalpa : Along with imagination of attributes.

Saviśeṣa aneka-śarīra-ekajīva-vāda : The *Vedāntic* theory that holds that *Hiraṇyagarbha* creates the world — while other *Jīvas* are just an appearance.

Siddhāntaleśasaṁgraha : The *Vedāntic* work compiled by Appaya Dīkṣita.

Siddhi Kāṇḍa : One of the chapters of *Brahmasiddhi.*

Skaṁbha Sūkta : One of the philosophical hymns of the *Ṛgveda.*

Smṛti : *Vedic* scriptures.

Sparśa : The origin of all mental elements.

Sphoṭa : The impression produced on the mind on hearing the sound of a word.

Sṛṣṭi : Creation.

Sṛṣṭi-Dṛṣṭi-vāda : The *Vedāntic* theory which holds that the world exists as it is already there.

Śruti : The *Vedic* scriptures.

Sthiti : One of the chapters of the *Yoga-Vāsiṣṭha.*

Śuka : Mythological character.

Sūkta : Hymns of the *Ṛgveda.*

Śūnyavāda : Nāgārjuna's theory that the nature of the Ultimate Reality is unutterable/Nihilism.

Śūnyavādin : The holder of *Śūnyavāda.*

Suṣupti : Deep sleep.

Svābhāvika bhedābhedavāda : Doctrine of difference and non-difference both being natural.

Svarūpa-lakṣaṇa : The Ultimate definition which explains the true nature of the thing.

Tad Ekaṁ : Only Ultimate Reality.

Tamas : One of the attributes of *Prakṛti.*

Tarka Kāṇḍa : One of the chapters of *Brahmasiddhi.*

Taṭastha lakṣaṇa : An indefinite definition.

Tathāgata : Lord Buddha.

Tat-tvam-asi : Thou art that/one of the *Mahāvākyas* of the *Upaniṣads.*

Tattvopaplava : The work composed on *Cārvāka* System.

Teja : Light/one of the gross elements.

Triṁśikā : 30 verses of the *Vijñaptimātratāsiddhi.*

Trisvabhāva : Three types of nature according to the *Vijñānavāda.*

Trisvabhāvanirdeśa : The work composed by Vasubandu.

Tṛṣṇā : Desire.

Udāharaṇa : Illustration/one of the five 'limbs' of *Nyāya* syllogism.

Upādāna : Material.

Upādāna Kāraṇa : Material cause.

Upadeśasāhasrī : The composition of Śaṅkara.

Upādhi : Limiting adjunct.

Upanaya : One of the five limbs of the *Nyāya* Syllogism/derivation.

Upāsanā : Worship of God.

Utpatti : Origination.

Utpatti Prakaraṇa : One of the chapters of the *Yoga-Vāsiṣṭha.*

Vaibhāṣika : One of the Schools of Buddhism.

Vairāgya : Detachment.

Vaiśeṣika : One of the Indian Systems of thought.

Varṇa : Caste.

Vāsanā : Residual impression.

Vastutantra : Dependent on the nature of the object being scrutinized.

Vāyu : Air/one of the gross elements.

Vedanā : Feeling.

Vijñāna : Cognition.

Vijñānavāda : Subjective Idealism of Buddhism.

Viñānavādin : The holder of *Vijñānavāda*.

Vijñapti : Sensation.

Vijñaptimātratāsiddhi : The work composed by Vasubandhu.

Vikṣepa Śakti : Projecting power of *Māyā*.

Viṁśatikā : 20 verses of the *Vijñaptimātratāsiddhi*.

Viṁśatikāvṛtti : Commentary composed on the *Vijñaptimātratāsiddhi*.

Vipāka : Result of deeds.

Vivaraṇa : The *Vedāntic* concept presented by Prakāśātman.

Vivaraṇaprameyasaṁgraha: The work composed by Prakāśātman.

Vivartavāda : Śaṅkara's theory of illusion.

Vivartopādāna kāraṇa : Materialistic cause of the *Vivarta*.

Vyakti : Individual.

Vyavahāra : Phenomenal dealings.

Vyāvahārika Sattā : Phenomenal/empirical existence.

Vyaṣṭi-Avidyā : Nescience of an individual soul.

Vyaṣṭi-Jīva : Individual soul.

Vyavasthā : Arrangement/ordered difference.

Yogācāra: One of the schools of Buddhism propounding Subjective Idealism.

Select Bibliography

General Books

Atreya, B.L., *Yoga Vāsiṣṭha and its Philosophy* (Lectures), 1932, The Benares Hindu University.

Belvalkar, S.K., *History of Indian Philosophy (Creative Period)*, Second edition, 1974, Oriental Reprint.

Chatterjee, Ashok Kumar, *The Yogācāra Idealism*, Second edition, 1975, Motilal Banarsidass.

Dagobert, Runes (ed.), *The Dictionary of Philosophy*, Fourth edition, 1942, New York.

Dasgupta, S.N. *History of Indian Philosophy*, 1975, Motilal Banarsidass.

Dasgupta, S.N., *Indian Idealism*, Cambridge University Press.

Datta, D.M., *The Chief Currents of Contemporary Philosophy*. Second edition, 1961, The University of Calcutta.

Deussen, Paul, *The Philosophy of the Upaniṣads*, Reprint, 1980, Motilal Banarsidass.

Durant, Will, *Pleasures of Philosophy*, 1952.

Ewing, A.C., *Idealism: A Critical Survey*, Third edition, 1961, Methuen & Co. Ltd.

Hasurkar, S.S., *Vācaspati Miśra on Advaita Vedānta*, 1958, Mithila Institute, Darbhanga.

Hiriyanna, M. *Outlines of Indian Philosophy*, Fourth Impression, 1958, George Allen & Unwin.

Hume, Robert Ernest, *The Thirteen Principal Upaniṣads*, Fifth impression, 1962, Oxford University Press.

James, Mark Baldwin (ed.), *The Dictionary of Philosophy and Psychology*, 1940, Peter Smith, New York.

Joad, C.E.M., *Guide to Philosophy*, 1946, Victor Gollander Ltd. London.

Keith, A.B., *Religion and Philosophy of the Veda and the Upaniṣads*, vol. 32, 1970, Motilal Banarsidass.

Kochumutton, Thomas A., *A Buddhist Doctrine of Experience*, First edition, 1982, Motilal Banarsidass.

Mahadevan, T.M.P., *Gauḍapāda: A Study in Early Advaita*, Third edition, 1960, University of Madras.

Mahadevan, T.M.P., *The Philosophy of Advaita*, Fourth edition, 1976, Arnold-Heinneman.

Mainkar, T.G., *The Vāsiṣṭha Rāmāyaṇa — A Study*, 1977, Meharchand Lachhmandas.

Mehta, N.D., *Siddhāntabheda, Sujña Gokulji Zāla Vedānta*, Prize Essay, 1894.

Murti, T.R.V., *The Central Philosophy of Buddhism*, 1955, George Allen & Unwin.

Potter, Karl H. (ed.), *Encyclopedia of Indian Philosophies*, Vol. III, 1981, Motilal Banarsidass.

Potter, Karl H., *Presuppositions of Indian Philosophy*, 1965, Prentice-Hall of India (Private Ltd.), New Delhi.

Radhakrishnan, *Indian Philosophy*, Vol. I, Eighth Impression, 1958, George Allen & Unwin.

Radhakrishnan (ed.), *The Principal Upaṇisads*, 1953, George Allen & Unwin.

Radhakrishnan (ed.), *History of Philosophy: Eastern and Western*, 1952, George Allen & Unwin.

Raju, P.T., *Idealistic thought of India*, 1973, Johnson Reprint Corporation, New York, London.

Ranade, R.D., *A Constructive Survey of Upaniṣadic Philosophy*, 1926, Oriental Book Agency, Poona.

Raval, C.V., *Śaṅkarācārya Nuṁ Tattvajñāna,* First edition, 1974, University Granth Nirman Board, Ahmedabad.

Sharma, Chandradhar, *A Critical Survey of Indian Philosophy,* 1976, Motilal Banarsidass.

Shastri, Prabhudata, *Doctrine of Māyā,* 1911, Luzac.

Shourie, Arun, *Hinduism: Essence and Consequence,* 1979, Vikas Publishing House, U.P.

Sinha, Jadunath, *History of Indian Philosophy,* 1956, Sinha Publishing House, Calcutta.

Sinha, Jadunath, *Introduction to Philosophy,* Fourth edition 1964, Sinha Publishing House, Calcutta.

Sinha, Jadunath, *Indian Realism,* Reprinted, 1972, Motilal Banarsidass.

Sircar, Mahendranath, *The System of Vedāntic thought and culture,* Second edition, 1975, Oriental Books Reprint, New Delhi.

Sogan, Yamakami, *Systems of Buddhistic thought,* 1912, University of Calcutta.

Solomon, E.A., *Avidyā, A problem of Truth and Reality,* First edition, 1969, Gujarat University, Ahmedabad.

Solomon, E.A., *Indian Dialectics,* Vol. I & II, First edition, 1978. Gujarat Vidya Sabha, Ahmedabad.

Stcherbatsky, Th.F., *Buddhist Logic,* 1962, Dover Publications, New York.

Basic Books

Advaitasiddhi, ed. by Sasti N.S. Anantakrishna, 1982. Parimal Publication.

Advaitabrahmasiddhi, ed. by Pt. Vaman Shastri, 1981. Parimal Publication.

Āgamaśāstra of Gauḍapāda, ed. by Vidhushekhar Bhattacarya, 1943. University of Calcutta.

Ālaṁbanaparīkṣā and Vṛtti, ed. by Aiyaswami N. Sastri 1942. *The Adyar Library Series*-32.

Brahamasiddhi, ed. by Kuppuswami P. Sastri, 1937, Madras Government Press.

The Brahma-Sūtra-Śāṅkara Bhāṣya with Commentaries, First edition, 1981, Parimal Publications.

Iśādi Upaniṣad with Śāṅkarabhāṣya, Reprint, 1978, Motilal Banarsidass.

Madhyantavibhāgasūtrabhāṣya, ed. by Vidhushekhar Bhattacharya Tucci, Part-I, 1939, *Calcutta Oriental Series*, N-24.

Mūla-Madhyamaka Kārikā, ed. by Hermabanath, Chatterjee, 1959, Calcutta.

Mūla-Madhyamaka Kārikā, ed. by J.W. Jong, 1977, The Adyar Library and Research Centre.

Mūla Madhyamaka Kārikā of Nāgārjuna with Prasannapāda Vṛtti of Candrakīrti, ed. by Louis de La-vallee Pousain, 1903. St. Petersbourg (Bibliotheca Buddhica-IV).

Naiṣkarmyasiddhi, ed. by G.A. Jacob, *Bombay Sanskrit and Prakrit Series*-XXXVIII, 1925.

Pañcadaśī (Gujarati edition), First edition, Sastuṁ Sāhitya Vardhaka Kāryālaya.

Pañcapādikā, ed. by Ramshastri Bhagavatacarya, 1948, Kashi.

Ṛksūktaśatī, ed. by H.D. Velankar, 1972, Bharatiya Vidya Bhavan.

Śabdakalpadruma, 1961, Motilal Banarsidass.

Saddharmālaṅkāvatārasūtra, ed. by Sitansusekhar Bagchi, 1963, Buddhist Sanskrit text. N-3 The Mithila Institute.

Sarvadarśanasaṁgraha, 1906, Anandasrama Sanskrit Granthavali-5.

Siddhāntabindu, ed. by Abhyankar Shastri Vasudeva, Second edition, 1962, Bhandarkar Oriental Research Institute.

Siddhāntabindu, ed. by P.C. Divanji, 1933, Baroda Oriental Institute.

Siddhāntaleśasaṁgraha, 1916, Chawkhamba Sanskrit Series, Benaras.

Trisvabhāvanirdeśa of Vasubandhu, S. Mukhopadhyaya, 1939, Visvabharati Series-4, Calcutta.

Vivekacūḍāmaṇi, tr. by P. Śaṅkaranārāyaṇa 1979, Bharatiya Vidya Bhavan.

Vijñaptimātratāsiddhi, ed. by K.N. Chatterjee, First edition, 1980, Kishor Vidya Niketan, Varanasi.

Vivaraṇaprameyasaṁgraha, V.S., 1969, Acyuta Grantha Mala Karyalaya, Kashi.

Vedānta Kalpalatikā, ed. by R.D. Karmarkar, 1962, Bhandarkar Oriental Research Institute.

Vedāntasiddhāntādarśa, 1943, Kashi.

Vedānta Siddhānta Muktāvalī, tr. by Arthur Venis, 1975, Chawkhamba Orientalia, Varanasi.

The Yoga-Vāsiṣṭha of Vālmiki with Tātparyaprakāśa, ed. by Vasudeva Laxman Sastri Panikar, 1981, Munshiram Manoharlal Publishers Pvt Ltd.

Journals

Annals of the Bhandarkar Oriental Research Institute, Vol. XXXIII, 1952. "Study of Śaṅkarācārya", Ingalls H.H. Daniel.

Journal of Indian Philosophy, vol. V, Sep./Dec. 1977, "Problems and Justificnations of the theory of "Dṛṣṭi-Sṛṣṭi" — Das Umeshchandra, D. Reidel Publishing Company, Holland, U.S.A.

Index